Omolade M

Release Planning of Software Systems

Omolade Moshood Saliu

Release Planning of Software Systems

A Decision Support Approach

VDM Verlag Dr. Müller

Impressum/Imprint (nur für Deutschland/ only for Germany)
Bibliografische Information der Deutschen Nationalbibliothek: Die Deutsche Nationalbibliothek
verzeichnet diese Publikation in der Deutschen Nationalbibliografie; detaillierte bibliografische
Daten sind im Internet über http://dnb.d-nb.de abrufbar.
Alle in diesem Buch genannten Marken und Produktnamen unterliegen warenzeichen-, marken-
oder patentrechtlichem Schutz bzw. sind Warenzeichen oder eingetragene Warenzeichen der
jeweiligen Inhaber. Die Wiedergabe von Marken, Produktnamen, Gebrauchsnamen,
Handelsnamen, Warenbezeichnungen u.s.w. in diesem Werk berechtigt auch ohne besondere
Kennzeichnung nicht zu der Annahme, dass solche Namen im Sinne der Warenzeichen- und
Markenschutzgesetzgebung als frei zu betrachten wären und daher von jedermann benutzt
werden dürften.

Coverbild: www.purestockx.com

Verlag: VDM Verlag Dr. Müller Aktiengesellschaft & Co. KG
Dudweiler Landstr. 99, 66123 Saarbrücken, Deutschland
Telefon +49 681 9100-698, Telefax +49 681 9100-988, Email: info@vdm-verlag.de
Zugl.: Calgary, University of Calgary, Diss., 2007

Herstellung in Deutschland:
Schaltungsdienst Lange o.H.G., Berlin
Books on Demand GmbH, Norderstedt
Reha GmbH, Saarbrücken
Amazon Distribution GmbH, Leipzig
ISBN: 978-3-639-14953-1

Imprint (only for USA, GB)
Bibliographic information published by the Deutsche Nationalbibliothek: The Deutsche
Nationalbibliothek lists this publication in the Deutsche Nationalbibliografie; detailed
bibliographic data are available in the Internet at http://dnb.d-nb.de.
Any brand names and product names mentioned in this book are subject to trademark, brand or
patent protection and are trademarks or registered trademarks of their respective holders. The use
of brand names, product names, common names, trade names, product descriptions etc. even
without a particular marking in this works is in no way to be construed to mean that such names
may be regarded as unrestricted in respect of trademark and brand protection legislation and
could thus be used by anyone.

Cover image: www.purestockx.com

Publisher:
VDM Verlag Dr. Müller Aktiengesellschaft & Co. KG
Dudweiler Landstr. 99, 66123 Saarbrücken, Germany
Phone +49 681 9100-698, Fax +49 681 9100-988, Email: info@vdm-publishing.com
Calgary, University of Calgary, Diss., 2007

Printed in the U.S.A.
Printed in the U.K. by (see last page)
ISBN: 978-3-639-14953-1

Acknowledgments

Foremost, I thank God Almighty –the Lord of the worlds, sustainer of the heavens and the earths– for giving me the talents and abilities that have allowed me to complete this work.

This work would not have been possible without the support of many exceptional people to whom I am grateful. I am greatly indebted to my supervisor, Dr. Günther Ruhe, for his support and guidance throughout the years. With the way Günther believes so strongly in me, I never had to search for motivation! Throughout my research, Günther continued to challenge my thoughts and consistently inspired me to always push myself to be the best I can be, even as he never hesitated to support me as I traveled the world presenting the work in this book at several international venues.

To my supervisory committee – Dr. Rob Walker and Dr. Jörg Denzinger – and my examining committee – Dr. Rick Kazman, Dr. Dietmar Pfahl, and Dr. Abraham Fapojuwo, I say thank you for patiently reading through this work and providing invaluable feedback.

I appreciate the support of wonderful individuals in the organizations I have visited for collaboration: Puneet Kapur, Kenton Smith and Andrew Smith (Chartwell Technology Inc), Chad Clarke and Joseph Momoh (Trema Labs Inc), Peter McCurdy (Nortel Networks), Mikael Lindvall, Chris Ackermann, and Patricia Costa (Fraunhofer USA Inc), Eric (Expert Decisions).

I would forever be thankful to my very loving siblings and undeniably supportive family. Thanks, mom and dad, for the love and support that only a parent can give. I could not dare to start listing names of several wonderful friends that have encouraged me all the way. With all due respect to everyone that has contributed one way or another I could not fail to mention Idowu, Nazeef, Malik & Ugo. Thanks guys for making Calgary home. Many thanks to Raheem for painstakingly reviewing drafts of my papers and sharing great ideas. I appreciate the engaging discussions with members of the Software Engineering Decision Support Laboratory and would like to thank An for being such a great research collaborator.

My appreciation goes to my lovely wife, Folasade. Every day, I thank God for giving you as the ultimate gift to me and for the invaluable love that we share. Thanks sweetheart for your understanding, putting up with my absences, and making me complete.

This research was funded by the Natural Sciences and Engineering Research Council of Canada (NSERC) and the Alberta Informatics Circles of Research Excellence (iCORE). I thank these funding agencies for allowing me give my best to the PhD research without worrying about finances.

This book is dedicated to my parents whose support never wanes

AND

To my wife, Folasade, the most wonderful partner I could ever wish for

Table of Contents

List of Tables

List of Figures

Glossary of Terms

The following is a glossary of useful terminologies that would facilitate the understanding of this book.

Terms	Definition
ε-Constraint method	A method for solving multi-objective optimization problems in which one objective function is taken as *primary objective* to be optimized, while all other objectives are converted into (in)equality constraints.
AHP	Analytical hierarchy process: an MCDA approach that uses pair-wise comparison together with expert judgments to measure qualitative criteria.
Bi-objective optimization	A special case of multi-objective optimization in which there are only two objective functions to optimize.
Business perspectives of planning	Everything that has to do with satisfying the business concerns of stakeholders, expected returns on investment, resources required to implement features and the available resource capacities.
Cognitive complexity	Complexity that results from the inability to completely formalize a problem, which implies that human judgment is required to address some aspects of the problem.
Computational complexity	Complexity that results from the need for near-optimal solutions to a problem, which limits the capability of relying on pure human intuition and experience.
Coupling interdependency	Type of interdependency in which two features must be assigned jointly to the same release.
Decision making	The entire process of making a choice among a number of alternatives.
Decision Support	A broad and generic term that covers all aspects related to supporting people in making decisions. It constitutes part of the decision making process.
EBEAM	Expert-based evaluation of architectures for modifiability: a framework for evaluating software architectural designs for modifiability.
ELECTRE IS	An MCDA method for supporting the problem of selecting one alternative solution from a given finite set of alternatives, especially in situations where we are dealing with imperfect knowledge.

EoM	Ease of modification: measures the ability to add new features or changes to the components of a system quickly.
FDIA	Feature-driven impact analysis: identification of the set of software entities (or components) that need to be changed to implement a new feature in an existing system.
Feature coupling	See the definition of "Interrelatedness of features" and that of SD-coupling. All three share same contextual meaning.
Feature interdependency	Refers to the manner in which features relate to and affect each other.
Features	A logical unit of behavior that is specified by a set of functional and quality requirements. In other words, features are abstractions or groupings from requirements that both customers and developers understand.
Framework	A set of ideas, conditions, or assumptions that determine how something will be approached, perceived, or understood.
GQM	Goal question metric: an approach for metrics definition, which defines measurement on three levels.
ILOG CPLEX	Optimization engine offered by ILOG Inc. for solving linear, mixed-integer and quadratic programming problems.
Impact analysis	The process involved in identifying the entities or elements of an existing software system that will be affected by a change, before the actual change is made.
Interrelated features	Two features are said to be interrelated if there exists overlaps in the components that would implement the two features in the existing system. In essence, interrelatedness refers to a situation in which two features are implemented by similar components.
Level of satisfaction of SD-coupling	A measure of similarity between the set of SD-coupling identified in the release planning problem and the set of SD-coupling fulfilled in a release plan.
Market-driven products	Software products that are not developed for specific customers, but the general market, e.g. Windows operating system.
MAUT	Multiple attribute utility theory: is an MCDA approach that assigns a utility value to each action to reflect the preferability of the action.
MCDA	Multi-criteria decision analysis: a process that helps in making decisions with regards to choosing, ranking or sorting alternatives. It basically deals with representation of preferences.
Modifiability	Modifiability is the ease with which a software system can be adapted to changes in the functional specification, in the environment, or in the requirements.

Multi-objective optimization	Multi-objective optimization is the process of optimizing a collection of objective functions simultaneously.
NASA	National aeronautics and space administration: an agency of the US government, responsible for the nation's public space program, and also for long-term civilian and military aerospace research.
Pareto-optimal solutions	Pareto-optimal solutions (also called non-dominated solutions or non-inferior solutions) are solutions to a multi-objective optimization problem in which no increase can be obtained in the values of any of the objectives without causing a simultaneous decrease in the values of the remaining objectives (i.e. for a maximization problem).
PD-coupling	Problem domain coupling: coupling interdependency that is related to the functionality of the system. PD-coupling can be extracted from description of features in requirements specifications.
Precedence interdependency	Type of interdependency in which a particular feature f_i must be released not later than another feature f_j in that order.
Primary objective	Using the ε-Constraint method to solve a bi-objective optimization problem, the *primary objective* refers to the objective function chosen to be optimized, while the second objective is used as a constraint.
Prioritization	Prioritization guides decisions about analyzing features to discover their order of importance for implementation.
Quality of solution	A measure of the level of optimality of the generated release plans.
RDIA	Requirements-driven impact analysis (see the definition of FDIA)
Release	A collection of new and/or changed features that form new versions of an evolving product; it is a software milestone that is set for distribution.
Release Planning decision framework	The process, context, and environment in which release planning decisions are carried out.
ReleasePlanner®	A commercial tool for software release planning that is offered by Expert Decisions Inc.
Requirements	This pertains to all the important behavioral characteristics expected of a system that are captured in a requirements document.
Requirements interdependency	See definition of feature interdependency.
RDIA	Requirements-driven impact analysis (see the definition of FDIA).
SD-coupling	Solution domain coupling: coupling interdependency that is extracted from the overlap in the implementation of the coupled features. (see also the definition of interrelated features).

Software configuration	Refers to the current state of a software system and the interrelationship between the constituent components. It includes source code, data files and documentation.
Software evolution	The tendency of software to change overtime.
SoRPES	Software Release Planning with Existing System-awareness: A decision support technique for software release planning that addresses both business and technical concerns.
Stakeholder	Stakeholder refers to anyone that influences or is influenced by the project plan. This includes customers, various types of users, developers, testers, project managers (decision-makers), and so on.
Stakeholder priorities	The set of priorities assigned to features by the stakeholders. This can be in terms of values, return on investment, urgency, and so on.
Strength of SD-coupling	The strength of SD-coupling between any pair of features refers to the degree of coupling that exists between the two features.
Structural diversity of plans	The degree to which two release plans are different in terms of the different releases to which each feature is assigned.
Technical constraints	A measure that differentiates between features that involve difficult and complex changes to the existing system and those that involve simple and small changes. In essence, it reflects the challenges associated with adding features the existing system.
Technical perspective	Technical perspective of release planning captures views development team that would implement the features. This also includes the potential challenges associated with adding features to the existing system.
TSAFE	Tactical separation assisted flight environment: A prototype software system specified by NASA Ames Research Center. TSAFE is used for checking conformance of aircraft flights to their flight plans and also to predict future trajectories.
Version	A small change to a software configuration. These minor changes are typically implemented while a system is in operation.
XoM	eXtent of Modification: a measure of the degree of changes required in components that would be modified to add a feature to an existing system.

List of Symbols

The following is a list of symbols in the book and the sections first mentioned.

Symbol	Definition	Reference
CL_e	Confidence level: the confidence that the expert e has in making judgments about certain objects e.g. architectural design	Sect. 4.4.4
CR_e	Consistency ratio: the accuracy of the pair-wise comparisons carried out by an expert e	Sect. 4.4.4
$V_e(z)$	A vector of relative contribution of all the characteristics $z \in Z$ from the perspective of expert e	Sect. 4.4.3
W_e	The relative weight of importance assigned to expert e	Sect. 4.4.4
$V(z)$	The overall vector of relative contribution of all the characteristics $z \in Z$ from the perspectives of all the experts	Sect. 4.4.5
$\phi_e(z,n)$	Matrix of the relative modifiability of each architectural design candidate n in the column with respect to the characteristics z in the row, according to expert e	Sect. 4.5.2
$W_{e,n}$	The weight of importance assigned to expert e based on his familiarity with architectural design candidate n	Sect. 4.5.3
$DF_{e,z}$	Domain familiarity: a measure of the level of familiarity that expert e exhibits relative to the architectural design candidate z	Sect. 4.5.3
$CR_{e,z}$	Consistency ratio: the accuracy of the pair-wise comparisons carried out by an expert e on design characteristic z	Sect. 4.5.3
$\theta(z,n)$	Aggregated matrix of the relative modifiability of each architectural design candidate n in the column with respect to the characteristics z in the row, from the perspectives of all the experts	Sect. 4.6.1
$EoM(n)$	The ease of modification of architectural design candidate n	Sect. 4.6.2
F	Set of software features	Sect. 5.3.1
f_i	A software feature	Sect. 5.3.1
c_m	The components of a system S	Sect. 5.3.1
Φ_i	Set of components to modify for the implementation of feature f_i	Sect. 5.3.1
$H(X, \xi)$	A hypergraph that consists of a set of vertices or nodes X and a set of hyperedges ξ	Sect. 5.3.2
$\Phi_x \in adj(\Phi_y)$	Hyperedges x and y are adjacent if their intersection is non-empty	Sect. 5.3.2
d_2	2nd order degree of a hyperedge, which is the number of other hyperedges that it has at least one vertex in common with	Sect. 5.3.2
$|F|$	The cardinality of the set F of features, which is a count of the number of features in the set	Sect. 5.3.3

$\Omega(i,j)$	Collection of components that appear in the intersection of the two adjacent hyperedges Φ_i and Φ_j in the hypergraph	Sect. 5.3.3
$\theta(i,j)$	The strength of SD-coupling between any pair of features i and j	Sect. 5.3.4
$sv(i)$	The system value assigned to a feature f_i based on the number of other features that it shares impacted components with	Sect. 5.3.6
$x(i)$	Decision variables of an optimization model, which determines whether a feature f_i assigned to a release or postponed	Sect. 5.4.2
K	A finite number of releases to be planned ahead	Sect. 5.4.2
$r(i,t)$	The amount of resource of type $t \in T$ required for the implementation of the feature f_i	Sect. 5.4.2
$r_{max}(k,t)$	The amount of resources type $t \in T$ available in release $k \in K$	Sect. 5.4.2
$(i,j) \in P$	Precedence constraints: indicates that feature f_i must be implemented before feature f_j	Sect. 5.4.2
$(i,j) \in C$	Problem domain coupling: indicates that the two features f_i and f_j must be implemented together in the same release	Sect. 5.4.2
s_p	The stakeholder p	Sect. 5.4.2
$v_{i,h}$	Expected value of the feature f_i according to stakeholder s_h	Sect. 5.4.2
$bv(i)$	Aggregated business value for feature f_i by all the stakeholders	Sect. 5.4.2
σ_k	The importance attached to a release k.	Sect. 5.4.2
$F_i(x)$	Objective functions	Sect. 5.4.2
Υ	Vector of objective functions (a point in the objective space)	Sect. 5.5
ε_i	Constraint limits for the ε-Constraint method	Sect. 5.5.1
μ_x^α	Level of satisfaction of SD-coupling by the plan x at threshold α	Sect. 5.4.4
x^*	A Pareto-optimal solution	Sect. 5.5
$XoM(c_m, f_i)$	Extent of modification required component c_m to implement f_i	Sect 6.3
$tc(i)$	Technical constraints of implementing f_i in the existing system	Sect. 6.3.3
β_k	The technical constraints threshold for release k	Sect. 6.4
τ_k	The maximal possible technical constraints, a percentage of this constitutes the β_k	Sect. 6.4

CHAPTER ONE

INTRODUCTION

Research is like a walk in the forest, only you are not sure the path
you are taking is going to get you home.
- Bradford Clark

1.1 Background

Incremental software development offers sequential releases of software systems, with new functionalities added in each increment. Using the incremental development process, a software vendor can deliver features of a system in different releases. This approach to software development allows customers to receive parts of a system early – a situation that enables customers to derive value early and provide feedback to the development team. Another advantage of incremental development is that it allows for better reaction to changes in the requirements of a product. Deciding what features to include in a release and in what order to include them depends on a number of factors that interact in complex ways. These factors include conflicting stakeholders interests, resource availability, schedule and other project constraints, which means only a subset of the features can be implemented [112].

A major problem faced by companies developing or maintaining large and complex systems is that of deciding which features should go into which releases of the software system [9], [124]. One of the main goals of software release planning is to address this problem. Release planning for incremental development can be approached from two dimensions: *what to release* and *when to release*. In this book, we discuss *what to release* decisions in terms of which new features or change requests should be assigned and implemented in which releases of a software system. Release Planning is a key determining factor of the success of a software product, and it also determines which customer gets what features at what particular time [23]. Release planning generalizes the ordinary prioritization of features [132], because the selection and assignment of features to releases must generally be preceded by feature prioritization [23].

Although incremental software development has been around for a long time [94], planning of multiple releases in an incremental development environment is a relatively new practice [62]. In the literature, the scope of release planning is often limited to just the next release [9], except for the works discussed by Greer and Ruhe [62] and Ruhe and Ngo-The [133].

Several reasons contribute to the need for a more systematic release planning. In the sequel we outline some of these reasons.

1.1.1 Mismatch Customer Satisfaction

The Standish Group [149] began its CHAOS research in 1994 and have concentrated on tracking software project successes and failures. In the 2002 Standish Group's report, it was observed that mismatch of customer satisfaction with the functionality of delivered software is still one of the main reasons that many software projects fail to achieve their stated objectives. It is straightforward to assume that mismatched customer satisfaction would definitely occur if the stakeholders are not sufficiently involved in selecting features for implementation. In order to develop a system that meets customer needs, clear requirements must be defined, and customers must be given the chance to specify their release preferences or priorities for the desired features.

1.1.2 Budget and Schedule Overrun

In 1995, The Standish Group CHAOS report showed that the average US software project overran its scheduled time by 190%, its budgeted costs by 222%, and delivered only 60% of the planned functionalities. According to their later reports, improving trends were observed over time. Even then, the 2004 Standish Group CHAOS report still shows a relatively low success rate with an estimated 71% projects either failed completely or were challenged (i.e. they were completed with exceeded budget and schedule estimates, and had less functionalities than originally requested), with 56% cost overrun and 84% scheduled time overrun. Even though planning releases may not "always" guarantee success, refusing to plan is definitely a recipe for failure – a popular adage says *"If you fail to plan, you plan to fail!"* A good release plan must result from analysis of the available resource capacities and ensures that features are assigned to releases within those capacities. This is essential, if the feasibility of the project and its success within budget and schedule would have a chance. A systematic release planning technique would ensure that the less important features are left until later, and if the schedule or budget is not sufficient, the least important features are the ones most likely to be omitted.

1.1.3 State of the Practice

Several industrial studies have revealed that practitioners typically take *ad hoc* approaches to release planning, without sound models and methodologies. This is the case even when planning for several hundreds of features. For instance, Karlsson and Ryan [76] and Lehtola *et al.* [99] observed during their industrial studies that most organizations select requirements (or features) informally.

According to the capability maturity model integration (CMMI) [31], the project management process area involves the planning, monitoring, and controlling activities. The CMMI recommends that the planning process should establish and maintain plans that define project activities [31]. This process includes developing the project plan, involving stakeholders appropriately, obtaining commitment to the plan, and maintaining the plan. Similarly, guidelines and standards (such as IEEE/EIA 12207.0) exist for the planning process in principle. But these standards and maturity models do not explain how to operationally assign features to releases to ensure maximal business values. Also, not much is known about how to effectively and efficiently perform the release planning process.

1.1.4 Lack of Consideration for the Existing Software Systems

Software development mostly proceeds as a series of changes to a base set of software components or modules. This series of changes includes the addition of new features, removal of defects detected during operational usage of the system, deleting unwanted features, and so on. Regardless of which type of changes is being made, the evolution activities are achieved by modifying the existing components of the software system. This implies that developers would want to find out what components or modules they would need to modify to implement a feature. In this case, release planning would be more challenging because the design decisions already implemented in the existing architecture of the system restrict its ability to accommodate future sequence of releases easily. Release planning in this context must take into consideration the operating environment and quality of existing components of the software system. This aspect of planning is extremely important since it is not possible to add new functionalities or change existing functionalities without proper knowledge of their impact.

In addition, some of the features to be implemented overlap in the components that would implement them in the existing system (*see* Definition 1.1). It would be desirable to cluster interrelated features together in the same release. This could help to reduce the cognitive complexity associated with understanding the implementation of features, thereby resulting in reduced development effort. By implementing interrelated features together, it may be possible to also avoid unplanned dependency among code elements, which could result from haphazard implementation of features [59]. As far as we know, there is no release planning technique that takes advantage of the *interrelatedness* between features. However, assigning interrelated features in the same release would reduce the cognitive complexity associated with understanding the implementation of features.

DEFINITION 1.1 (INTERRELATEDNESS OF FEATURES)

Two features are said to be interrelated if there exist overlaps in the components that would implement these features in the existing system. □

1.2 Research Problem

A program only stops to evolve when it is no longer used [64]. According to Lehman's "laws of software evolution" [96], software systems must be continually adapted, or they become progressively less satisfactory to use in their environment. Therefore, an operational system always has the tendency to evolve, because of the need to extend functionality of the system by adding new features or removing defects discovered during operation of the software. The new features originate from stakeholders who have diverse interests and all want their needs to be met, in spite of resource and other project constraints. The features (or requirements) to be planned could represent customer wishes derived from perceived market needs, or product requirements that the development company considers worthwhile to pursue [112]. Because most software systems are already operational, the new set of features is expected to be integrated into the existing architecture of the system.

In order to formally state the research problem addressed in this book, we define the following fundamental concepts:

- *Let a release be a software milestone that consists of a collection of features that form new versions of an evolving system.*
- *Let S be an existing system that consists of components* [*] $C = \{c_1, c_2, ..., c_m\}$.
- *Let* $Q = \{s_1, s_2, ..., s_p\}$ *be the set of stakeholders requesting the features.*
- *Let* $F = \{f_1, f_2, ..., f_n\}$ *represent the set of software features requested by the stakeholders.*

---

[*] The granularity of components is not pre-defined here. Components could be subsystems, modules, files, classes, or packages. We leave this up to the discretion of the software engineer.

- Let $V = \{v_{11}, \ldots, v_{1p}, v_{21}, \ldots, v_{2p}, v_{n1}, \ldots, v_{np}\}$ be the set of priorities assigned to the features by the stakeholders.

- Let $R = \{r_1, r_2, \ldots, r_T\}$ be the set of different resource types required for implementing the features.

- Let $K = \{k_1, k_2, \ldots, k_K\}$ be the set of release milestones in which the requested features are to be delivered.

- Let each release $k \in K$ have an associated total value, which is a function of the priorities of the features that are assigned to release k.

Based on the above fundamentals, we formally define the problem of planning the next releases of existing software systems as follows:

> "Given a set of features F with associated sets of priorities V and a set R of T resource types required for implementing the features, find an assignment of the features to a sequence of releases k_1, k_2, … , k_K such that the implementation of F in the set of components C of S is feasible, and the total value of the releases are maximized while keeping most of the p important stakeholders satisfied."

The term "feasible" in the problem definition pertains to the realization of the objectives of maximizing values, while ensuring that the constraints are not violated. From the business perspective, these constraints include efforts, schedule, and budget, while from the technical perspective the constraints include risk, dependencies between the features, and the dependency between the features and the existing system.

Given our formal description of the problem in the context of existing software systems, any solution to the problem of release planning needs to answer these three broad research questions:

1. How can we quantify the impact of adding a feature to an existing system?
2. How can we model interrelated features?

3. What is a good[†] formulation that can inform an effective solution to the release planning problem?

1.3 Research Motivation

This research is motivated by the need for a more systematic release planning, as outlined in Section 1.1. Also, an industrial study by Carlshamre *et al.* [24] concluded that the dependencies between requirements and the existing code base is not well understood. Thus, it is important to be able to extract useful information from the dependency between features and the components that would implement them in the existing system, and also use such information in release planning decisions.

Release planning for large software systems is complex from a business perspective. The business perspective captures the concerns of business stakeholders that include users, customers, management, marketing departments (in case of market-driven products), and so on. In this perspective, there are several stakeholders with diverse and often conflicting interests to be considered as well as resource and schedule constraints. From a technical perspective, this complexity is further aggravated by the dependencies between features and the existing code base, and also by the need to consider interrelatedness of features. The technical perspective reflects the views of the development team that includes architects, designers, and developers.

Because of the foregoing, an ad hoc approach would fail to generate optimal/feasible release plans. To the best of our knowledge, no published release planning technique addresses these concerns.

[†] A good solution must address both the business and the technical concerns.

1.4 Research Contributions

In this work, we propose a decision support technique for planning releases of software systems. The decision support technique is based on a bi-objective optimization model for release planning that would take advantage of the potential synergy in the implementation of features as one objective. This first objective leads to features that share maximal interrelatedness being assigned to the same release. The second objective of the model aims to assign features to releases in a way that maximizes the priorities given to the features by the stakeholders.

This research presents a number of significant contributions to the field of software engineering. The key contributions and findings from the research are as follows:

1. **Decision-Centric Framework for Release Planning:** We introduce a decision-centric framework for release planning that addresses both business and technical concerns. The proposed framework is flexible and the implementation of the individual process elements is customizable to different organizations and project contexts.

2. **Evaluation of Architectural Design for Modifiability:** We propose an expert-judgment technique known as EBEAM (Expert-Based Evaluation of Architectures for Modifiability) for evaluating the modifiability of software architectural designs. The design and development of EBEAM involves an exploratory study to investigate the characteristics that influence the modifiability of software architectural designs. We develop EBEAM as an evaluation method that can transform the judgment of experts into measurable quantities. EBEAM also presents a new weighting scheme for assigning importance to experts. We report a case study that uses EBEAM to evaluate the architectural designs of a prototype system for NASA flight assistance known as TSAFE (Tactical Separation Assisted Flight Environment).

3. **Incorporating Stakeholders' Concerns:** We model the different views of stakeholders in an optimization model. By involving stakeholders and allowing them to specify their priorities for different features and aggregating these priorities in a systematic manner, it is possible to strike a balanced and acceptable compromise in feature selection and assignment. This would likely result in developing products that satisfy a broad range of stakeholders and avoid mismatched customer satisfaction.

4. **Quantifying Feature Interrelatedness:** We propose an approach to quantify the interrelatedness of features using impact analysis data. Taking advantage of this interrelatedness during implementation would help the developers to reduce the cognitive complexity associated with understanding the implementation of features.

5. **Bi-Objective Release Planning Model:** We formulate the release planning problem as a bi-objective optimization problem that would take advantage of the interrelatedness of features as one objective. This first objective leads to features that share maximal implementation-related dependency being assigned to the same release. The second objective of the model aims to assign features to releases in a way that maximizes the priorities attached to the features by the stakeholders

6. **Decision Support for Release Planning:** We develop a decision support technique known as SoRPES (Software Release Planning with Existing System-awareness). SoRPES extends the bi-objective release planning model to include the *technical constraints* associated with implementing features in the existing system. The technical constraints aims to treat features that involve difficult and complex changes to the existing system differently from those involving simple and small changes.

7. **Empirical Validation:** We conduct empirical validation of the SoRPES technique that showed the potential of SoRPES to generate results that are as good as (or even better than) a similar technique that is based on single objective

optimization, both in terms of quality of solutions and implementation synergy among features.

8. **Prototype Tool:** We provide a proof-of-concept implementation of the key components of the SoRPES technique. This initial prototype can serve as a basis for the development of a full-fledged decision support tool that is based on the proposed SoRPES technique.

1.5 Organization of the Book

This book is further organized as follows (see Figure 1.1):

- Chapter 2 explores the background to this work and presents a survey of related topics.

- Chapter 3 presents the framework for release planning. The framework uses results from impact analysis and component evaluation to support and guide release planning decisions.

- Chapter 4 presents an expert-based technique for modifiability evaluation of software architectural designs.

- Chapter 5 discusses an approach to detect and quantify feature interrelatedness and the implications for release planning decisions. The approach is based on the assumed effort savings to be derived from extracting the interrelatedness between the features.

- Chapter 6 presents the SoRPES decision support technique which is an instantiation implementation of the framework proposed in Chapter 3.

- Chapter 7 discusses empirical studies to validate the proposed SoRPES technique.

- Chapter 8 summarizes the book, discusses the limitations and contributions of this work and outlines directions for future research.

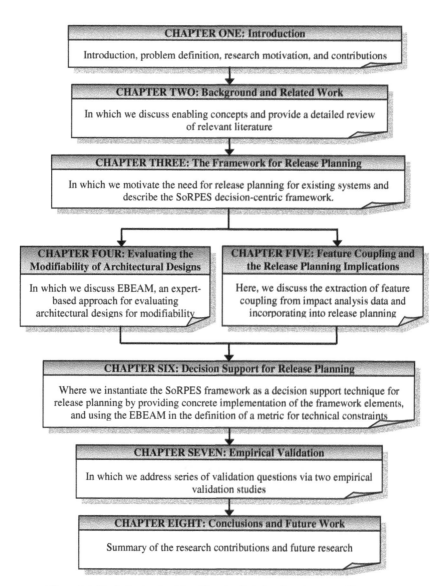

Figure 1.1: Book Navigation Map Showing Relationships between Chapters

CHAPTER TWO

RESEARCH FOUNDATION AND LITERATURE REVIEW

*Research is seeing what everybody has seen, and thinking what
nobody else has thought.*
- Albert Szent-Gyorgy

2.1 Introduction

In this chapter, we present an overview of existing work on software release planning. We discuss enabling concepts that are considered fundamental to the research. For each concept, we discuss the background and then present a survey of related work. Our emphasis in the survey is on existing release planning techniques.

2.2 Software Release Planning

2.2.1 Background

Investigating the *what-to-release* decision in release planning can be approached from different perspectives. In [134], we have identified two fundamental approaches: 1) the *art*, and 2) the *science* based planning of releases. The art of release planning mainly relies on human intuition, communication and capabilities to negotiate between conflicting objectives and constraints. The science of release planning involves formalization of the problem and applying computational algorithms to generate solutions.

The art and science of release planning complement each other. The art-based approach does not cope well with the complexity of release planning problems, especially when the number of factors to consider grows. The science-based approach copes better with complexity but cannot evaluate the problem with the same cognitive abilities as the human decision maker. [134]

We present a survey of existing work in release planning. Where applicable, we state which of the two approaches is adopted.

2.2.2 Related Work

Industrial studies by Lehtola et al. [99] and Karlsson and Ryan [76] show that practitioners mostly follow the art-based approach to release planning. They perform release planning in an *ad hoc* manner using a simple spreadsheet. Nonetheless, a number of techniques for release planning have been proposed in the literature – some techniques are targeted at the release planning problem, while others are simply requirements prioritization and selection techniques. These approaches include: Estimation-Based Management Framework for Enhancive Maintenance (EMFEM[§]) [121], Incremental Funding Method (IFM) [39], Cost-Value Approach for Prioritizing Requirements (COVAP[§]) [76], Optimizing Value and Cost in Requirements Analysis (OVAC[§]) [75], Provotype [23], The Next Release Problem (NRP[§]) [9], Planning Software Evolution with Risk Management (PSERM[§]) [61], Hybrid Intelligence in Software Release Planning (EVOLVE*) [133], and Flexible Release Planning using Integer Linear Programming (FRP[§]) [5]. We will succinctly discuss some of these approaches.

ENFEM proposed by Penny [121] is a high-level framework for planning enhancive software maintenance. Penny's approach focuses on release monitoring by ensuring balance between required effort and available effort, as project implementation progresses.

[§] The abbreviations used here are merely for convenience; the techniques were not originally named as such.

Denne and Cleland-Huang proposed the IFM in [39] as a data-driven and financially-informed approach for software release planning. IFM focuses release planning decisions on revenue projections. That is, it concentrates on the rate at which value is returned to the customer. IFM decomposes the system into units of functionality called minimum marketable features (MMF), which is defined as small self-contained features that can be delivered quickly and that can provide market value to the customer. The main thrust of IFM is the sequencing of features by their values, which could be measured in terms of revenue generation, cost savings, and so on. Once the MMFs have been identified, the costs and projected revenues are analyzed over the number of periods established by the business. Developers estimate cost and effort for developing each MMF while business stakeholders estimate each MMF's revenue. The authors equally identified the presence of dependencies between elements to be developed in what they term "precursor" relationship – this is what we generally refer to as precedence relationship that requires a feature to be developed before another.

Karlsson and Ryan's COVAP [76] is essentially a requirements prioritization approach that is discussed in the context of release planning. This approach ranks requirements in two dimensions: according to their relative value to the customer and their estimated cost of implementation. The relative value and relative cost of requirements to the customers are determined by using the pair-wise comparison of the Analytic Hierarchy Process (AHP) [136], this implies that the method only deals with comparisons between requirements and not the actual value or cost. These relative measures form the basis for prioritization of requirements for an onward selection from the pool, based on their rankings.

Jung's OVAC [75] is an extension of the cost-value approach discussed by Karlsson and Ryan [76]. Jung argued that ordinary inspection to perform pair-wise comparison of requirements using AHP can be very complex as the number of requirements grows larger. Hence, it is important to deal with such complexity by using optimization techniques. The resulting cost-value model was also formulated as a variant of the 0/1 knapsack problem with multiple objective. Just like COVAP, the goal is to select features that give maximum value for minimum cost, and within allowable cost limits.

Carlshmare [23] developed a release planning tool that was aimed at understanding the nature of release planning from the perspectives of industrial planner. The tool known as "Provotype" is based on the formulation of the release planning problem as a binary knapsack problem. The objective function and constraints were based on value of requirements and estimated resource demands respectively, while making sure interdependencies are accounted for. A preliminary empirical study on Provotype was conducted with release planners in the industry as a means of learning about release planning. According to Carlshamre, the preliminary study revealed that *"...release planners would not be interested in one optimal solution...by some magical algorithms"*, but providing a set of near-optimal solutions would suffice. The study also discovered that cost and value are not sufficient in determining the goodness of a solution.

The NRP [9] formulated the release planning problem as a variant of the 0/1 knapsack problem. As a variant of the 0/1 knapsack problem, the release planning problem was classified as an NP-hard problem. By its NP-hardness, the release planning problem would not be amenable to solutions by polynomial time algorithms. At the core of their method is the assignment of weights to customers based on their importance to the software company; the objective is to find a subset of customers whose features are to be satisfied within available cost. Bagnall and colleagues [9] investigate the applicability of a variety of solution algorithms to the resulting optimization model. These algorithms include: integer programming, greedy algorithms, and local search-based algorithms (specifically, hill climbing and simulated annealing). While experimenting with the algorithms, Bagnall and his colleagues found that integer programming proved sufficient for finding optimal solutions to smaller size problems but could fail to yield such optimal solutions in reasonable time for larger size problems, while simulated annealing found good quality solutions (possibly sub-optimal) on larger size problems. The authors also considered precedence dependencies among features which require that certain features must be implemented before another.

In a recent work, Zhang et al. [169] attempts to extend the NRP proposed by Bagnall *et al.* [9]. Zhang et al. [169] adopted the same planning parameters as those for NRP and formulated the release panning problem as a bi-objective optimization problem that is focused exclusively on optimizing value and cost, but ignores several other release planning parameters and constraints.

EVOLVE* proposed by Ruhe and Ngo-The [133] facilitates the involvement of stakeholders in the release planning process. The goal is to generate release plans that offer high-level of satisfaction among the different stakeholders. It also accounts for the dependencies between features as well as other constraints that restrict the amount of features that can be selected for implementation. EVOLVE* formulates the release planning problem as an optimization problem. Also, EVOLVE* focuses on offering higher flexibility in the number of releases to be planned ahead. Despite the formulation of release planning as a single-objective optimization problem, EVOLVE* emphasizes the need for human decision makers to further analyze resulting solutions.

FRP [5] formulates release planning as an optimization problem based on integer linear programming. The focus is to select features with maximal project revenues subject to the available resources. The FRP introduces release planning flexibility in order to cope with deadline extensions, hiring of external resources when needed, and allowing team transfers across different phases of the feature implementation.

In general, the software release planning problem is closely related to the problem of requirements prioritization. In the event that we do not need to consider many impacting factors other than cost and value, as well as not planning for more than one release ahead, pure prioritization of features would suffice. It simply boils down to selecting the top-most subset of the features for implementation. A comparative analysis of the most important and representative requirements prioritization techniques is discussed by Karlsson *et al.* [77], where they found the AHP to be the most promising requirements prioritization technique.

2.2.3 Comparing the Existing Release Planning Techniques

Here, we identify the most relevant dimensions of release planning to be considered when developing a technique to address the problem of release planning, and then compare the existing techniques based on these key dimensions.

2.2.3.1 Release Planning Dimensions

1. Scope of Planning

It has been observed that planning for only one release (i.e. next one) is not enough [23], because dissatisfactions are likely to arise. Some stakeholders would be disappointed seeing their highly ranked features not in the next release, especially if there are no planned schedules to have such needs met in the future. It is a good idea to plan two or more releases in advance, depending on increment interval (i.e. release calendar or milestones). During implementation, some of the features requested could be dropped and yet some others could be added. Because of these possible changes, it does not make sense to plan too many releases ahead.

2. Time Horizon of Planning

The time horizon of planning refers to the time interval required for a product or part of a product to be released – in essence, the release cycle. There are two fundamental types of release planning problems: (i) release planning with fixed and pre-determined time interval for implementation, and (ii) planning with flexible intervals. In the second problem type, the decision about the length of the interval to implement all the assigned features is not pre-determined. Most release planning approaches available today focus on fixed release cycles.

3. Objectives of Planning

A release planning technique must have an approximate definition of objectives. Typically, it is a mixture of different aspects such as value, urgency, risk, satisfaction/dissatisfaction, return on investment, and interrelatedness of features. A good formulation of the release planning problem should bring these different aspects together in a balanced way.

4. Stakeholders Involvement

A stakeholder is any individual or organization that has interest in a software development project. Stakeholders can be end users, developers, customers, testers, project managers, and management. Involvement of stakeholders is of vital importance for the development of feasible and high-quality release plans that address real customer needs.

5. Prioritization Mechanism

Prioritization mechanism refers to the formulated scheme for assigning relative importance to features. This includes addressing the question about the appropriate scale and granularity of priority data required. To address the problem of mismatch customer satisfaction, stakeholder preferences for features must constitute part of the prioritization scheme.

6. Interdependency Constraints

Even when characterized by features that are independent of each other, the release planning problem is a difficult problem [23]. However, most features in release planning share one form of dependency or the other. An industrial study of requirements repositories in a Telecommunication domain by Carlshamre et al. [23] concluded that, only a few sets of requirements were singular or independent of each other. Given this conclusion, it is important for release planning techniques to consider the interdependencies between features. For example, there could be coupling interdependency in which case two or more features must be implemented together in the same release, and the precedence interdependency in which case a feature x must be implemented before feature y or vice-versa. Coupling interdependency could be due to relatedness in the functionalities provided by the features or interrelatedness of features based on the components that would be modified to add the features to the existing system.

7. Resource Constraints

To implements features that are assigned in a release plan, several resource types are required. The need for release planning is partly necessitated because there are mostly less resources available. For any release plan to be feasible, the release planning technique must assign features within available resource capacities. The resource constraints could be in form of insufficient budget, effort, and so on.

8. Technical Constraints

Release planning is a central activity to the evolution of software products [137]. Release planning to select and assign features into increments may not be feasible without considering the effects of the pre-existing design of an evolving system. The sources of information from the existing system may be the existing architecture, code base, change repository and defect history, and so on. Technical constraints should be derived from impact analysis of the features on the existing system, the ease with which the system can be modified to add the features, the extent of modification that would be needed in the system when adding the feature. The technical constraints must be defined in such a way that we can distinguish between features that are difficult and complex to add from those that are simple and easy to add to the existing system.

9. *Character and Quality of Solutions*

This dimension addresses the question of what is considered and accepted to be a good solution of the problem. The range is quite large – a single solution versus a set of alternative solutions? Rather, do we adopt an *ad hoc* solution that does not guarantee feasibility in terms of the constraints or a solution approach that satisfies all (or most) of the constraints? Another issue to consider is whether a release planning technique generates solutions with undefined quality or solutions that achieve a predefined level of optimality.

10. *Tool Support*

Release planning is a human and knowledge intensive process, which has a number of tedious tasks like resource estimation, conflicting stakeholder concerns, release plan generation, and decision evaluation. The overheads of such computationally complex tasks call for tool support that would be of great value to the project manager.

2.2.3.2 *Comparing the Techniques*

The release planning techniques that we evaluate here are those discussed in the related work above. These techniques are considered to be representative of the current state-of-the-art-and-practice in software release planning. Table 2.1 gives a summary of the release planning techniques and their contributions to the different dimensions.

From Table 2.1, it can be seen that the major problem with the existing release planning techniques is the lack of consideration for the technical constraints. The technical constraint is due to the pre-existing design, which could restrict the type of features that can be easily added. The only attempt in [61] assumes that the operational risk of features resulting in system failure can be assigned probabilistic values by the development team. In the context of evolving systems, where there is a pre-existing design, it is not a realistic assumption to plan the next releases without considering the existing system. This constitutes one of the major gaps that we address.

Table 2.1: The comparison of various release planning methodologies

Techniques / Dimension	PSERM [61]	ENFEM [121]	NRP [9]	OVAC [75]	COVAP [76]	IFM [39]	EVOLVE* [133]	FRP [5]
Scope	1 release	1 release	1 release	1 release	1 release	Chunks of small releases	Several releases planned ahead	1 release
Time horizon	Fixed release	Fixed release	Fixed release	Fixed release	Fixed release	Fixed release	Fixed release	Flexible release
Objectives	Based on benefit of system changes	Based on benefit of features to customers	Based on weight of customers	Based on value of requirements	Based on customer satisfaction	Based on return on investment	Based on value, urgency, stakeholders weights and satisfaction	Based on expected revenue
Stakeholders involvement	Project manager	Developers, project management	Project manager, customer	Involvement of project manager is implied	Project manager, customer, users	All major stakeholders	All major stakeholders	Product or project managers
Prioritization mechanism	Optimization	No defined prioritization scheme	Optimization	Optimization	AHP	IFM Heuristics	Stakeholders prioritize features; Optimization heuristics used to balance conflicts	optimization
Interdependency constraints	Not available	Not available	precedence	Not available	Not available	Precedence (precursor)	Coupling and precedence	Precedence
Resource constraints	Cost, risk	Effort	Cost	Cost	Cost	Cost, time-to-market	Effort, risk, schedule	Effort
Technical constraints	Operational risk	Not available	Not available	Not available	Not available	Not available	Not available	Not available
Character and quality of solutions	One solution plan	One solution plan	One solution plan by any chosen search algorithm	One solution plan	One solution plan	One plan spanning many release periods	Alternative solutions within qualified range of optimality	One solution plan
Tool support	Not available	Time-tracking system	Not available	Not available	Not available	Partially available	ReleasePlanner	ReqMan

2.3 Software Components Characterization

2.3.1 Background

Any attempt to account for the influence of the existing system on release planning decisions must examine the current state of the components that constitute the existing system. Examining the current state of the components requires the characterization of the components based on the factors that determine the ease with which the components can be modified to accommodate new features. In the sequel, we give an overview of relevant research concerned with the characterization of existing software systems.

2.3.2 Related Work

Several researchers have explored product release histories in order to derive quality measures that could be relevant in characterizing existing software systems. Notables in this regard include the modeling of code decay by Eick *et al.* [47], the work of Gall *et al.* [55],[56] on identifying change patterns in evolving products, Mockus and Weiss [111] risk prediction model via characterization of the system, and the classification scheme developed by Porter and Selby [123]. The findings from these works show the relationships they share with the topic of this research. For example, Eick *et al.* [47] and Lehman [97] observed that, as the code base of a system evolves through releases it begins to decay, which implies that current and/or future changes to the code are difficult to make. The difficulty in changing decayed code has also been noted as affecting three aspects of product evolution [60] [157], namely: (1) increased cost of implementing a change, (2) increased time to complete a change, and (3) reduced quality of the changed product. In concluding their study on fault-proneness of software components over several releases, Ohlsson *et al.* [118] stated that the ability to identify parts of a system that need improvement makes planning and managing for the next release easier and more predictable.

Based on the results of some of these studies, it is imperative that release planning for next releases of existing systems would need to build on ideas from system component characterization, such as to enable analysis of the current state of the existing system.

2.4 Evaluation of Software Architectural Designs

2.4.1 Background

There is no universally accepted definition of what constitutes software architectures [8],[58]. For instance, some school of thoughts agree that design patterns constitute part of software architectural designs while others refer to design patterns as part of detailed design. According to Kazman [80], the Software Engineering Institute (SEI) have collected over 60 definitions of software architecture. In discussing software architectural designs, we adopt as a guide, the most widely used definition of software architecture in the literature:

> *Software architecture of a program or computer system is the structure or structures of the system, which comprise software components, the externally visible properties of those components, and the relationships among them* [11].

To determine how the characteristics of architectural designs compare to the desired characteristics of a system, techniques for evaluating architectural designs are important. Architecture evaluation can be performed at different stages in the development life cycle. Lindvall et al. [106] distinguishes between early and late software architecture evaluation. Early evaluation is carried out on architectures that are yet to be implemented. These architectures are typically a description of the system to be built. Although, it is impossible to fully understand the actual design characteristics of a system until it is built and tested, a model of the system can help characterize the architectural design for evaluation purposes. On the other hand, late evaluation is used to evaluate software architectures once an implemented version of the system exists. Late architecture evaluation is useful because it helps in identifying deficiencies in the existing architecture, and guides the reconstruction of the architecture to address these deficiencies. An example of a late architecture evaluation method and tool is the Software Architecture Visualization and Evaluation (SAVE) [110].

Abowd et al. [1] categorize existing architecture evaluation methods into two –
questioning and *measuring* techniques. Questioning techniques generate qualitative
questions to be asked about architecture, while measuring techniques are based on
quantitative measurements on the architecture to determine a specific quality attribute.
Instead of providing ways to generate questions that should be asked about an
architectural design, the measuring techniques provide answers to existing questions that
the evaluation team already has about particular qualities of the architecture. Questioning
techniques include scenarios, checklists, and questionnaires, while measuring techniques
include metrics, simulations, prototypes and experiences.

2.4.2 Related Work

Most of the existing works on architecture evaluation are based on questioning
techniques, with scenarios being the most widely used questioning technique. Scenarios
are used to capture events that could happen during the life of a system. Some of the
architectural evaluation techniques that are based on questioning techniques include: the
Architecture Tradeoff Analysis Method (ATAM) [84], Cost-Benefit Analysis Method
(CBAM) [81], Active Reviews for Intermediate Design (ARID) [43], Scenario-based
Architecture Analysis Method (SAAM) [83] and its variants, Architecture-Level
Prediction of Software Maintenance (ALPSM) [13], Software Architecture Evaluation
Model (SAEM) [45], and Architecture Level Modifiability Analysis (ALMA) [14]. Each
technique has different views about architecture evaluation and presents different
approaches to assessing architectural designs. Measuring techniques for architecture
evaluation are relatively rare, though. Shereshevsky et al. [145] and Lindvall et al. [106]
are two examples of research in this area. Existing measuring techniques use coupling or
cohesion measures or both, as the basis for their evaluation. Measurement-based
techniques have some limitations: they are always strongly dependent on the context, it is
difficult to determine the right set of metrics, and the interpretation of pure measurement
data is often unclear (what does it mean if a value is 4 instead of 5). For a more detailed
discussion of existing evaluation techniques in the literature, the reader should refer to the

survey by Dobrica and Niemela [43] which discusses various early evaluation techniques, and the comparison framework by Babar et al. [8] and Kazman et al. [82].

2.5 Software Change Impact Analysis

2.5.1 Background

Several definitions exist for impact analysis in the literature. According to Arnold and Bohner [7], impact analysis refers to the activity of identifying the entities or elements of an existing software system that will be affected by a change - or the activity of identifying the possible consequences of a change - before the actual change is made [125]. In the context of requirements, Lindvall [103] defines requirements-driven impact analysis (RDIA) as "the identification of the set of software entities that need to be changed to implement a new requirement in an existing system." Both definitions capture the core issue, which is the identification of entities that would change. However, the definition given by Lindvall [103] is of higher interest in our context, because it inherently requires traceability from the new requirements to the entities that would change in the existing system. This is the type of impact analysis that we desire when planning the releases of systems that are developed incrementally, over several releases.

In the real world of software evolution, changes affect both the component to be changed and also affect the other components that interact with the changing components. Change impact analysis also involves the identification of the likely ripple effects of software changes [170]. Impact analysis techniques require a starting point for a change to be located in the system, and all the other dependencies can be traced to discover what other components to change together with the starting component.

Impact analysis constitutes a part of change planning, and the output from such impact analysis has been identified to be a useful input to many project planning activities [105]. The change management process, as described by Lock and Kontoya [107] (see Figure

26

2.1), shows release planning as part of the activities that constitute change management in evolving software systems. Whenever a developer is given a piece of change task, and the developer is asked to evaluate what is required to accomplish the change task, Arnold and Bohner [7] opines that the programmer would be expected to provide answers to the following issues: 1) difficulty assessment, 2) effort estimate, and 3) risk assessment.

Certain forms of relationships exist among these three top issues. Because a "hard to perform" change task would be expected to be "more complicated" and also expected to require "much effort" to accomplish. Therefore, these assessments are fundamental to the planning of software releases.

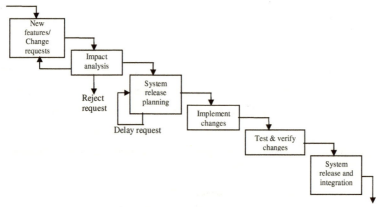

Figure 2.1: The Change Management Process [107]

2.5.2 Related Work

Early work on impact analysis began in the 1980's and concentrated on ripple effects of changes [148]. The software change impact analysis literature contains several techniques. For a detailed overview of the research results in this area, Bohner and Arnold [16] provides a good collection of papers. Most of these impact analysis techniques concentrate on analyzing the source code of a system.

There is an emerging research direction in automated change impact analysis. This involves mining the repositories of software projects to determine dependencies among source code entities. Gall *et al.* [55] is one of the early research in this direction. Gall *et al.* [55] studied the change patterns among different modules of a system in order to determine logical dependencies between the module using historical co-change. The research was based on the assumption that the modules that changed together in the past have a tendency to change together in the future. Hassan *et al.* [68],[69] studied change propagation and complexity of the software development process using data from software repositories. Ying *et al.* [167] and Zimmermann *et al.* [171] applied data mining techniques to explore version histories to discover change patterns, in order to predict and suggest the likely change entities to the developers. According to Gall *et al.* [55] mining the repositories of software projects would help in discovering couplings that static analysis of source codes could not reveal. In order to predict the risk involved in implementing a feature in existing system, Walker *et al.* [158] analyzed past change histories and current structure of software systems to estimate the probability of change propagation.

In the context of software release planning, it is important to have traceability from the requested features to the initial set of components of the existing system that would be impacted directly. From this starting point, change impact analysis could then analyze ripple effects to identify other components that are indirectly impacted but would need to be changed. The change impact analysis literature discussed above presupposes that a particular set of primary starting-point components is already known in the existing system, and we are only left with the task of identifying other components that would co-change with the starting-point. Pfleeger and Bohner [122] identified the importance of traceability from requirements to code for application in impact analysis. Lindvall and Sandahl [105] carried out an empirical study to determine the effectiveness of software developers in identifying both starting-point as well as the other co-changing components, based on pure experience. They concluded that software engineers are fairly able to identify components that would be impacted by the features to be implemented. Based on their study on impact analysis, Jonsson and Lindvall also concluded in [73] that *"interviewing knowledgeable developers is probably the most common way to acquire information about likely effects of new or changed requirements..."*

The automated aspect of RDIA (and analogously feature-driven impact analysis (FDIA)) cannot replace human experts, but could only serve to complement their ability to discover more indirectly impacted components. This is because logical co-changes may be amenable to automated detection, but automated traceability from new features to directly impacted components of existing system would be difficult since these features would not have been envisaged when naming program segments and architectures. Thus, traceability of features to primary components impacted would still require manual intervention.

In contrast to the literature discussed here, this book does not discuss a new technique for feature-driven impact analysis. Neither have we attempted to recommend or validate any of these existing techniques. Instead we rely on existing impact analysis techniques in order to determine the effects that feature impacts have on release planning decisions. Thus, any of the existing techniques for impact analysis would suffice.

2.6 Feature Interaction Management

2.6.1 Background

The essence of feature interaction management (and analogously, requirements interaction management) is to analyze the degree to which a system can satisfy multiple features (or requirements) at the same time [129]. Turner [155] observed that features interact in the problem domain because they share requirements or depend on each other for services, but interact in the solution domain because they share subsystems, modules, and so on [156]. Both feature interaction management [22],[85] and requirements interaction management [51],[129] share similar goals, which are to detect possible interactions between features or requirements and providing methodologies for resolving the interactions [156]. Research in feature interactions is aimed at detecting and resolving interactions like duplication, redundancy, inconsistency, vagueness in specification, incompatibility, conflicts, deadlocks, and incorrect order of execution.

2.6.2 Related Work

The bulk of prior studies on feature interaction started from the telecommunications domain. This is probably due to the nature of services provided in telecommunication systems, because these services tend to cause interaction challenges [63],[155]. Features of a telecommunication service are said to interact if one feature affects or changes the functionalities (or services) of another feature [4],[85]. Keck and Kuehn [85] and Calder et al. [22] present comprehensive surveys on existing research results on feature interactions. In most of these studies, the focus of interactions detection is based on the properties of the features, the services rendered by the features, or the behavioral descriptions of the features [22]. Some other prior studies have looked at interactions from the general requirements engineering perspective without necessarily focusing on telecommunications systems. Robinson et al. [129] presents a comprehensive collection of research results on interactions from the requirements engineering perspective.

Most of the existing interaction detection techniques focus on requirements engineering and design phases of system development. Only a few of the existing techniques consider interactions during implementation (e.g. [109]), and even those are based on the behavioral aspects of the implemented features. The behavioral aspects of a feature can be observed when the features are actually running in their environment [22]. Metger [109] discussed an interaction detection technique that refines requirements into tasks that are assumed to exhibit the behaviors expected from the requirements. Such interactions could be in terms of resources (i.e. physical elements that the system uses to fulfill its requirements) that the features share. This sort of interaction occurs, for example, when features compete for bandwidth on a network during execution.

In contrast to our work, none of these existing works on feature (or requirements) interaction management are targeted at supporting release planning decisions [24].

2.7 Decision Support

2.7.1 Background

Decision-making is concerned with the entire process of making choices among a set of alternatives. According to Keeney [87], a decision problem does not even arise until we have alternative choices to make. In an attempt to provide ideas that are most useful for guiding decision-making, Keeney [86] came up with eight key elements for making smart choices. These key elements are as follows [86]:

1. *Problem*: Define the decision problem so as to solve the right problem.
2. *Objectives*: Clarify what is to be achieved with the decision.
3. *Alternatives*: Create alternatives to choose from.
4. *Consequences*: Describe how well each alternative meets the stated objectives.
5. *Tradeoffs*: Make compromises when it is not possible to achieve all the objectives at once.
6. *Uncertainty*: Identify and quantify the uncertainties affecting the decision.
7. *Risk tolerance:* Account for the risks associated with the decision.
8. *Linked decisions*: Plan ahead by coordinating current and future decisions.

These key elements would apply to any kind of decision making problem, without necessarily enforcing the formalization or non-formalization of the decision problem. Besides, most practical decision problems can be analyzed and solved without necessarily going through the full range of the eight elements. The most important of these elements is to identify the right decision problem, and then create the objectives and alternatives.

As observed by Keeney [86], if the objectives and alternatives are inadequate, then we would most probably be led to a poor decision.

There are different types of decision making strategies, namely: normative, descriptive, and prescriptive strategies. We discuss these strategies next.

2.7.1.1 Normative Decision-Making

Normative decision-making (also called rational decision making) is concerned with identifying the best decision to take, assuming an ideal decision maker exists who is fully informed, who is able to compute with perfect accuracy, and who is fully rational. According to Simon [147] normative decision-making embodies rational behavior that is represented by a decision maker who has a *"well-organized and stable system of preferences and a skill in computation that enables him to calculate, for the alternative courses of action that are available to him, which of these will permit him to reach the highest attainable point on his preference scale"*. In the domain of normative decision-making appear theoretical multiple criteria decision analysis (MCDA) [50],[53] approaches like: 1) the multiple attribute utility theory (MAUT) [88] that assigns a utility value to each action to reflect the preferability of the action, 2) the analytical hierarchy process (AHP) [136] that uses pairwise comparison together with expert judgments to measure qualitative or intangible criteria.

2.7.1.2 Descriptive Decision-Making

Descriptive decision-making (also called Naturalistic decision-making), on the other hand, realizes the obvious fact that people do not typically behave in optimal ways, thereby attempting to describe what people will actually do by capturing the psychological impact and processes underlying actual observed behavior. One central theme of the descriptive decision-making literature is the idea of "Bounded Rationality", also known as "Limited Rationality" that was first proposed by Simon [147]. The basic principle of bounded rationality is that all intended rational behaviors occur within constraints, which stem from human "physiological and psychological limitations" regarding the extent of information that a human is capable of dealing with. Rather than aim at optimizing a solution, descriptive decision-making has a goal of "satisficing" which implies that "good enough" solutions would suffice. According to Simon [147], accepting good enough solutions is not an indication that "less" is preferred to "more", but that there is no choice.

2.7.1.3 Prescriptive Decision-Making

According to Stuart [152], a third classifier has recently been introduced – the prescriptive decision-making. Prescriptive decision-making is based on both the strong theoretical foundation of normative theory in combination with the observations of descriptive theory. A prescriptive decision model is one that can and should be used by a decision maker, and which is tuned to both the specific situation and needs of the decision maker [152].

2.7.2 Decision-Support – The Software Engineering Perspectives

The software engineering life cycle is composed of several activities from requirements elicitation to evolution of the operational system. At every stage of the life cycle, a broad range of decisions have to be made. According to Strigini [151], important decisions in the software industry mostly depend on subjective judgments, because we lack mathematical models of product behavior that are available in more traditional engineering disciplines. Typically, difficulties in software engineering decision problems arise from these important aspects [131]:

- Software is developed, and not produced or manufactured. And most development techniques are human-based, which implies that decision experiences cannot easily be transferred across projects.
- The discipline itself is experimental, which implies that experiences are constantly gained from development projects.
- It is difficult to predict the effects of actions and decisions.

These difficulties have motivated the advocates of the decision-based paradigm for software engineering. Wild et al. [160] discussed the need to model the software development process as a set of decisions in which each decision relates to a development problem activity.

One may be tempted to say that software engineering decision-making problems mostly fall within the realm of the descriptive rather than the normative decisions, but in reality they could be amenable to either normative or descriptive decisions, or both. The reasons for this are not far-fetched, because most real-world software engineering problems, if not all, can be found somewhere between the two extreme cases of completely structured and unstructured decisions. Also, there are always technical as well as human factors to deal with in software engineering problems [44]. The structured part of a software engineering problem may be amenable to automated solution, while the unstructured aspects of the problem could be tackled by human decision makers.

The nature of software engineering problems has implications for the kind of decision support that would be appropriate [23]. Especially, the inability of humans to cope well with complex decisions involving competing and conflicting goals in software engineering suggests the need for supplementary decision support [131]. As a result, Ruhe [131] proposes a marriage between computational and human intelligence to support decision-making in software engineering. The application of such a hybrid approach to specific problems in software engineering is beginning to gain ground in the software engineering community. For instance, Donzelli [44] recently proposed a hybrid process modeling approach to decision support for software project management.

2.7.3 Decision Support for Software Release Planning

Release planning decisions exhibit difficulties that characterize decision-making in natural settings. Considering problems involving several hundreds of features, a large number of widely distributed stakeholders, and several project constraints, it becomes very hard to find appropriate solutions without intelligent decision support.

Experience with release planning reveals that the difficulty of the problem results from two aspects: 1) *cognitive complexity* owing to the ill-defined nature of the problem which limits the ability to completely formalize the problem, and 2) *computational complexity* relating to the concern for at least a near-optimal selection and assignment of features to releases, which limits the capability of relying on pure human experience and intuition. Thus, any attempt to model the release planning problem would essentially be an approximation of reality, because tacit judgment and knowledge will always influence the actual decisions.

2.7.4 Related Work

To support release planning decisions, different strategies have been applied. In extreme programming (XP), for example, release planning decision-making is treated as a human-centered problem using a descriptive decision-making strategy. However, other researchers have followed the normative decision-making strategy in solving the same problem of release planning. Noteworthy in this category include Bagnall [9] and Jung [75]. More recently is the adoption of the hybrid intelligence by Ruhe and Ngo-The [133] and our earlier work [134], [141], which employed the prescriptive decision-making strategy to provide decision support for software release planning.

To address the uncertainties in release planning [79], it is suggested in [113] to provide support in the form of alternative solutions, and to also support the decision maker in the selection of an appropriate solution from the alternatives. The idea of providing alternative solutions is fundamental, because there are always uncertainties in software engineering. Providing alternative solutions would enable the decision maker to have the opportunity to perform tradeoff analysis. Tradeoff analysis is essential during decision making, because the decision maker could evaluate the extent to which each alternative solution conforms to the expected goal of the project. Our work is built on this foundation.

2.8 Summary

In this chapter, we discussed the current state-of-the-art and state-of-the-practice in software release planning. To be able to appropriate decisions support for software release planning, we have discussed enabling concepts that form the basis for providing such support. We discussed impact analysis that would be helpful in estimating the amount of work required to add a feature to an existing system. We have presented existing research in software components characterization, which is important for quantitatively ranking the components, based on the ease with which they can be modified to add features. Feature interaction is closely related to the type of interdependency and interrelatedness that we consider in release planning. As a result, we have discussed existing research in feature interaction. To provide appropriate support for release planning decisions, it is important to explore the paradigm of software engineering decision support. In this chapter, we discussed all these enabling concepts and the existing literature on the presented concepts.

CHAPTER THREE

THE FRAMEWORK FOR RELEASE PLANNING OF
SOFTWARE SYSTEMS

It is better not to proceed at all, than to proceed without a method.
- René Descartes

3.1 Introduction

This chapter makes the case for release planning decisions to be partly driven by the technical concerns of an existing system, rather than exclusively by the business concerns. We characterize the release planning problem and propose a release planning framework for software systems. The framework is motivated by the need to focus on both the business perspectives of release planning as well as the technical perspectives. The rest of the chapter discusses the proposed framework. A concrete implementation is presented in subsequent chapters.

3.2 Existing System-Driven Release Planning – The Preliminaries

Release planning involves deciding what new features or change requests to implement in which releases of a software system. Several planning parameters influence the assignment of features to releases. These parameters include the priorities of features, stakeholders concerns, delivery time of the product, resource demands, feature interdependencies, and interrelatedness of features [24],[133],[141]. Analysis of the release planning literature in Chapter 2 reveals the lack of support for existing software systems when selecting and assigning features to future releases.

In defining the objective of planning, most of the existing release planning techniques focus on the priorities of features from the business perspective as the major planning parameter [142]. Meanwhile, results from industrial studies reported in [24] showed that features share other form of relationships that should be considered when planning software releases, especially as it concerns the relationships between the features to be added and the existing system. Unfortunately, none of the existing release planning techniques has looked into this aspect of planning.

To fill this gap, this research develops a release planning technique for software systems that is partly driven by the existing system. This technique is an instance of the framework called SoRPES (**So**ftware **R**elease **P**lanning with **E**xisting **S**ystem-awareness), which we present in this chapter. We have put forward the initial arguments for this framework in [135],[138],[141].

3.3 Formal Problem Definition

Recall from Section 1.2 that, for a formal definition of the release planning problem, we can make the following assumptions:

1. A set F of features $f_1, f_2, ..., f_n$ are to be integrated into an existing software system S, to produce new releases of the system.

2. A set V of priorities $v_{11}, ..., v_{1p}, v_{21}, ..., v_{2p}, v_{n1}, ..., v_{np}$ are assigned to the features by the stakeholders.

3. The software system S is made up of m components $c_1, c_2, ..., c_m$.

4. In order to add the features, a subset of these components would have to be modified and a set R of T different types of resources would be needed.

5. There are p stakeholders with diverse interests in the software system, who all want their needs met. It is often the case that stakeholder interests would conflict especially for market-driven software products.

6. In order to deliver value early to the stakeholders, an incremental delivery strategy is adopted, and the features are delivered in K different releases.

7. Each release $k \in K$ has an associated total value, which is a function of the priorities of the features that are assigned to release k.

Given these assumptions, the release planning problem is restated as follows:

> *"Given a set of features F with associated sets of priorities V and resource types T required for implementing the features, find an assignment of the features to a sequence of releases k_1, k_2, ... , k_K such that the implementation of F in the set of components C of S is feasible, and the total value of the releases are maximized while keeping most of the p important stakeholders satisfied."*

The term "feasible" in the problem definition means all constraints are preserved. From the business perspective, these constraints include effort, schedule, and budget, while from the technical perspective the constraints include risk and the dependency between features and the existing system.

3.4 Research Objectives

The overarching goal of this research is to *provide a release planning decision framework that addresses both business and technical concerns.* This is expected to address the problem presented above and the following three corresponding research questions [RQ] (already outlined in Chapter 1):

[RQ1]: How can we quantify the impact of adding a feature to an existing system?

[RQ2]: How can we model interrelated features?

[RQ3]: What is a good formulation that can inform an effective solution to the release planning problem?

To achieve this goal in a more systematic manner, we break down these research questions into 6 research objectives. These objectives are a further refinement of the 3 research problems into achievable goals. Thus, our work aims to:

Objective 1: **Develop a decision-centric framework that addresses both business and technical concerns of release planning.** It is important to develop a decision-centric framework that includes all the concerns in release planning decisions. The framework should be flexible and the implementation of the framework should be customizable to different organizations and project contexts. Otherwise, the framework becomes difficult to adopt. This concerns all 3 research questions raised above.

Objective 2: **Investigate the constraints that the design decisions in an existing system exert on the implementation of new or changed features.** To make good release planning decisions, two things need to be clear. First, it is necessary to understand how much existing components must change to accommodate a feature. This involves impact analysis to identify components that would be affected by the new feature. Second, it is important to determine the difficulty associated with implementing the features in the existing system. *This objective addresses research question* [RQ1].

Objective 3: **Develop a technique to detect and quantify the interrelatedness of features.** Certain features could be implemented by modifying similar components of the existing system. The development team would rather have such features assigned to the same release. The implication of this is that it would reduce the cognitive complexity associated with understanding the features during implementation. It is important to develop a technique for model this interrelatedness of features using the overlaps in their implementation. In addition, the implications of this interrelatedness of features for release planning decisions need to be investigated. *This objective addresses research question* [RQ2].

Objective 4: **Provide a theoretical foundation for modeling the release planning problem in a way that can underlie the design of a decision support system.** It is important to investigate a suitable model for release planning to deal with the computational complexity associated with planning releases of large software systems. The formalized description should consider both business and technical concerns. *This objective partly addresses research question [RQ3].*

Objective 5: **Design a decision support technique that supports release planning decision making.** In order to support the decision maker during the release planning process, it is important to provide a decision support technique. This decision support technique should address both the computational complexity and cognitive complexity associated with release planning decision making. *This objective partly addresses research question [RQ3].*

Objective 6: **Evaluate the decision support technique in order to determine its applicability.** The developed decision support technique has to be empirically validated in order to determine its usefulness in supporting real-life release planning decisions and how it will actually be used in practice. *This objective partly addresses research question [RQ3].*

The completion of *Objective 1* means to outline the process, context, and environment in which release planning decisions are made. This defines the framework within which the other five objectives are realized. We present this framework next and discuss its constituents.

3.5 Decision-Centric Framework for Release Planning

This section presents a decision-centric framework for release planning known as SoRPES. This framework shown in Figure 3.1 establishes release planning in the context of software engineering decision support. The SoRPES framework is flexible and the implementation is customizable to different organizations and project contexts.

In the SoRPES framework, we have identified ten key process elements based on the findings from our analysis of release planning literature in [142] and the industrial experience reports on the state of the practice by Carlshamre [23], Lehtola *et al.* [99], and Regnell *et al.* [126]. The process elements represent release planning activities indicated by the rounded rectangles, and intermediate output from each activity indicated by the ovals. The three roles that contribute to the process and products of release planning are identified: project manager and development team; stakeholders that are not in project management or development role; and the support environment. Activities occur directly under the roles that are involved. For example, the roles indicated as project manager/development team and stakeholders are involved in the elicitation of features, while the support environment maintains the features. We briefly describe the activities involved in the process elements in the sequel.

P1: Feature elicitation

This refers to the process of collecting the set of features requested. The most important issue here is that features extracted from the customer and technical requirements should be described such that they are understandable, consistent, and correct. Collecting meaningful features is a complex problem that is not studied in this research. Christel and Chang [27] contains an overview of the issues involved in the elicitation of features. One of the most important goals of elicitation of features is to determine the problem that needs to be solved [116]. Nuseibeh and Easterbrook [116] discuss existing elicitation techniques in the requirements engineering literature. These existing techniques for feature (or requirements) elicitation would suffice.

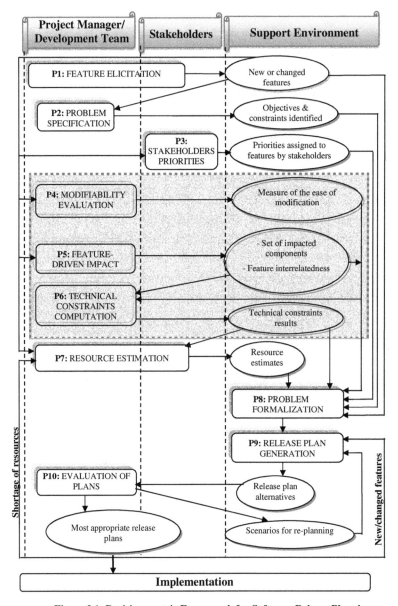

Figure 3.1: Decision-centric Framework for Software Release Planning

P2: Problem specification

In order to solve the right problem, it is important to define the release planning problem appropriately. In specifying the problem, the goal of planning should be clearly defined. This includes a specification of the number of releases to be planned ahead and the objective of planning from the business perspective, and the nature of the prioritization scheme to be used. The prioritization scheme may be defined in terms of the stakeholder expectations in form of value, urgency, return on investment, or other priority schemes. Essentially, it depends on the project and the stakeholders involved. The constraints that emanate from the business concerns (e.g. resource and schedule constraints) should be specified here. We discuss problem specification for release planning in Chapter 5 and Chapter 6.

P3: Stakeholders voting

Often, different stakeholders have diverse interests in a software project, especially for a market-driven software product. The stakeholders have various business concerns and should be invited to participate in the planning process through the identification and assignment of priorities to the features. Since the stakeholders decide the success criteria for the software product, it is essential to have the stakeholders vote on the features. In Chapter 5 and Chapter 6, we address these issues by defining as part of the objective functions, a value function that aggregates the business concerns of the stakeholders.

P4: Modifiability assessment

The goal of modifiability assessment is to measure the ease of modification (EoM) of the components of existing systems. This is a prerequisite for determining the relative ease of modifying the components for adding a new feature. In Chapter 4, we discuss a technique for evaluating the modifiability of architectural designs in general. Then, we apply this technique to evaluate components of the existing system, since a more fine-grained component-level assessment is required for release planning. Chapter 6 discusses this component-level assessment of modifiability.

P5: Feature-driven impact analysis (FDIA)

Feature-driven impact analysis (FDIA) refers to the identification of components to be modified when adding a given feature. This research does not propose any impact analysis technique, because the impact analysis literature contains several techniques, any of which could be adopted. We have discussed the impact analysis literature in Chapter 2.

However, Chapter 5 uses the results from impact analysis to detect the interrelatedness of features. Recall that two features are interrelated if to implement them, we need to touch on a common subset of components. The goal of determining interrelatedness of features is to assist the developers, by reducing the effort they need to modify the impacted components. In order to achieve this, it is important to develop a measure of this interrelatedness and incorporate it into release planning decision making. The detection and integration of the interrelatedness of features into formalized release planning models is the subject of Chapter 5.

P6: Technical constraints computation

A technical constraint is a measure of the restrictions that the pre-existing design of a system imposes on adding new features. To calculate the technical constraints, we need the results from the modifiability of components and the FDIA of the features. We also require a measure of the eXtent of Modification (XoM) required in these components in order to add a feature. The metrics to assess the technical constraints of a feature is an aggregation of both the EoM and XoM over all components to be modified to add a feature. We discuss these metrics in Chapter 6. During release planning, the technical constraints differentiate between features that involve difficult and complex changes to the existing system and those involving simple and small changes. In Chapter 6, we present a formal model to incorporate the technical constraints into the release planning decision.

P7: Resource estimation

Estimating likely amount of effort, schedule, and cost to implement the features is important. This process element is crucial to the success of release planning. It is essential to match the resource requirements of the features with the available resources. Accurate resource estimation has remained a challenge in software engineering [3]. Proposing a resource estimation technique is outside the scope of this research. The huge literature on resource estimation offers several estimation techniques that could be adopted. Thus, any of the existing techniques used by a development organization would suffice. A survey of resource estimation in software engineering is presented by Briand and Wieczorek [20], while more focused surveys on software effort estimation can be found in Jørgensen and Shepperd [74] and Saliu and Ahmed [139].

P8: Problem Modeling and Formalization

A formal description of the problem would help address the computational complexity of the problem. Without a formal description, it would be challenging to make good release planning decisions in a project with thousands of features, tens of thousands of existing components, hundreds of constraints, and tens of stakeholders. In most cases, the model would involve objective functions that seek to maximize parameters that capture both business and technical concerns. This formal description of the problem should integrate the results of all the preceding process elements. In Chapter 5, we present a bi-objective optimization model for software release planning. An extension to this model that incorporates the technical constraints of implementing the features is discussed in Chapter 6.

P9: Release plan generation

Release plan generation is based on solutions to the optimization models developed in the preceding process element, P8. The result of release plan generation is an assignment of features to consecutive releases. The generation of release plans must respect the project constraints, for the release plans to be feasible. This aspect of the SoRPES framework is addressed in Chapter 5 and Chapter 6.

P10: Evaluation of release plans

The release plans generated by solving the optimization models is essentially a first step in supporting release planning decision making. To determine whether the plans match the project goals, the decision maker needs support in evaluating the release plans. The evaluation scheme should be guided by the project goals and other issues that are of concern to the decision maker, but which could not be formally modeled. An unsatisfactory set of plans could lead to re-planning scenarios through a reformulation of the problem. While we hinted on this aspect of the research in Chapter 5, we provide greater detail in Chapter 6.

3.6 Summary

We have discussed a decision support framework proposed for software release planning. The framework provides an environment to integrate business concerns with technical concerns in order to define feasible release plans. In this chapter, we have presented an overview of the process elements that constitute the SoRPES framework. The different process elements in SoRPES can be realized through different concrete implementation strategies. Our main focus in this book is to provide a decision support technique that consists of concrete implementations of these process elements. This work gives particular attention to the impact of the existing system (i.e. process elements P4, P5, and P6), as this has been largely ignored in the literature. The existing system dimension is captured in the shaded region of Figure 3.1. The rest of the book presents an instantiation of the framework, in which we have proposed approaches to provide a concrete implementation of the different aspects.

CHAPTER FOUR

EVALUATING THE MODIFIABILITY OF SOFTWARE ARCHITECTURAL DESIGNS

You cannot control what you cannot measure.
- Tom DeMarco

4.1 Introduction

In this chapter, we present an architectural design evaluation technique called EBEAM (Expert-Based Evaluation of Architecture for Modifiability) that assists experts in articulating their knowledge of architectural designs and expressing the knowledge in measurable terms. EBEAM supports the evaluation of different architectural design versions for modifiability. In addition, EBEAM supports relative comparison between these design versions and the target design. We develop EBEAM as a generalized technique that is reusable for evaluating other architectural design attributes, apart from modifiability. We discuss EBEAM in detail and report on a case study that investigates its applicability. We also present another empirical study to validate the results of the evaluations made using EBEAM.

4.2 Evaluating Software Architectural Designs

According to Lehman's laws of software evolution [96], software systems must be continually adapted, or they become progressively less satisfactory to use in their environment. Therefore, we often need to extend the functionalities of an operational system by adding new features or removing defects discovered during usage of the software system [64]. The ease of adding features in the system depends on the modifiability of its architectural design. Bengtsson [14] defines modifiability as:

> *"Modifiability is the ease with which a system can be adapted to changes in the functional specification, in the environment, or in the requirements".*

Improving the modifiability of an architectural design implies that future changes will take less time and will be less costly to implement. When compared to a less modifiable design, the architectural design with improved modifiability will allow for smoother evolution. Thus, new upgraded versions of the system can be delivered earlier to the customers. Software that lacks modifiability is sometimes re-architected in order to increase the modifiability. Typically, re-architecting does not necessarily add user value, because it does not provide new functionalities. Since re-architecting could also be expensive, it is desirable to have a technique to assess whether the re-architected software achieves the desired improvement in modifiability. It is also important to assess the potential improvement in modifiability, in case there are several candidate architectures available that address the improvements in different ways. Information about the modifiability would also be useful for determining the amount of effort required and the risks involved in implementing new features.

In the literature, there are several objective metrics that are defined on architectural design characteristics in order to correlate them with quality attributes (e.g. modifiability) [89]. Such correlation has been met with several limitations [89].

For several reasons, using only architectural design metrics is not sufficient for measuring the improvement in modifiability. First, architectural design metrics have not been able to combine measures for architectural design characteristics, because of the problem of aggregating measures that are based on different scales. Second, several aspects of software architectures are difficult to measure, and can only be assessed by the experts that designed the architectures. For example, it is difficult to measure how well the names of components convey their role in the system, but an expert could answer such a question. A major problem, however, pertains to how experts can be systematically involved. One option is to have a review and evaluation of the architectural design candidates by experts, but it is difficult and expensive to hire experts in the field for architectural reviews (especially for small projects). The current architects (and other people in the development team) understand the system and the various architectural design candidates, but are somewhat biased, especially if they contributed to the definitions of the various candidates.

Given the aforementioned difficulties, it is important to have a methodology that assists experts in articulating their knowledge of an architectural design and expressing this knowledge in measurable terms, and also in relation to another architectural version of the same system. We develop an evaluation technique named EBEAM (Expert-Based Evaluation of Architecture for Modifiability) that assists experts in articulating their knowledge of architectural design candidates in a systematic manner.

We focus on the modifiability of architectural designs, because it has a significant effect on the overall system costs. The same technique could be used for any other attribute desired of an architectural design. The case study described in this chapter, examines the particular case when a redesign and reimplementation of a software architectural design have been conducted. Nevertheless, EBEAM can also be used earlier in the lifecycle when changes have yet to be conducted. During the case study, we used EBEAM to evaluate the improvement of the new version of a system relative to the old version, and also in relation to the overall architectural goals (i.e. the target design).

The results obtained from EBEAM can be used to determine the level of improvement in the modifiability of the architectural design, and whether the improvement is close to the target architectural goals. This information together with information about the (actual or estimated) cost to achieve the improvement can be used to determine the cost for further improvement.

4.3 Overview of the EBEAM

EBEAM is a three-stage evaluation technique that is based on a systematic elicitation of the judgment from experts and transforming the results into quantitative measures. We adopt and adapt the analytic hierarchy process (AHP) [136] as part of our three-stage approach to help experts articulate their judgments. EBEAM allows the participation of multiple experts in the evaluation process. Li and Smidts [100] discusses the importance of using multiple experts in making judgments.

The activities involved in the three stages of EBEAM, shown in Figure 4.1, are as follows:

Stage I: Evaluation of Design Characteristics

This stage of EBEAM requires experts that are knowledgeable in architectural design to identify the characteristics that influence the modifiability of architectural designs. Then, these experts evaluate and rank the relative importance of these characteristics to modifiability. Using aggregation schemes established in the literature and discussed by Forman and Peniwati [54] and Clemen and Winkler [29], we combine the judgments made by all the different experts into a unified measure. Any expert that has knowledge and experience in architectural designs could participate in this phase. Thus, the experts do not necessarily have to be familiar with the candidate architectural designs. This model can be improved over time by having more experts add their knowledge and experience to it.

Stage II: Evaluation of Architectural Designs

In Stage II, the experts with knowledge about the candidate architectural designs (we refer to them as the local experts) individually compare each candidate in relation to the other candidates or the specific architectural goals or both. This comparison is performed based on how the candidate architectural designs handle each of the characteristics evaluated in the first stage. By using the knowledge and experience of the local experts, we can evaluate important characteristics that are difficult or even impossible to measure objectively. This is further simplified because we use relative measures instead of absolute measures.

Stage III: Overall Architectural Modifiability Evaluation

In Stage III, we consolidate the results from the general experts in Stage I with the judgments from the local experts in Stage II to produce the relative modifiability of the architectural designs. The consolidation approach we adopt aims to reduce the bias from local experts.

It should be noted that there can be overlap between the general experts and the local experts, because some experts could posses both general architectural design knowledge as well as the knowledge about the specific architectural design candidates.

We have published an earlier version of this evaluation technique in [141]. EBEAM builds on the idea in this previous work, but focuses on software architectures and uses a more fine-grained set of architectural design characteristics. The previous work also involves a straightforward application of the AHP. On the other hand, EBEAM defines a new 3-stage process that adapts the AHP, especially with regards to the aggregation of the judgments from multiple experts. The EBEAM also introduces a new and more robust weighting scheme that considers the consistency in the judgments made by each expert and their familiarity/confidence in making the judgments.

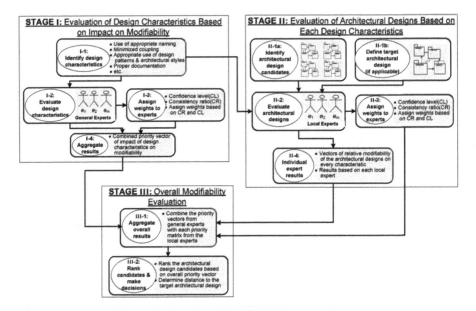

Figure 4.1: Overview of the EBEAM Framework

4.4 STAGE I: Evaluation of Design Characteristics

This stage is concerned with the identification of the design characteristics that contribute to modifiability and also the evaluation of their relative contributions.

4.4.1 Identifying Design Characteristics (I-1)

Every major post-implementation activity (e.g. implementing change requests) requires that the technical development team first develops an understanding of the existing architectural design. An architectural design that adheres to tested design principles and practices would facilitate this understanding to a higher degree than would an architectural design that does not follow such principles. These design principles (e.g. minimized coupling), when adhered to, can result in an architectural design that facilitates understandability. We focused on adherence to design principles as a way to measure the goodness of an architectural design. Because irrespective of the domain of a software system, adherence to characteristics of good and tested design principles and practices may result in a more modifiable system.

The first task is to identify the desired characteristics of software architectural designs that could be considered good practices. There are several software architectural design ideas that are considered to be good practices [48]. There are also discussion forums (e.g. Hacknot [66]) where software architectural design experts discuss the characteristics that a good software architectural design should possess.

There is no doubt that there is a long list of architectural design characteristics to explore [89]. In the process of coming up with the characteristics of a good architectural design, we explored the vast literature on software architectural design, extracted the generally accepted architectural design practices and refined the resulting set. In order to achieve this, we organized two workshops involving participants drawn from experienced architectural designers and researchers at the Fraunhofer Center in Maryland (FC-MD). The first workshop resulted in an initial list that we later used to conduct a pilot study on architectural evaluation. During the second workshop, we discussed the results of the pilot study, identified the coverage and applicability of the initial list of characteristics, and refined the characteristics. The final list of characteristics is based on experiences of the software developers, existing software architectural design literature, and experiences of the researchers involved in the study. Some of the characteristics that made the initial list, but were later excluded are: size of the system, size of files, size of folders making up the system, and use of less complex algorithms. A discussion of their exclusion appears in Section 4.4.2. The chosen design characteristics that influence modifiability include the following:

4.4.1.1 Use of Appropriate and Representative Naming

The names of the components, classes, methods, parameters, attributes, and all other constructs of a system should closely correspond to the functionality and the roles they represent in the system. Appropriate naming allows programmers to quickly understand the structure of a software system, identify components and their responsibilities, and relationships of a component with other components. The importance of using representative naming is discussed in [48].

4.4.1.2 Minimized Coupling

Coupling is a measure of the interdependence between entities in a system e.g. components, classes, modules, and so on. It measures the number of connections from and to a component [71]. The quality of a component increases as component coupling decreases [42]. Tight coupling can magnify the implementation effort of new features since the dependencies to the rest of the program can lead to ripple effects [165]. Tight coupling also makes it difficult to comprehend the role of a component.

A special case of coupling is the coupling to Libraries. It is important to encourage reuse of libraries to prevent the re-implementation of functionality that the components in the library provide. However, coupling from libraries and other common components and functions to application-specific components must be avoided.

4.4.1.3 Minimized Coupling to COTS (including Languages)

Another special case of coupling is the coupling to COTS components and coupling to programming languages and vendor unique libraries. While it is desirable to reuse such components, it is often important that the COTS components are wrapped so that the coupling is to the wrapper rather than to the COTS component itself. High direct coupling to COTS components can create problems with modifiability, since replacing the COTS component increases with increased coupling. This characteristic, for example, is motivated by a recent project at FC-MD in which coupling to COTS was analyzed [150].

4.4.1.4 Maximized Cohesion

Cohesion is the strength or logical unit of software components [93]. Entities that provide a certain function should be bundled together to facilitate programmers' identification of components (classes and packages) that are related to each other. Even if we do not desire coupling, it is a known fact that we cannot live without coupling. It is better to have couplings inside components than couplings between components. Couplings inside components could indicate the coming together of related classes, which inherently translates to high cohesion.

Even though there are definitions for how to measure cohesion, it requires an expert to judge whether the right components are grouped together, especially from the perspective of functionality.

4.4.1.5 Appropriate use of Design Patterns and Architectural Styles

Design patterns represent frequently used ways to combine classes or associate objects to achieve a certain purpose [57]. Most software developers agree on the benefits of design patterns and try to build software based on them to provide an easily modifiable software system. Nevertheless, incorrect implementation of design patterns leads to confusion, because developers tend to make wrong assumptions that the existence of a design pattern means the pattern has been implemented correctly. If design patterns are not implemented correctly, the software architecture may be difficult to understand and it may not readily accommodate future changes. For example, empirical studies in [71] indicate that the goal of developing a modifiable system based on design patterns is seldom reached because of incorrect implementation.

One of the questions requiring difficult decisions when building the architectural design of a system is the selection and use of appropriate architectural style(s) [143]. Architectural styles constrain the roles of architectural elements (i.e. components, connectors, and data) that may be used to compose a system or subsystem, and also the pattern of relationships among the elements [144]. Examples of architectural styles include pipe and filter model, layered model, and client-server. Decisions on architectural styles choices determine the suitability of the architecture in addressing the problem and affect the desired functionality and performance [143].

The need to choose appropriate style and the correct implementation thereof is of high interest from modifiability perspective; using appropriate architectural styles helps to understand the roles of the components and how they interact.

Appropriate usage of architectural styles and design patterns is difficult to measure, but an expert who knows about the roles of the system components and how they interact can determine whether suitable patterns are used.

4.4.1.6 *Proper Use of Information Hiding (including Interfaces)*

One major criterion suggested for decomposing systems into modules is the information hiding principle [119]. In making design decisions, this principle requires that, "system details that are likely to change independently should be the secrets of separate modules; the only assumptions that should appear in the interfaces between modules are those that are considered unlikely to change [120]." In essence, it requires hiding design decisions to protect other parts of a software architectural design from changing, if the design decisions change. Proper use of information hiding ensures that changes are easier to perform because the changes are typically local rather than global. Although, applying this principle perfectly is not always easy, because of the difficulty of estimating the likelihood of change [120].

The use of interfaces also facilitates reuse because in order to use the component only the interface class needs to be understood. In addition, it is a good design practice to maintain narrow interfaces. We define narrow interfaces by three criteria: 1) low number of available methods, 2) low number of parameters, and 3) use of simple parameters. Even though some rules of thumbs, such as the ones above, do exist, it is difficult to measure these characteristics. Notwithstanding, an expert can determine not only whether the size, but also whether the structure of the interface is appropriate.

4.4.1.7 Maximized Modularity

Modularization is one of the techniques proposed for the structural decomposition of software systems. The goal of modularization is to allow modules to be designed and revised independently [120], thereby improving the ease of change. A proper modular structure facilitates change, because it isolates some changes to a small part of a software system [119]. Measuring modularity is difficult; at the same time an expert with knowledge about the software system can recognize whether the system is decomposed into appropriate modules.

4.4.1.8 Minimized Duplication and Redundancy

Each design problem is expected to be solved once, instead of providing different solution instances for the same problem. Such duplication may cause unnecessary overhead of understanding two or more different solutions [66]. There are many reasons why duplicated functionality decreases modifiability. One reason is that it takes less effort to make a change in one place than in many places. Another reason is that it is easy to forget changing many different but similar design decisions. In addition, when there are many instances of the same entity, it is confusing and difficult to understand why they all exist and which one to use. It is also difficult to maintain consistency between the different solutions [66]. Several duplications could exist in an architectural design, including duplication of algorithms.

4.4.1.9 Minimized Concurrency and Threads

A system that only has one thread is easier to understand than a system with many threads and concurrent processes. Implementing concurrency and threads makes the design difficult to understand, because there are a lot of codes that distract from the implementation of the functionalities. We may not be able to avoid this kind of implementation mechanisms for some problems, but it constitutes a good design principle to reduce their usage as much as possible [66]. Concurrency is not bad, but the constructs for implementing concurrency could make it difficult to understand the design.

4.4.1.10 Proper Documentation

Documentation plays an important role for modifiability because it facilitates understanding of the architectural design. According to Clements and colleagues [30], an architecture must be documented in order for the architecture to achieve its effectiveness. Documentation provides explanations about the design in a way that enables designers new to the design or code base of the system to get a good overview quickly. Documentation provides clarifications on design decisions already made, which could help during modification tasks, thereby increasing the ease of modification by enhancing understandability.

4.4.2 Comments on the Excluded Characteristics

A number of software design characteristics were not included in this list for various reasons. We did not include size as an attribute of modifiability because size can be seen as an effect of other characteristics. Modifiability can be increased by adding comments, by using longer and more expressive names, and by dividing complex algorithms into smaller pieces, but all these could also increase the size. On the other hand, getting rid of duplications often means decreased size. Thus, an increase in size may not necessarily mean that the code resulting from the design would be more difficult to modify.

We have also not included number of files and number of folders, because redesigning a system to increase modifiability often means adding more structures, classes, files, etc. Since our interest is to compare two or more architectural design versions of the same system, we believe size, number of files and folders may not really change much, and even if they change it will not have big relative impact on the modifiability of the system.

By comparing two versions of a system, we also avoid other context-oriented characteristics such as non-real-time versus real-time systems and non-embedded versus embedded systems. These factors definitely have huge impact on modifiability, but they are irrelevant when comparing two version of the same system. By comparing two versions of the same system, we also avoid discussions regarding essential and accidental complexity [21]. The essential complexity relates to the complexity of the problem to be solved, while accidental complexity relates to the complexity of the solution. Accidental complexity refers to the extra complexity in the solution to a design problem, which results from the specific design approach adopted in solving a problem. A good design is expected to minimize accidental complexity. Thus, focusing our characteristics selection on good design principles subsumes minimization of accidental complexity. On the other hand, the unavoidable software complexity resulting from the nature of the problem being solved is an essential complexity [21].

Thus, it is safe to conclude that the set of characteristics we have selected and refined would apply to any type of system, as long as we are evaluating different design versions of the same system.

4.4.3 Evaluating Design Characteristics (I-2)

4.4.3.1 Definition of Goal and Alternatives

To evaluate the contribution of design characteristics to modifiability, EBEAM first structures the problem in a hierarchical form as shown in Figure 4.2. At the top is the goal; that is the relative contribution of the design characteristics to modifiability. In the middle layer are the architectural design characteristics that contribute to the goal (in AHP, they are also known as the criteria). The experts (i.e. $e_1, e_2, ..., e_m$) that would evaluate the relative contribution of each characteristic to the goal are represented in the third layer. We adopt this hierarchical structuring from the AHP, but adapted the evaluation process using a new aggregation and weighting scheme for the participating experts.

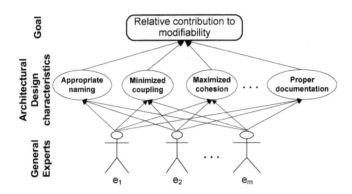

Figure 4.2: Evaluation of Architectural Design Characteristics

4.4.3.2 Prioritization of Design Characteristics

Each expert, selected according to their general knowledge and experience in architectural designs, performs pair-wise comparison between the design characteristics. Pair-wise comparison is carried out to determine which of the characteristics contribute more to modifiability than another. The weighting scale used for the purpose of this pair-wise comparison is shown in Table 4.1. Since we have 10 characteristics, we need a 10 x 10 matrix that contains the list of these characteristics in the rows and columns. This matrix enables us to relatively compare each characteristic from the row to all the other characteristics in the column. For each pair of design characteristics (starting with "appropriate and representative naming" and "minimized coupling", for example) their relative contribution to modifiability is described by the "intensity of contribution". Using the comparison scale in Table 4.1 (adapted from AHP [136]), the expert inserts into the comparison matrix, the number representing his chosen importance intensity in the cell that appears in the intersection of the two properties being compared. The question the expert is asking herself or himself while comparing each pair of characteristics to get the intensity of importance value is: *"How does characteristic-i (row) contribute to the modifiability of software designs when compared to characteristic-j (column)?"*

Table 4.1: Scale for Pair-wise Comparison of Architectural Design Characteristics

Intensity of contribution	Definition	Explanation
1	Equal contribution	The two characteristics (i and j) are of equal importance
3	Moderate contribution	Experience slightly favor one characteristic over another
5	Strong contribution	Experience strongly favors one characteristic over another
7	Very strong contribution	A characteristic is strongly favored and its dominance demonstrated in practice
9	Extreme contribution	The evidence favoring one over another is of highest possible order of affirmation
2, 4, 6, 8	Intermediate values between two adjacent judgments	When compromise is needed
Reciprocals	If characteristic i has one of the above numbers assigned to it when compared with characteristic j, then j has the reciprocal value when compared with i	

On completing the pair-wise comparison, the aggregated eigenvalues computation establishes a *priority vector*, $V_e(z)$ $(1 \leq z \leq Z)$, $(0 \leq V_e(z) \leq 1)$, which represents the relative contribution of all the Z characteristics from the perspective of each expert e. It is guaranteed that the entries in the vector $V_e(z)$ satisfy $\sum_{z=1...Z} V_e(z) = 1$.

4.4.4 Assigning weights to experts (I-3)

Having different knowledge and experience in architectural design research and practice, the general experts would be expected to exhibit different confidence levels (CL_e) in making judgments on the characteristics. Each expert is asked to rate his confidence level (CL_e) in making the judgments on a scale of 1 (Lowest) to 9 (Highest). Their confidence level (CL_e) shows the extent to which their judgments can be trusted. But given that a highly confident expert might not be necessarily consistent when making the comparison judgments, we also need to consider the consistency of the comparisons that an expert makes. The consistency ratio (CR_e) for an expert e defines the accuracy of the pair-wise comparisons carried out by the expert. The lower the CR_e of expert e, the higher the accuracy of the judgment s(he) made. A consistency ratio of 0.10 or less is considered acceptable [136].

We derive the weight of the experts by integrating both CL_e and CR_e. The consequence of this premise is that the more confident an expert is about his ability to make judgment on the characteristics, and the more consistent he performs the relative comparison tasks, the more the influence he wields in determining the overall contribution of each characteristic to modifiability. We employ the consistency formulae discussed in [136] to compute the consistency ratio from the comparison matrix prepared by each expert. Because a lower CR_e is desirable, we use $1-CR_e$ as a multiplicative factor of the confidence level, so that we do not penalize a highly consistent expert. To consider the impact an expert has on the final priority vector, we compute the weight W_e $(1 \leq e \leq E)$ for each expert using the formula:

$$W_e = \frac{CL_e(1-CR_e)}{\sum_{e=1...E} CL_e(1-CR_e)} \qquad (4.1)$$

where $(0 \leq W_e \leq 1)$. The weights of all the experts satisfy $\sum_{e=1...E} W_e = 1$.

4.4.5 Aggregating the contribution of design characteristics to modifiability (I-4)

In this step, we aggregate the different priority vectors resulting from the evaluation of all the experts. This results in a single overall vector of relative contribution of each characteristic from the perspectives of all the experts. During this aggregation procedure, the weight of each expert is a multiplicative weighting factor of the vectors of relative contribution of the characteristics, as given in Equation (4.2).

$$V(z) = \sum_{e=1...E} V_e(z) \cdot W_e ; \qquad 1 \leq z \leq Z \tag{4.2}$$

This type of aggregation scheme is referred to as the weighted arithmetic mean of priorities (AIP) [54]. There are evidences in the literature to support the fact that weighted linear combination of the judgment of experts, such as the one in Equation(4.2), performs better than other more mathematically complex aggregation methods [29]. Besides, they are more easily understood.

4.5 STAGE II: Evaluation of Architectural Designs

In this stage of EBEAM, we evaluate the relative modifiability of the architectural design candidates, and their relative modifiability with respect to the target design.

4.5.1 Identify architectural design candidates and define the target design (II-1)

The first task here is to identify the architectural design candidates, which are different design versions of the same system. If applicable, the software architects also define a specification of the target architectural design. Lindvall et al. [106] discusses the idea of specifying a target (or ideal) design for an existing system architecture. For example, existing versions of the design for Client-Server architecture may currently allow direct communication between the clients and the server. In an ideal case, the target design specification could be defined such that no Client component except the Mediator should be allowed to contact the Server directly. Such a target design may define some goals that are yet to be implemented in the existing design versions, probably due to a lack of resources.

4.5.2 Evaluation of design candidates for a fixed characteristic (II-2)

Each local expert with knowledge of the architectural candidates performs relative pair-wise comparison of the architectural design candidates and the target design with respect to each of the design characteristics (In AHP, the architectural design candidates and the target design would be known as the alternatives to compare). The goal is to evaluate the relative ease of modification of any pair of candidates being compared based on the manner the architectural design candidates handle the characteristic under consideration. We structure the problem (similar to the one for the design characteristics) as shown in Figure 4.3. The question to ask when comparing two designs, based on the characteristic under consideration, is of the following form: "How much easier to modify would design-i be when compared to design-j, if we only consider their use of *minimized coupling?*" The same question applies to all the other characteristics that contribute to modifiability. The rating scale used is given in Table 4.2.

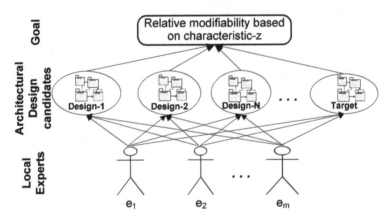

Figure 4.3: Evaluation of Architectural Designs

Table 4.2: Scale for Pair-wise Comparison of Architectural Designs

Intensity of contribution	Definition	Explanation

1	Equal contribution	The two architectural designs (i and j) are of equal importance
3	Moderate contribution	Experience slightly favor one architectural design over another
5	Strong contribution	Experience strongly favors one architectural design over another
7	Very strong contribution	An architectural design is strongly favored and its dominance is demonstrated in practice
9	Extreme contribution	The evidence favoring one architectural design over another is of highest possible order of affirmation
2, 4, 6, 8	Intermediate values between two adjacent judgments	When compromise is needed
Reciprocals	If architectural design i has one of the above numbers assigned to it when compared with architectural design j, then j has the reciprocal value when compared with i	

Each local expert develops one comparison matrix for each characteristic on which the candidates are compared. It should be noted that the target design (if applicable) also constitutes one of the candidates, for comparison purposes. For each of these matrices developed we also compute the consistency ratio for the purpose of assigning weights during aggregation. During this step, we also compute the priority vector for each comparison matrix developed. The priority vector shows the relative modifiability of the candidate designs based on each characteristic, and from the perspective of each expert.

Let us suppose we have N architectural design candidates (including the target design) to compare. Combining all the priority vectors for one expert would result in a Z x N matrix that shows, for every entry (z, n), the relative modifiability of each design in column n with respect to the attribute in row z. Higher value in a cell of the matrix translates to higher modifiability of the design in the column relative to other design candidates, and consequently the easier it is to modify the design. The matrix by each expert e is described by:

$$\phi_e(z,n); \quad 1 \le e \le E, 1 \le n \le N, 1 \le z \le Z \tag{4.3}$$

where each row z (representing one characteristic) in the priority matrix $\phi_e(z,n)$ for each expert e must satisfy the inequality $\sum_{n=1\ldots N} \phi_e(z,n) = 1$.

4.5.3 Computing the weight for local experts (II-3)

For the purpose of aggregating the judgment by all the experts, weights must be assigned to the experts to reflect the influence that each expert wields on the final matrix. The process of weight assignment is similar to the one described by Equation (4.1). One difference here is that, we replace confidence level in Equation (4.1) with a measure of domain familiarity (DF). Also, the DF is assessed on per-design basis for each expert e (i.e. $DF_{e,n}$) – an expert maybe more familiar with one architectural design candidate than the other. Thus, he could specify different familiarity level for different design candidates on a scale of 1 (lowest) to 9 (highest). Also, from the previous step, it is clear that the CR is also derived on per-characteristic basis for each expert (i.e. $CR_{e,z}$), because each expert develops one comparison matrix for each characteristic. Thus, a CR must be computed for each comparison matrix. As a result, the weight $W_{e,n}$ for each expert e on design n is computed as:

$$W_{e,n} = \frac{DF_{e,n}(1-CR_{e,z})}{\sum_{e=1\ldots E} DF_{e,n}(1-CR_{e,z})} \tag{4.4}$$

where $1 \le n \le N, \quad 1 \le z \le Z$.

Equation (4.4) shows that we derive the relative weight of each expert for specific characteristic and on specific design candidate during aggregation.

4.6 STAGE III: Overall Modifiability Evaluation

During this stage of EBEAM, we consolidate the results from the local experts with the judgment from the general experts (i.e. results from Stage I) to produce the relative modifiability of the architectural design candidates, and their closeness to the target design.

4.6.1 Combining the design modifiability matrices of all experts (III-1)

Using the priority matrix (i.e. described by Equation (4.3)) developed by each expert, we have to combine all their priority matrices into a single aggregated matrix, in order to establish the overall relative priorities of the design candidates from the perspectives of all the experts. Unlike the aggregation carried out in Stage I (*see* Equation (4.2)), the aggregation required here is a little tricky. First, because we have to combine design modifiability matrices and not vectors. Second, because we have to consider the weighting vector $W_{e,n}$ defined in Equation (4.4), and also augment it with the priority vector $V(z)$ of the characteristics. The combined matrix is described by:

$$\theta(z,n) = \sum_e V(z) \cdot \phi_e(n,z) \cdot W_{e,n} \tag{4.5}$$

Since we are combining matrices and vectors, we perform a cell by cell computation. This explains the weighting scheme described by Equation (4.4). On expanding Equation (4.5) further, the resulting priority matrix $\theta(z,n)$ is given by:

$$\theta(z,n) = V(z) \cdot \left[\frac{\sum_{e=1\ldots E} \phi_e(n,z) \cdot DF_{e,n}(1-CR_{e,z})}{\sum_{e=1\ldots E} DF_{e,n}(1-CR_{e,z})} \right] \tag{4.6}$$

where $1 \le n \le N$, $1 \le z \le Z$.

Now, we have a Z x N priority matrix that aggregates the judgment of all the experts. From this priority matrix, we can determine the overall relative modifiability of each design candidate in terms of each characteristic that contributes to modifiability. The information derived from here is useful in helping us determine which subset of characteristics is actually contributing to the low modifiability of a design. Such information could assist architects when making refactoring or redesign decisions.

4.6.2 Rank architectural designs (III-2)

4.6.2.1 Rank the designs based on modifiability values

We derive a priority vector from the aggregated priority matrix $\theta(z,n)$ developed in the previous step by summing over each column (i.e. each column represent a design candidate) of the matrix. The higher the priority value assigned to a design, the easier it is to modify the design relative to the other candidates, and consequently the higher the modifiability of the design. Thus, we define the ease of modification (EoM) based on these modifiability values, as follows:

$$EoM(n) = \sum_{z=1\ldots Z} \theta(z,n) \tag{4.7}$$

where $\theta(z,n)$ is the Z by N matrix described by Equation (4.6). Each entry in the modifiability vector is normalized, where $0 \le EoM(n) \le 1$ and $\sum_n EoM(n) = 1$.

While $\theta(z,n)$ gives the overall modifiability of each design with respect to each of the characteristics, the EoM(n) gives the overall modifiability over all the characteristics. All the design candidates can then be ranked based on their modifiability values.

4.6.2.2 Determine the distance from the Target-Design

To measure the distance from the target, we *idealize* the modifiability values in the priority matrix $\theta(z,n)$ and also in the priority vector EoM(n). By idealizing, we mean selecting the design with the largest modifiability value (i.e. definitely the Target Design) and dividing all the other values in the priority matrix (respectively the priority vector) by this largest value. Thus, the Target Design now has a modifiability value 1, then the modifiability value for every other design candidate would be proportionately less than 1. These idealized priorities can help in road mapping, as we would be able to measure how far we are from the goal specified for the target design. For instance, if the Target Design has modifiability value of 1 on a specific characteristic, and the best design version has a modifiability value of 0.75 on the same characteristic, it implies that the best of the design versions has achieved 75% of the goal defined for that design characteristic.

However, if there is no target architectural design specified for the system, we simply exclude Target Design from consideration in the EBEAM evaluation process. Thus, the modifiability evaluation is conducted relative to the available design versions.

4.7 CASE STUDY: The Application of EBEAM to TSAFE Designs

The application of EBEAM to a real life software project was conducted at the Fraunhofer Center Maryland (FC-MD) in the summer of 2006. We used EBEAM to evaluate the architectural design versions of the air traffic control piece of software – the Tactical Separation Assisted Flight Environment (TSAFE) system. We discuss the study in details.

4.7.1 Context

The system under consideration is a prototype of the Tactical Separation Assisted Flight Environment (TSAFE) software system defined by NASA Ames Research Center [49] and implemented by Dennis [40]. This implementation was later turned into a testbed by FC-MD [104]. TSAFE was proposed as a principal component of a larger Automated Airspace Computing system that shifts the burden from human controllers to computers. The TSAFE prototype checks conformance of aircraft flights to their flight plans, predicts future trajectories, and displays results on a geographical map. We refer to this original prototype as TSAFE I. Figure 4.4 shows the high level structure of TSAFE I with its four main components: the client, the parser, the database, and the engine. TSAFE runs in two independent threads: the parsing thread and the main thread. In the parsing thread, the parser reads data from a radar feed, extracts flight information, and sends it to the database component. In the main thread, a timer in the client component initiates the process of updating the flight data every 3 seconds. The client requests data from the database and sends it to the engine component for computation. The engine sends the computation results to the client to be displayed on a graphical user interface.

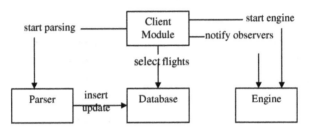

Figure 4.4: Conceptual View of TSAFE I

Since TSAFE I was a prototype, it only implemented the most basic functions from the original NASA description [49]. An earlier analysis study was conducted at Fraunhofer Center Maryland (FC-MD) using TSAFE I as the basis for an experimental software testbed [2]. During the experimental study, new set of features that would be required in TSAFE in the future were described. These features are related to demands that would be placed on TSAFE I when operating in a real environment.

After several analyses conducted during the experiments in [2], it was discovered that it would be difficult to incorporate the new set of features into TSAFE I because the architecture is not easily modifiable. This prompted the need to redesign the system in order to fix the modifiability problems and then create structures to accommodate the implementation of the change requests. The newly created design of TSAFE is now referred to as TSAFE II. Both TSAFE I and TSAFE II have different structures but their external graphical user interface (GUI) and behavior are identical. Details regarding how the new architectural design was created from the old design are discussed in [2]. The high-level design models of TSAFE I and TSAFE II are given by Figure A.1 and Figure A.2 in Appendix A.

During the design of TSAFE II, the designers focused on improving the manner in which a subset of design characteristics (i.e. naming, coupling, cohesion, and use of design patterns) is handled. Having completed the design of TSAFE II, it is important to be able to show whether there is improvement in modifiability. It is also necessary to show the extent of the improvement, and in terms of which design characteristics. In addition, it is desirable to determine how the current versions of the architectural designs measure up to the target design. With these issues under consideration, EBEAM was seen as a systematic method that could help with the evaluation and communication of results to third party. Most importantly, EBEAM could generate quantitative measures without ignoring the knowledge and experience of the local experts.

4.7.2 Evaluating TSAFE Designs using EBEAM

The goal of this evaluation is to compare the architectural designs of TSAFE I and TSAFE II with respect to modifiability. Apart from comparing the two implemented design versions (i.e. TSAFE I and TSAFE II), it is important to determine how close the current designs are to realizing the projected design goals in terms of other design characteristics. The projected design goals are encapsulated in a conceptual design known as the Target-TSAFE. In order to perform the modifiability evaluation using EBEAM, we treat all the three designs (TSAFE I, TSAFE II, and Target-TSAFE) as candidate designs. From the evaluation results, we can determine the relative modifiability of the two versions as well as their closeness to the target architecture design in terms of all the design characteristics.

During the case study, three experts participated in Stage I of the EBEAM evaluation process. The requirements for selecting these experts were based on their experience in architectural design in general. With their experiences, these experts could evaluate the relative contribution of the design characteristics to modifiability, without having particular design candidates on mind. For Stage II, only two experts that are familiar with the TSAFE system and its different design versions participated. These two experts (i.e. Architect-1 and Architect-2) compared the three candidate designs to evaluate the relative modifiability of TSAFE I and TSAFE II, and the closeness of the two versions to the Target-TSAFE. The two experts that evaluated the design candidates in Stage II also participated in the evaluation of the design characteristics in Stage I. The participation of these experts in both stages is not a requirement. In fact, it would be more desirable to have the local experts participate only in the evaluation of architectural design candidates to reduce bias. For the case study, however, there were not enough independent experts for Stage 1 of the evaluation process. This is not a limitation of the EBEAM technique.

4.7.3 Results and Discussions

4.7.3.1 Results from Stage I: Contribution of design characteristics to modifiability

On completing the first stage of the evaluation, the priority vectors resulting from each of the three experts, which show the relative contribution of design characteristics to modifiability, are given in Table 4.3. We have not included the comparison matrix completed by each expert or the process of computing the priority vectors, because they adhere to the EBEAM process. In Table 4.3, the columns named "Rank" represent the relative ranking of the contribution of each design characteristic to modifiability, based on each expert's evaluation. For example, Expert e_1 ranked "minimized concurrency and threads" as the most important characteristic that determines how modifiable an architectural design would be, while ranking "minimized duplication" as the least important characteristic. The results in Table 4.3 show that the experts do not completely agree on how each attribute relatively contribute to modifiability. However, a perfect correlation is not expected, because EBEAM is supposed to support the experts in articulating their individual knowledge and experience, which we cannot expect to be the same. Although, some levels of agreements exist. For example, the results from expert e_2 and expert e_3 agree that "minimized coupling" contributes to ease of modification the most. The results from expert e_1 almost agree with this ranking as well, as expert e_1 also ranked minimized coupling as the second most important characteristic.

The consistency ratio (CR_e), confidence level (CL_e), and the weight computed for each expert e are also given in Table 4.3. This weight is computed for each expert using Equation (4.1). Although expert e_1 and e_3 claimed to exhibit the same confidence level, but expert e_1 achieved a higher CR when performing the evaluation of the design characteristics. The higher CR for e_1 indicates that we can trust the judgments of expert e_1 more than the judgments of expert e_3, which invariably translates to the higher weight assigned to e_1. Expert e_2 has the lowest weight because the expert has lower CL and lower CR than the other two experts. The weights are used in the aggregation scheme for unifying the different priority vectors from each expert's evaluation into a single priority vector. The resulting priority vector shows the relative contribution of each architectural design characteristic to modifiability. The aggregation scheme is defined in Equation (4.2).

The priority vector reflecting the aggregated views of all the experts is also shown in Table 4.3. For easy interpretation, we also present the priority vectors as percentages. The percentages enable us to reason in terms of what percentage of the relative modifiability values that a specific characteristic assumes. The column named "Rank" in the aggregated result represents the relative ranking of each characteristic based on their impact on modifiability (note: we have sorted Table 4.3 according to these final rankings). The aggregated result ranked "minimized coupling" as the architectural design characteristic that has the highest contribution to the modifiability of architectural designs (i.e. rank R(1)). The interpretation is that, if only one choice is possible, all the experts agree that they would rather select an architectural design that minimizes coupling over another design that minimizes duplication. The reasoning supporting such decision is that, it would be easier to modify a candidate with minimized coupling than another without minimized coupling, but which exhibits minimized duplication. The final aggregated priority vector given here would be used in Stage III when aggregating the results with those from TSAFE designs evaluation.

Our interpretation of results here should be treated with caution, however, because it only reflects the judgment of the participating experts based on their experience. It could turn out to be different ranking if the evaluation is performed by different architectural design experts. For the purpose of our study, this is not a limitation, because the experts have been drawn from the same environment where we need the results to evaluate specific design candidates.

Table 4.3: Contribution of the Characteristics to Modifiability from the Perspectives of the 3 Participating Experts

z	Design Characteristics	Expert (e_1)		Expert (e_2)		Expert (e_3)		Aggregated Result		
		Priority Vector $V_1(z)$	Rank	Priority Vector $V_2(z)$	Rank	Priority Vector $V_3(z)$	Rank	Priority Vector $V(z)$	Priority Vector (%)	Rank
1	Minimized coupling	0.1591	R(2)	0.2345	R(1)	0.2564	R(1)	0.2151	21.51%	R(1)
2	Maximized cohesion	0.1441	R(3)	0.1925	R(2)	0.1233	R(4)	0.1513	15.13%	R(2)
3	Maximized modularity	0.1092	R(6)	0.1294	R(4)	0.1438	R(3)	0.1271	12.71%	R(3)
4	Minimized concurrency and threads	0.1709	R(1)	0.0433	R(6)	0.0856	R(6)	0.1036	10.36%	R(4)
5	Proper information hiding (including interfaces)	0.0309	R(9)	0.1050	R(5)	0.1743	R(2)	0.1024	10.24%	R(5)
6	Appropriate use of design patterns and architectural styles	0.1108	R(5)	0.0402	R(7)	0.0993	R(5)	0.0858	8.58%	R(6)
7	Minimized coupling to COTS (including language)	0.0537	R(8)	0.1766	R(3)	0.0209	R(10)	0.0789	7.89%	R(7)
8	Proper documentation	0.1387	R(4)	0.0219	R(10)	0.0261	R(9)	0.0651	6.51%	R(8)
9	Use of proper and representative naming	0.0655	R(7)	0.0276	R(9)	0.0363	R(7)	0.0442	4.42%	R(9)
10	Minimized duplication	0.0172	R(10)	0.0292	R(8)	0.0340	R(8)	0.0266	2.66%	R(10)
	Confidence Level - CL =	8		7		8				
	Consistency Ratio - CR =	0.0494		0.0976		0.0836				
	(1-CR) =	0.9506		0.9024		0.9164				
	CL*(1-CR)	7.6048		6.3168		7.3312				
	$W_e =$	0.35783		0.29722		0.34495				

4.7.3.2 Results from Stage II: Evaluation of TSAFE designs

Results from the evaluation of TSAFE architectural designs, according to the perspectives of the two architects (i.e. the local experts), is given as part of Table 4.4. Table 4.4 also contains the results of the consistency ratios ($CR_{e,z}$). The $CR_{e,z}$ is computed for each expert, using each comparison matrix developed for the design candidates with respect to each characteristic. In the last row of the table, we have the domain familiarity of each architect with respect to each of the design candidates. The $DF_{e,n}$ entries show that the architects claimed the same level of familiarity on all the design candidates, but their consistency ratio for each comparison would ensure the architects do not have the same influence on the overall modifiability result. In addition, Table 4.4 has a column named "Priorities of Design Characteristics". This column represents the overall priority vector shown in Table 4.3 which already unifies the design experts' evaluation of the relative contribution of each characteristic to modifiability. This overall priority vector would be used as a multiplicative factor of each of the priority matrices from the architects' evaluation of the design candidates.

Table 4.4: Evaluation of TSAFE Designs from the Perspectives of the 2 Architects

z	Design Characteristics	Architect-1 (e_1)					Architect-2 (e_2)					Priorities of Design Characteristics V(z)
		TSAFE I	TSAFE II	Target TSAFE	Consistency Ratio (CR)	1-CR	TSAFE I	TSAFE II	Target TSAFE	Consistency Ratio (CR)	1-CR	
1	Minimized coupling	0.0567	0.2946	0.6486	0.0701	0.9299	0.0548	0.3583	0.5869	0.0320	0.9680	0.2151
2	Maximized cohesion	0.0869	0.2737	0.6393	0.0466	0.9534	0.0548	0.3583	0.5869	0.0320	0.9680	0.1513
3	Maximized modularity	0.1111	0.4444	0.4444	0.0000	1.0000	0.0581	0.2299	0.7120	0.1453	0.8547	0.1271
4	Minimized concurrency and threads	0.3333	0.3333	0.3333	0.0000	1.0000	0.1250	0.1250	0.7500	0.0000	1.0000	0.1036
5	Proper information hiding (including interfaces)	0.1226	0.3202	0.5571	0.0158	0.9842	0.0543	0.3059	0.6399	0.0944	0.9056	0.1024
6	Appropriate use of design patterns and architectural styles	0.1096	0.3092	0.5813	0.0032	0.9968	0.0556	0.2424	0.7020	0.1867	0.8133	0.0858
7	Minimized coupling to COTS (including language)	0.3333	0.3333	0.3333	0.0000	1.0000	0.2500	0.2500	0.5000	0.0000	1.0000	0.0789
8	Proper documentation	0.2000	0.2000	0.6000	0.0000	1.0000	0.1111	0.1111	0.7778	0.0000	1.0000	0.0651
9	Use of proper and representative naming	0.0819	0.3431	0.5750	0.0251	0.9749	0.0577	0.3468	0.5955	0.0188	0.9812	0.0442
10	Minimized duplication	0.3333	0.3333	0.3333	0.0000	1.0000	0.0605	0.2009	0.7386	0.1460	0.8540	0.0266
	Domain Familiarity (DF)	8	8	8			8	8	8			

In Table 4.4, there are two Z x N priority matrices with each of the matrices representing the result from one architect. Every entry (z,n) in each priority matrix represents the relative modifiability of the architectural design candidate in column n with respect to the characteristic in row z. This priority matrix is described by Equation (4.3). For example, looking at the entries for "minimized coupling" in the first row for Architect-1, the architect evaluated the modifiability of TSAFE I as having a value of 0.0567 compared to the modifiability of TSAFE II that stands at 0.2946, and that of Target-TSAFE which is 0.6486.

These modifiability values have been evaluated with respect to the way in which the architectural design candidates handle "minimized coupling" from the perspective of Architect-1. But what do the numbers really mean? In a simple term, suppose Architect-1 is given 100 points to distribute among the three candidates based on the way the candidates handled coupling, TSAFE I would receive 5.67% while TSAFE II and Target-TSAFE would receive 29.46% and 64.86% respectively. Therefore, TSAFE II is a major improvement over TSAFE I and it is more modifiable than TSAFE I in terms of reduced coupling. Notwithstanding the improved modifiability of TSAFE II, it is still far from the Target TSAFE design in terms of minimizing coupling in the architecture. This implies that Architect-I knows that the coupling would still need to be reduced considerably in order to achieve the target coupling level envisaged for the Target-TSAFE. For example, suppose we have client/server architecture and TSAFE II implements it in such a way that there are bi-directional calls between the server and the client components, but the target is to have just the client call the server for services rather than allowing bi-directional calls. Then, it would be necessary to reduce the coupling in TSAFE II by a factor of 2 in order to attain the objectives defined for Target TSAFE. This interpretation is straightforward because the values derived by the architect for each of the candidates evaluated are relative to one another. Similar interpretation applies to all the other entries in the two priority matrices.

4.7.3.3 Results from Stage III: Overall Modifiability of TSAFE designs

To aggregate the views of the architects, as reflected in Table 4.4, we combine the priority matrices, the priority of design characteristics, the consistency ratios, and the domain familiarity using Equation (4.6). Instead of giving the raw values as matrices and vectors, we present the results as figures to ease understanding. Figure 4.5 shows the aggregated result that represents the relative modifiability of each candidate with respect to each architectural design characteristic. Figure 4.5 generally shows that TSAFE II constitutes a major improvement over TSAFE I across all the design characteristics, but TSAFE II still falls short of the specification envisaged for the Target TSAFE. This evaluation does not end only in the design comparisons, as it also allows us to know what characteristics of the design to focus on when making refactoring or redesign decisions.

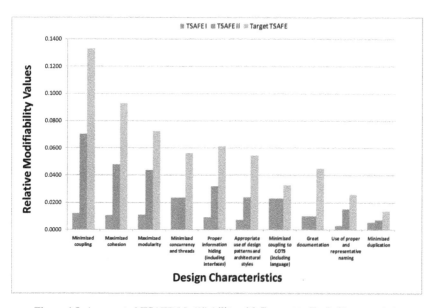

Figure 4.5: Aggregated TSAFE Modifiability with Respect to Each Characteristic

Looking at the first characteristic (i.e. minimized coupling) in Figure 4.5, for example, TSAFE II has achieved a major improvement over TSAFE I, but it is still far from achieving the target design in terms of coupling. But looking at the 4th characteristic (i.e. minimized concurrency and threads) TSAFE II is not any better than TSAFE I based on the evaluation of both architects. In addition, the two TSAFE design versions are not yet close to the Target-TSAFE design in terms of their use of minimized concurrency and threads. The two TSAFE versions are also not better than each other in terms of documentation and coupling to COTS.

Figure 4.6 shows the final overall modifiability values that are computed from the fine-grained values given in Figure 4.5, using Equation (4.7). The figure gives a more coarse-grained evaluation that allows us to easily rank the architectural designs and make decisions about which design is more modifiable overall, without looking at each design characteristic. This is more useful when we only have to choose from a set of candidate designs, regardless of the fine-grained information on the design characteristics.

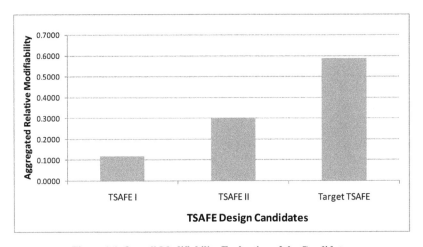

Figure 4.6: Overall Modifiability Evaluation of the Candidates

The radar diagram in Figure 4.7 is the transformation of the aggregated modifiability result shown in Figure 4.5 into its idealized form, as discussed in Section 4.6.2.2. The Target TSAFE now represents the current goal, which is to attain a level 1 (i.e. 100%) on all design characteristics. The results shown in the radar diagram is useful for road mapping, since it is possible to determine how far we are from the goals specified for the target design. In Figure 4.7, the target architectural design (Target-TSAFE) is used as a reference. For instance, the radar diagram shows TSAFE II to be in the mid-way to achieving the specified goal in terms of maximized cohesion. Coupling to COTS is the design characteristic for which the current versions of the architectural designs have made the most improvement in terms of modifiability. Conversely, there is still no proper documentation available for TSAFE II. Documentation remains the characteristic for which the current design is farthest from reaching the target design goals.

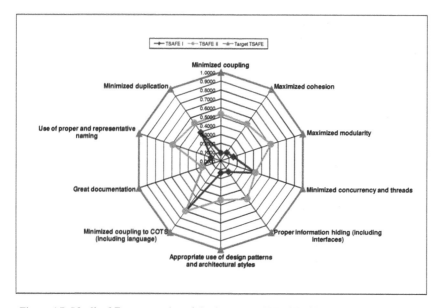

Figure 4.7: Idealized Representation of the Aggregated Modifiability with Respect to Each Characteristic

4.8 Empirical Validation of the Results from Expert Judgment

The goal of this empirical validation is to verify the efficacy of EBEAM in assisting the experts to correctly articulate their knowledge of architectural designs. We defined and selected some architectural design metrics, collected data on the design candidates in terms of the metrics, and compared the results with the results from expert judgment. This empirical validation study was conducted in Fall 2007; about 3 months after the case study in which the experts articulated their knowledge of the architectural designs using EBEAM and results collected. This implies that the results from design metrics were not available during the case study discussed above, thereby reducing the possibility of the metrics results introducing bias into the judgments of the experts.

4.8.1 Defining and selecting the objective metrics

Several design metrics have been discussed in the literature. For objective metrics collection, we chose a subset of the design characteristics discussed in Section 4.4.1. We only chose a subset of the characteristics, because it is not possible to define objective metrics on most of the characteristics. Since we only need the objective metrics for validation purposes, it is not even necessary to define metrics on all the characteristics. The design characteristics we have chosen include coupling, duplication, and information hiding/interfaces. These metrics can be computed from the unified modeling language (UML) models, except for measure of duplication that requires specialized tools. In the sequel, we discuss the metrics we have defined and those we have selected for use in this study.

4.8.1.1 Coupling metrics

Although there are many existing coupling metrics [18], we focus on defining metrics that can easily be captured at both coarse-grained and fine-grained levels. The two coupling metrics provided here are based on measuring the relationship between elements that belong to different components/modules of a software system. It should be noted that we use the terms module and component interchangeably.

1.   High-Level System Coupling Metric

This metric is aimed at capturing the number of calls that exist between all the components of the architectural design of a system. The metric does not consider the individual classes in the components. The purpose is to have a high-level view of the number of components as well as the number of relationships that exist among them. The system coupling metric (SCM) is measured as a count of the number of directional inter-component references. We do not ignore the direction of the arrows because we want to capture the number of components as well as the different calls that exist.

From the UML model of TSAFE I in Figure A.1 (see Appendix A), we compute the SCM(TSAFE I) = 9, while UML model in Figure A.2 (Appendix A) gives SCM(TSAFE II) = 4. These values are computed by adding all the arrows in each UML model. For example, we have just three components in TSAFE II, but the Client and the Server components are involved in bi-directional calls for services. These coupling measures do not include the number of coupling to libraries. The lower the value of SCM the easier to modify the corresponding architectural design candidate is assumed to be, and vice versa. According to the results here, TSAFE II is more modifiable than TSAFE I.

2.   Fan-in/Fan-out metric

The Fan-in/Fan-out coupling metric proposed by Henry and Kafura [70] is a directional measure of coupling. The fan-in/fan-out captures the inbound and outbound relationship to and from the elements in a component. Given a component C, the fan-in is the number of components that call it and the number of global data elements (or libraries) from which C retrieves information. The fan-out for a component C is the number of components called by C, including the number of data elements (or libraries) that C alters.

The results of the fan-in/fan-out metrics for each component of TSAFE I and TSAFE II as computed from the low level views captured in Figure A.3 and Figure A.4 (see Appendix A) are given in Table 4.5. The lower the value of fan-in/fan-out the easier it is to modify the components as well as the corresponding architectural design of the system, and vice versa.

Table 4.5: Coupling Measures for TSAFE I & TSAFE II

TSAFE I				TSAFE II		
Components	Fan-in	Fan-out		Components	Fan-in	Fan-out
Main	0	10		Main	0	5
Client	1	6		Client	3	2
Engine	12	0		Server	5	1
Database	10	0				
Feed	4	11				

4.8.1.2 Interfaces metrics

We define two metrics for interfaces. The first metric is the number of interfaces (NOI) which counts the number of classes from different components that directly assess classes in a particular component C. The second metric is the classes calling interfaces (CCI) which is a count of the classes in a component that directly assess the classes in other components. The NOI and CCI calculation for each component C and the sum for the entire system for TSAFE I and TSAFE II appear in Table 4.6. The interface metrics was computed from the low level views of the UML models of the architectural design shown in Figure A.3 and Figure A.4 (Appendix A) for TSAFE I and TSAFE II respectively.

We compute the NOI metric for each component of both TSAFE I and TSAFE II. Suppose we consider the *Main* component of TSAFE I and that of TSAFE II, these two *Main* components do not receive any direct call from any class outside of it. Thus the NOI for the *Main* component of TSAFE I is 0 and that of TSAFE II is 0. We also compute the NOI for the rest of the components; the results appear in Table 4.6. We can see in Table 4.6, that the NOI(TSAFE I) = 10 and NOI(TSAFE II) = 5, respectively.

Table 4.6: Interfaces Measures for TSAFE I & TSAFE II

TSAFE I			TSAFE II		
Components	Number of Interfaces (NOI)	Classes Calling Interfaces (CCI)	Components	Number of Interfaces (NOI)	Classes Calling Interfaces (CCI)
Main	0	6	Main	0	1
Client	1	2	Client	2	2
Engine	5	0	Server	3	1
Database	1	0	**Total**	**5**	**4**
Feed	3	6			
Total	**10**	**14**			

In addition, we compute the CCI for both TSAFE I and TSAFE II. The results of the CCI also appear in Table 4.6. For example, if we look at the *Main* component in TSAFE I architectural design model in Figure A.3, we can see that 6 classes in the *Main* component call several other classes in the other components. On the other hand, the *Main* component of TSAFE II architectural design has only 1 class that issues calls to classes in the other components. The goal is always to try to minimize the total number of these calls in a system. For example, instead of 6 classes in the *Main* component directly accessing data from the classes in the other components of the system, it is better to provide one interface through which these communications can take place. Table 4.6 contains this measure for all the components in the system, where the total for all the components of TSAFE I is given as CCI(TSAFE I) = 14, and that of TSAFE II is given as CCI(TSAFE II) = 4.

The lower the total number of interfaces computed for an architectural design candidate, the easier it would be to modify the architectural design, and vice versa. Thus, TSAFE II is generally assumed to be more modifiable than TSAFE I according to the results.

4.8.1.3 Duplication

The tool we used to measure duplication in the code implementation of TSAFE I and TSAFE II is the Simian UI tool [146]. The Simian UI is a tool for finding and removing duplicated regions of code from within the Eclipse IDE. The measure is based on blocks that include more than 6 lines of code. For this measure, the result is that TSAFE I and TSAFE II contain the same amount of duplicated regions, namely 1321 blocks each.

4.8.2 Expert-judgment using EBEAM on selected design characteristics

Since we focused on defining metrics for 3 characteristics, it is important that we also choose the same 3 characteristics from the expert judgment evaluation using EBEAM.

The good thing about EBEAM is that, we can easily extract the judgment of the experts on a subset of the design characteristics, without requiring the experts to perform the evaluation all over. Although, the relative values obtained for each of the characteristics would be different from what we have in the results discussed in the case study, because the relative comparison would be based on just 3 characteristics and not on all 10 characteristics considered earlier. The result of the evaluation by each of the architects is shown in Table 4.7, while an aggregated result is shown in Table 4.8. Table 4.8 compares TSAFE I to TSAFE II with respect to each characteristic from modifiability perspective. Table 4.8 also shows the final overall modifiability of the two architectural designs, with TSAFE I having a relative modifiability value of 0.1517 while the relative modifiability value of TSAFE II is 0.8483. The result clearly shows that the modifiability, measured in this way, is higher for TSAFE II than for TSAFE I.

Table 4.7: Evaluation of TSAFE I and TSAFE II Designs on 3 Characteristics

Z	Design Characteristics	Architect-1 (e_1)		Architect-1 (e_2)		Priorities of Design Characteristics V(z)
		TSAFE I	TSAFE II	TSAFE I	TSAFE II	
1	Minimized coupling	0.1250	0.8750	0.1111	0.8889	0.6519
2	Proper information hiding (including interfaces)	0.2500	0.7500	0.1111	0.8889	0.2704
3	Minimized duplication	0.5000	0.5000	0.1667	0.8333	0.0777
	Priority Vector	0.1879	0.8121	0.1154	0.8846	

Table 4.8: Aggregated TSAFE Evaluation from all Architects

Attributes	TSAFE I	TSAFE II
Minimized coupling	0.0770	0.5749
Proper information hiding including interfaces	0.0488	0.2216
Minimized duplication	0.0259	0.0518
Final Priority Vector	**0.1517**	**0.8483**

4.8.3 Comparing the objective and subjective measures on TSAFE architectural designs

It is important that we have a basis for comparing the results from design metrics to those obtained from expert judgment. There is no straightforward way to accomplish this, because the results from the objective metrics defined on different characteristics are not on the same scale or unit, for all 3 characteristics considered. We do not have this problem with EBEAM, however. Notwithstanding, we can define approximate mappings that would ease the comparison. Table 4.9 contains all the modifiability results computed using design metrics. The reader should note that we sum up the fan-in/fan-out for each of the TSAFE architectural designs, because we need to compare the architectural designs and not the components that make up the designs. Although Henry and Kafura [70] did not perform such additions in their work.

Because the results from EBEAM are normalized measures (i.e. between 0 and 1), comparison between results from expert judgment and the metrics would only make sense if we normalize the results from design metrics. The easiest way to do this is to find the ratio of each architectural design measure relative to the measures within its metric category.

Table 4.9: TSAFE Evaluation using Metrics

Metrics	TSAFE I	TSAFE II
System Coupling Metric	9	4
Fan-in/Fan-out	54	16
Number of Interfaces	10	5
Classes calling interfaces	14	4
Duplication	1321	1321

Thus, given two architectural designs with values A and B, we would compute their metric values m(A) and m(B) using the following formulae:

$$m(A) = 1 - \left(\frac{A}{(A+B)} \right) \tag{4.8}$$

$$m(B) = 1 - \left(\frac{B}{(A+B)} \right) \tag{4.9}$$

In Equations (4.8) and (4.9), we subtract from 1 in order to change the interpretation of the metric values such that higher values mean higher modifiability, and vice-versa for lower values. This is necessary to ensure that the interpretation of results obtained using design metrics is consistent with those results obtained from expert-judgment using EBEAM. Recall that, assigning higher values to an architectural design on a particular characteristic in EBEAM implies higher relative modifiability on that characteristic. On applying Equations (4.8) and (4.9) to the measures given in Table 4.9, we obtained the results given in Table 4.10.

Table 4.10: Normalized Metrics for TSAFE Evaluation

Metrics	TSAFE I	TSAFE II
System Coupling Metric	0.3077	0.6923
Fan-in/Fan-out	0.2286	0.7714
Number of Interfaces	0.3333	0.6667
Classes calling interfaces	0.2222	0.7778
Duplication	0.5000	0.5000

To compare the results from objective and subjective measures, we can choose any of the two coupling metrics and any of the two interfaces metrics in Table 4.10 to represent the objective metrics for these two characteristics (i.e. coupling and interfaces). This decision is justified, because the results from different metrics that measures the same characteristic produced correlated results. For example, both system coupling metric (SCM) and fan-in/fan-out consistently ranked TSAFE II as better than TSAFE I in terms of reduced coupling. Thus, whether we discuss results in terms of SCM or in terms of fan-in/fan-out is immaterial; the relative preference between the candidates in terms of coupling remains the same. The same argument applies to the measures derived from number of interfaces (NOI) and classes calling interfaces (CCI), as both measures agree in their ranking of the two design candidates.

Now, suppose we choose SCM and NOI as the representative metrics for coupling and interfaces, respectively. Figure 4.8 shows the bar charts of the results from metric-based approach. It is easy to deduce the relative modifiability of the two architectural design candidates with respect to each characteristic. Except for duplication measures in which the two architectural designs perform equally, TSAFE II is clearly better than TSAFE I.

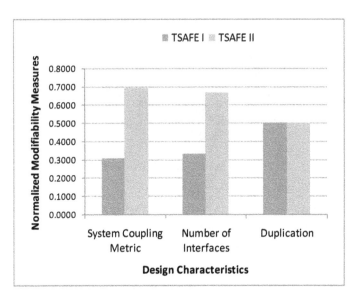

Figure 4.8: Metrics Results on TSAFE I and TSAFE II

Now, looking at the results from expert judgment using EBEAM (see Table 4.8), we see that the values for TSAFE I and TSAFE II fall between 0 and 1 for each characteristic. However, the modifiability values of the two architectural designs do not add to 1 for each characteristic, as we now have for the metrics results in Table 4.10. Thus, we need to apply Equations (4.8) and (4.9) to Table 4.8 without subtracting 1 from the results. The normalized results using the EBEAM are given in Table 4.11 with the corresponding bar chart in Figure 4.9.

Table 4.11: Normalized TSAFE Evaluation using EBEAM

Attributes	TSAFE I	TSAFE II
Minimized coupling	0.1181	0.8820
Proper information hiding (including interfaces)	0.1806	0.8195
Minimized duplication	0.3334	0.6667

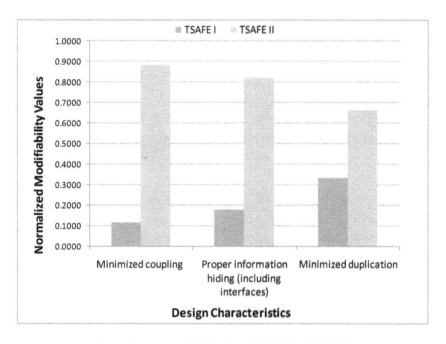

Figure 4.9: Results of EBEAM on TSAFE I and TSAFE II

The results shown for the metrics-based approach in Figure 4.8 and the results from EBEAM in Figure 4.9 are both consistent in their conclusions that TSAFE II is overall a superior architectural design candidate in terms of modifiability TSAFE I. Although the two figures reveal that we do not have perfect correlation in the exact values resulting from the two approaches in terms of each characteristic considered, but this should not be expected. The most important issue is whether EBEAM could assist expert in making consistent judgment that reflects reality. By consistently ranking the design candidates, EBEAM allows easy judgment between competing design candidates. Meanwhile, the difference in the conclusion drawn by expert assessment and design metrics with respect to duplication could be an indication of the limitation of human expert in coping with more fine-grained assessments. Especially, for a task as arduous as sifting through codes that implements a design to count duplicated entities, only a rough approximation could be expected from an expert, at the very best.

4.9 Applicability of the EBEAM Technique

Observations from the results obtained using both EBEAM and design metrics show that the two approaches are not competing, but rather complementary. Therefore, expert judgment can be employed to evaluate candidate architectures for characteristics that cannot be measured using metrics, and vice-versa. If there are no mechanisms to collect metrics, then expert judgment would suffice for evaluating all the architectural design characteristics. Especially, if all we have are high level architectural designs without the codes that implement the architectures, then it would be hard to even consider using some of the existing metrics. Example of this is the conceptual view of the target architectural design that we considered during the case study that we discuss in this chapter.

In fact, there are situations in which objective metrics exist for measuring specific characteristics, but such metrics may not be able to capture the detail meaning of the characteristics. If we consider characteristics like *use of proper and representative naming*, one could define a metric that uses the Thesaurus to check for appropriate naming. This type of metrics would only confirm the use of meaningful names, but it cannot measure whether such names are representative. During the case study presented earlier, the lead architect that worked on redesigning TSAFE I shared his experience on the use of representative naming. He discovered a particular component that was named "Feed" in TSAFE I, which took him several days to decipher what the component actually does. This component was later discovered to be a component that handles parsing tasks, which would have been easier to understand if named "Parser". The ease of modification of such component would be inhibited, because the naming convention is not representative of the tasks the component performs, even though the naming convention is meaningful. A metric would show the name "Feed" as proper because it is meaningful. It is only through expert judgment evaluation that we can establish whether the naming convention adopted across the architectural designs are representative. Closely related to this is the fact that we can easily determine whether documentation exists, but we cannot use metrics to determine how proper and useful the documentation is.

In concluding our discussions on EBEAM and the empirical studies presented, we summarize the benefits, limitations, and threats to validity of using the EBEAM for architectural design evaluation.

4.9.1 Benefits of EBEAM

The major benefit of the EBEAM technique presented in this chapter is that it does not just give a high level measure that simply identifies which architectural candidate is better than another. It also allows the architects to see which architectural characteristic needs to be re-examined in order to increase the modifiability of the candidate. It is not enough to say that an architecture restructuring has been performed and modifiability has been improved. It is important to know what aspects have been improved in the redesigned architecture. Thus, the results derived from EBEAM can serve as a pointer to what aspects of the existing architectural design require further improvement to increase modifiability.

Because of the flexibility and adaptability properties of EBEAM, the results from the Stage I (i.e. evaluating the contribution of characteristics to modifiability) can be updated with new knowledge and experience of new experts, whenever such become available. The new experts simply have to carry out their own evaluation, and the aggregated results are recomputed to accommodate the new knowledge.

There are several other benefits that would justify the use of EBEAM over design metrics. These benefits include the following:

- EBEAM is a generic modifiability evaluation technique that can be applied to any architectural design, regardless of the domain of the software system. Some metrics are not defined to be generic, and would work within certain programming paradigms only. For example, some metrics properties defined by Weyuker [159] have been found to be irrelevant to object-oriented design metrics, especially the structural metrics [6], [65]. There are hosts of other metrics that are targeted at only object-oriented designs, like those by Chidamber and Kemerer [26]. Metrics defined on datasets collected from a specific software product cannot always be generalized to other products, especially if the software products are from different domains.

- The results from EBEAM are based on ratio scale measures. The aggregation of the judgment of experts also retains ratio scale measures. The measures from EBEAM are also normalized relative measures that enable easy comparison of results. In the case of design metrics, however, raw measurements taken on different design characteristics would all be on different range of values and scales/units. Thus, it is not possible to aggregate these measures into a single measure in order to support decision making. And consequently, it complicates the comparison of different candidates using raw metric results [115]. Some metrics have been criticized in the literature because of the way the metrics assume measurement scale types [92] that contradict standard measurement practices [52],[92].

- EBEAM can easily be adopted and adapted to assess other architectural design attributes, even though we have developed it with modifiability as the focus. The experts only need to identify the characteristics that influence such attributes, and the nature of influence that each characteristic have on the attributes. Nevertheless, the evaluation process remains the same.

4.9.2 Limitations

We identified the following limitations of the EBEAM technique and threats to the experiments discussed in the case study:

- The EBEAM presents a repeatable evaluation process, but it does not guarantee that an expert will always give the same relative ranking to each characteristic and the architectural design candidates, if the expert is not consistent in his judgment. The consistency of an expert in making judgments depends on how focused the expert during the comparison procedures.

- We consider as an approximation the choice of design characteristics for evaluating modifiability. Modifiability would always be influenced by several other issues. But using this approximation for assessment would suffice for the task of comparing any two or more architectural design candidates.

- The EBEAM is a heavy-weight technique. Adopting EBEAM requires that software architects devote time to the process of articulating their knowledge.

- As part of EBEAM, experts are asked to rate their confidence level (CL) in making judgment on design characteristics and also their domain familiarity (DF) with the architectural design of the system being evaluated. Some experts may assign higher ratings for themselves on these two factors, even if they do not posses high CL or DF. This could happen if the experts do not want to reveal that they posses little knowledge of the design characteristics, and also little knowledge of the architectural design candidates. We cannot independently verify their ratings in this case, because it is difficult to ascertain that the ratings they give for CL and DF are consistently in sync with their levels of expertise.

4.10 Related Work

Most of the existing techniques for analyzing software architecture, which we have discussed in Chapter 2, are targeted at evaluating a single architecture [153]. These techniques are used to determine the suitability of architectural designs with respect to quality attributes of a system. The evaluation techniques could clarify whether a given architecture satisfies certain properties, but they do not directly result in criteria collation and analysis. EBEAM is useful for evaluating a single architecture from the perspective of a chosen quality attribute, and also useful for selecting among competing architectural design candidates.

While we require experts to answer questions about the goodness characteristics of architectural designs when making their judgments, the resulting judgments are transformed to measurable quantities to better support decision-making. Therefore, EBEAM is a bridge between measuring and questioning techniques (see Chapter 2 for a discussion of these techniques). By combining both measurement based approach and questioning based approach, we take advantage of the benefits that each approach has to offer. Each architectural design candidate can be compared based on quantitative results generated with respect to different design characteristics considered. Of all the existing techniques, the closest to EBEAM is the architecture evaluation technique proposed by Svahnberg et al. [153]. In contrast to our work, Svahnberg and his colleagues simply focused on comparing candidate architectures based on the presence of competing quality attributes. Their technique is mostly useful for early architectural design evaluation, and they do not support fine-grained evaluation based on selected characteristics. The EBEAM presented in this chapter is more general, because it can be used during both early and late phases of architectural designs.

4.11 Summary

In this chapter, we discussed an expert judgment-based technique (i.e. EBEAM) for evaluating the modifiability of software architectural designs. We have also reported a case study that uses EBEAM to evaluate the architectural designs of the prototype system for NASA flight assistance known as TSAFE (Tactical Separation Assisted Flight Environment). The architectural designs of TSAFE that were evaluated include the initial prototype, a redesigned version, and the target design. To validate the results obtained from EBEAM, we defined a set of design metrics, evaluated the modifiability of the architectural designs of TSAFE using these metrics, and compared the results. Both EBEAM and the metrics show correlation in their results.

The EBEAM is a three-stage evaluation technique that can be performed independently, depending on the relevance of the knowledge that a participating expert has at that stage of the evaluation process. The three-stage formulation of the technique ensures that, the bias of individual experts in the first stage of the assessment would not be propagated down to the subsequent stages of the evaluation process. While we acknowledge that the bias of the experts cannot be completely eliminated, reducing the bias is an initial attempt. We can only verify the extent to which bias influences results after an extensive longitudinal study involving the application of EBEAM to different projects, and also in different development environments.

In developing EBEAM, we have also proposed a new weighting scheme to assign importance to experts. The weighting scheme considers the consistency with which the experts make their judgments about the characteristics or the architectural candidates being compared. Our empirical study did not reveal how much influence the inclusion of the consistency of judgment exerts on the final results, because the consistency ratio of the experts that participated in the study at FC-MD was close. But this is not expected to be the case all of the time, because varying degrees of inconsistency could occur, especially when there are more experts involved.

The contributions of EBEAM that we have proposed in this chapter include:

1. Proposing architectural design evaluation technique (i.e. EBEAM) that assists experts in articulating their knowledge and experience, and transforming these into quantifiable results.

2. Combining measurement based approach with questioning based approach in EBEAM, thereby taking advantage of the benefits that each approach has to offer.

3. Conducting exploratory study involving detailed analyses of design characteristics that influence the modifiability of software architectural designs.

4. Describing the way EBEAM can be adopted for making architectural comparison and selection decisions.

5. Demonstrating the applicability of EBEAM in a case study using a prototype of the Tactical Separation Assisted Flight Environment (TSAFE) system defined by the NASA Ames Research Center [49] and implemented in [40].

6. Evaluating the correlation between the results obtained from expert judgment using EBEAM and the results from design metrics.

CHAPTER FIVE

FEATURE COUPLING VIA IMPACT ANALYSIS AND
THE IMPLICATIONS FOR RELEASE PLANNING

*Build for your team a feeling of oneness, of dependence on one another
and of strength to be derived by unity.*
- Vince Lombardi

5.1 Introduction

In this chapter, we discuss feature interdependency[**] that results from the overlap in the components that would implement features. The components that would implement the features are derived from change impact analysis. We discuss the integration of the results from feature coupling into a release planning strategy that encourages the assignment of features with maximal interrelatedness in the same release. This helps to avoid haphazard implementation of interrelated features. We present a release planning model that formulates the release planning problem as a bi-objective optimization problem. The model is aimed at optimizing the value of release plans from both business and technical perspectives. The work discussed in this chapter is partly based on the assumption that, if two features are highly interrelated, then it indicates the existence of coupling between the two features.

The questions addressed in this chapter are the following:

1. How do we detect and quantify the interrelatedness of features based on the overlaps in their implementation?

[**] Note: The interrelatedness of features, as defined in Chapter 1, is a form of interdependency that we refer to as solution domain interdependency (or feature coupling) in this chapter. Because it was too early to introduce these technical terms in Chapter 1, where they cannot be discussed in details, we defined interrelatedness in lieu. Henceforth, we use feature coupling (SD-coupling) or feature interdependency in solution domain interchangeably to mean the same thing as interrelatedness of features.

2. How do we employ the interrelatedness of features together with other planning parameters in order to make release planning decisions?

The main motivation for this chapter is the importance of maximizing the interrelatedness of the features assigned to the same release. In order to facilitate reuse and save on development resources, software developers would rather have features that share common implementation components assigned to the same release. By implementing such features together, developers may be able to implement several features more quickly. This is due to the reduced cognitive effort required to understand the implementation of the individual features, if they were to be implemented differently in different releases. Also, by implementing these features together it may be possible to avoid or at least reduce the negative effects of unplanned dependency (as discussed by Giroux and Robillard [59]), and to reduce implementation effort.

5.2 Classification of Feature Interdependency

The functionalities provided by a software system are derived from the domain of the problem through collection of new features or change requests or both. The users of a software system are primarily interested in the functionalities that the system offers. Software developers, on the other hand, examine features and change requests in terms of the development activities that are required to implement the features. Thus, the developers are responsible for exploring different solution possibilities in the solution space. We would refer to these two views as the perspectives of features of a software system in the *problem domain* and the *solution domain* respectively.

Given the two views above, it is expected that interdependencies between the features would exist in both domains. This is the case because features are merely the sets of requirements in the problem domain, while the implementation of features is their realization in the solution domain [63],[155]. Turner's research in feature engineering [155] observed that features interact in the problem domain because they share requirements or depend on each other for services, but interact in the solution domain because they share subsystems, modules, and so on [156]. This implies that interdependencies between features may be related to functionality or runtime-behavior of the system in the problem domain, while interdependencies between features in the solution domain are implementation-related. Functionality-related interdependency can be extracted from the description of the features in the requirements specification, while runtime-behavior-related interdependency can be detected during actual usage of a system or through scenarios describing usage patterns. On the other hand, solution domain interdependency refers to the implementation-related interdependency discovered during impact analysis and within the system design or code.

In Figure 5.1, we categorize interdependencies as either emanating from problem domain or solution domain, depending on the stage of the development process in which the interdependencies are discovered. Figure 5.1 is a high-level development or change management process. In the Figure 5.1, *requirements specification* contains the set of features and change requests, *impact analysis* identifies the components that would need to be modified in the existing system for each feature to be implemented, *release planning* assigns the features into different releases, *design & implementation* encompasses both development and testing activities, while *usage of the deployed system* refers to user interaction with the product.

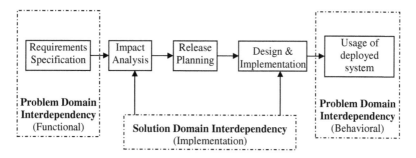

Figure 5.1: Overview of Feature Interdependency Classification

There are other more fine-grained classification schemes for requirements interdependencies in the literature [24], [34]. These classification schemes have so far not made any connection between interdependencies and the domain in which they exist. Besides, none of these classification schemes have investigated implementation-related interdependencies between features via change impact analysis. In a recent study by Zhang et al. [168], it was observed that most of the existing requirement interdependency approaches do not focus on the solution domain, as their views are essentially limited to the requirements phase of software development. Thus, there are still unanswered questions as to the nature of the roles played by requirements interdependencies in the solution domain [168]. Zhang et al. [168] states that, *"...if this question of interdependency in solution domain is not explicitly focused, we can never get a complete view of how requirement dependencies influence the whole process of software development."*

5.3 Feature Coupling via Change Impact Analysis

5.3.1 The Impact of Features on the Components of a System

Impact analysis is the process involved in identifying the entities or elements of an existing software system that will be affected by a change – or the activity of identifying the possible consequences of a change – before the actual change is made [7],[125]. These elements/entities of the existing system are the components that make up the system.

In most cases, implementation of a feature would require modification of one or more components. Even when we identify only one component as the impacted component, such components might interact with other components that would also have to be modified. We refer to feature-driven impact analysis (FDIA) as the process of identifying the component(s) of the existing system that would need to be modified directly or indirectly in order to implement each new or changed feature. Sometime the code that implements a feature may even be found in components that ordinarily seem to be unrelated to each other [164].

The input to the FDIA process is a set of features to be implemented together with the existing system to be modified [105]. The process of performing FDIA correctly has been found to largely depend on experience with the system and the change activities to be performed [105]. The technique we propose for determining solution domain coupling (or simply SD-coupling) is independent of the level of granularity at which components are defined. This ensures the scalability of the technique. The only constraint imposed is that the same granularity level of components must be defined across any given software project.

DEFINITION 5.1 (COMPONENTS)

Given an existing software system S and a set C of M components $C = \{c_1, c_2, \ldots, c_M\}$, the components $c_m \in C$ $(1 \leq m \leq M)$ of the system are the elements that constitute the building blocks of S. These components may be expressed in the form of subsystems, classes, methods, procedure, or files. □

DEFINITION 5.2 (SET OF IMPACTED COMPONENTS)

Given a set F of n features $F = \{f_1, f_2, \ldots, f_n\}$, the set of impacted components for a feature f_i $(1 \leq i \leq n)$ is the set of components $\Phi_i \subseteq C$ that would be modified when adding feature f_i in system S. □

The set of impacted components are derived via impact analysis of each feature on the components of the existing system. Since the components to be modified are associated with the features, we can infer the existence of SD-coupling between the features using the overlap in their set of impacted components. This inference is based on the assumption that there is a connection between the overlap of components and feature coupling. Precisely, given any two features f_i and f_j with corresponding sets of impacted components Φ_i and Φ_j respectively, the two features are SD-coupled if the intersection of Φ_i and Φ_j is non-empty.

5.3.2 Some Concepts from Hypergraph Theory

We adopt concepts from hypergraph theory to model the SD-coupling between features. Hypergraphs are generalizations of the usual graphs in the sense that edges are defined for subsets of vertices. Hypergraph theory offers supportive visualization and representation capabilities. We briefly discuss some useful concepts from hypergraph theory.

A hypergraph H(X, ξ) consists of a set of *vertices* or *nodes* X and a set of *hyperedges* ξ. Each hyperedge is a subset of X. We adopt our definitions of hypergraph concepts and its operations from [15] and [36].

DEFINITION 5.3 (HYPERGRAPH)

Let $X = \{x_1, x_2, \ldots, x_n\}$ *be a finite set of vertices, and let* $\xi = (\Phi_i \mid i \in I \text{ and } |\xi| = n)$ *be a family of non-empty subsets of X with*

$$\bigcup_{i \in I} \Phi_i = X \tag{5.1}$$

Then, H(X, ξ) is called a hypergraph. $\square$

To illustrate the concept of a hypergraph, we consider a sample set of four features f_1, f_2, f_3, f_4, where each feature respectively impacts the following sets of components of a given system:

$$\Phi_1 = \{c1, c3, c5, c7\},$$
$$\Phi_2 = \{c1, c3, c5\},$$
$$\Phi_3 = \{c1, c2\}, \text{ and}$$
$$\Phi_4 = \{c4, c6, c7\}.$$

For this example, the vertices are $X = C = \{c1, c2, c3, c4, c5, c6, c7\}$, and the collection of hyperedges are the impacted sets of components $\xi = (\Phi_1, \Phi_2, \Phi_3, \Phi_4)$. The corresponding hypergraph is represented in Figure 5.2.

Hypergraph of impacted components

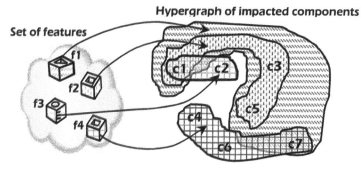

Figure 5.2: Mapping of Features to the Impacted Components in a Hypergraph $H(X, \xi)$

DEFINITION 5.4 (ADJACENT HYPEREDGES)
Two hyperedges are adjacent (denoted as $\Phi_x \in adj(\Phi_y)$) if their intersection is non-empty. □

In the example above, Φ_2 is adjacent to Φ_3 (denoted as $\Phi_2 \in adj(\Phi_3)$), but Φ_3 and Φ_4 are not adjacent hyperedges (i.e. $\Phi_4 \notin adj(\Phi_3)$).

DEFINITION 5.5 (2ND ORDER DEGREE OF A HYPEREDGE)
For any hypergraph $H(X, \xi)$, the 2nd order degree (d_2) of a hyperedge is the number of other hyperedges that it has at least one vertex in common with. □

In the example above, $d_2(\Phi_1) = 3$, $d_2(\Phi_2) = 2$, $d_2(\Phi_3) = 2$, $d_2(\Phi_4) = 1$.

5.3.3 Solution Domain Coupling (SD-coupling)

In order to compute the SD-coupling between features, the set of components that each feature impacts in the existing system must be determined. Determining the set of impacted components is a pre-processing step that is not part of our algorithms for SD-coupling. Dependency analysis tools [68], [158] or expert judgment-based techniques [103] could provide the set of impacted components. Dependency analysis tools are able to identify impacted components at more fine-grained levels, though. In the sequel, we define concepts employed in our models and algorithms for computing SD-coupling between features.

DEFINITION 5.6 (SET OF COMMON COMPONENTS)
Given a pair of features f_i and f_j with their corresponding sets of impacted components Φ_i and Φ_j, the set of common components between the two features (denoted $\Omega(i,j)$) is the collection of components that appear in the intersection of the two adjacent hyperedges Φ_i and Φ_j in the hypergraph. □

DEFINITION 5.7 (SD-COUPLING)
Given a pair of features f_i and f_j with corresponding sets of impacted components Φ_i and Φ_j, we say there is SD-coupling between the features if there exists an overlap in their sets of impacted components. That is, $\Phi_i \in adj(\Phi_j)$. □

DEFINITION 5.8 (SD-COUPLING MATRIX / FEATURE COUPLING MATRIX)
Given a collection of features $f_i \in F\,(1 \leq i \leq n)$ and their corresponding impacted components sets $\Phi_i \in \xi$, the SD-coupling matrix (feature coupling matrix) is a matrix of size $|F|$ x $|F|$ where $\Omega(i,j) = \Phi_i \cap \Phi_j$ if $\Phi_i \in adj(\Phi_j)$ and $\emptyset$ otherwise. □

Note that, $|F|$ in Definition 5.8 is the cardinality of the set F. The SD-coupling matrix contains all the sets of common components (i.e. $\Omega(i,j)$) between every pair of hyperedges in the hypergraph. The computation of the feature coupling matrix can be achieved using any of the existing algorithms for computing set intersections (e.g. [166]). The intersection algorithm takes collections of hyperedges as input and applies the adjacency operation $\Phi_i \in adj(\Phi_j)$ to obtain the SD-coupling matrix. Since the adjacency operation is commutative, that is $\Phi_2 \in adj(\Phi_5) = \Phi_5 \in adj(\Phi_2)$, we only need to fill up the upper or lower triangular matrix.

5.3.4 Strength of SD-coupling

A feature could share impacted components with one or more other features, but the number of such shared components would vary. The strength of SD-coupling between any pair of features refers to the degree of coupling that exists between the two features. We propose a metric for measuring the *Strength of SD-coupling* as follows.

DEFINITION 5.9 (STRENGTH OF SD-COUPLING)

Given a pair of features f_i and f_j with corresponding sets of impacted components Φ_i and Φ_j. Suppose $\Omega(i,j)$ is the set of common components between Φ_i and Φ_j, we define the strength of SD-coupling between f_i and f_j as:

$$\theta(i, j) = \frac{|\Omega(i, j)| \cdot \left(|\Phi_i| + |\Phi_j| \right)}{2 \left(|\Phi_i| \cdot |\Phi_j| \right)} \tag{5.2}$$

where $(0 \leq \theta(i, j) \leq 1)$. □

Equation (5.2) is based on the cardinality of the set of common components, and the cardinalities of the set of impacted components for each of the pair of features being evaluated. This metric is normalized to allow for meaningful comparisons. The higher the strength of SD-coupling, the more the two features are assumed to be interrelated. A perfect coupling exists between a pair of features if and only if the two features are realized by exactly the same set of components in the existing system. If this is the case, then we have $\theta(i,j) = 1$.

Algorithm 5.1 describes the procedure for calculating the *Strength of SD-coupling* between every pair of features. This algorithm issues a call to any algorithm that computes intersection of sets to generate the SD-coupling matrix. Then, it computes the ratio of the number of common components shared by any two features relative to the number of components required to implement each of both features respectively. The premise of these ratios is that, even if a pair of features f_i and f_j has the same number of common components as another pair of features f_x and f_y, the two different pairs should not necessarily have the same *Strength of SD-coupling*. That is, given that $|\Omega(i,j)| = |\Omega(x,y)|$ should not necessarily translate to $\theta(i,j) = \theta(x,y)$, because it is possible that $(|\Phi_i|, |\Phi_j|) \neq (|\Phi_x|, |\Phi_y|)$.

Algorithm 5.1: Coupling Strength
Input: A set of features F and a collection of hyperedges $\Phi_i \in \xi, \Phi$ and the SD-coupling matrix
Output: Strength of SD-coupling $\theta(i, j)$ between pair of features.

1. **Begin**
2. $\Omega(i, j) =$ ADJACENCY_ELEMENTS $(\Phi_1, \Phi_2,....,\Phi_n)$
3.   **For** i = 1 to n-1
4.   k = i + 1
5.   **For** j = k to n
6.   RCI=$\left|\Omega(i,j)\right|/\left|\Phi_i\right|$ /*Relative changes to f_i (RCI)*/
7.   RCJ=$\left|\Omega(i,j)\right|/\left|\Phi_j\right|$ /*Relative changes to f_j (RCJ)*/
8. $\theta(i, j) =$ (RCI + RCJ)/2
9.   **EndFor**
10.   **EndFor**
11. **Return** $\theta(i, j)$
12. **End**

5.3.5 Properties of the Strength of SD-coupling

We discuss the properties that characterize our measure of strength of SD-coupling. We derived our properties by analogy to the mathematical framework for software engineering measurements by Briand et al. [19], and ensuring that it adheres to the theoretical validation framework for software measurement developed by Kitchenham and Pfleeger [91].

5.3.5.1 Property 1: Nonnegativity.

According to our definition, the strength of coupling between a pair of features cannot be negative. Any pair of features would either share common components or not. That is,

$$\theta(i, j) \geq 0$$

5.3.5.2 Property 2: Null value.

The strength of SD-coupling between any pair of features is null, if the features do not share common components (i.e. their hyperedges are not adjacent).

$$\Omega(i, j) = \varnothing \implies \theta(i, j) = 0$$

5.3.5.3 Property 3: Symmetry.

The normalized strength of SD-coupling between a given pair of features is independent of the order of the index used to represent the coupling relationship between them.

$$\Omega(i, j) = \Omega(j, i)$$
$$\implies \theta(i, j) = \theta(j, i)$$

5.3.5.4 Property 4: Equality.

It is possible to have the same normalized strength of SD-coupling measures for distinct pairs of features, even when the number of common components is different. That is, given features $i_1, j_1, i_2, j_2, (i_1 \neq i_2; j_1 \neq j_2)$, it is possible to have:

$$\theta(i_1, j_1) = \theta(i_2, j_2)$$

This property holds, even if $\Omega(i_1, j_1) \neq \Omega(i_2, j_2)$.

5.3.6 System Value for Features

We assign a system value sv(i) to each feature f_i based on the number of other features with which the feature shares impacted components. It is desirable to implement the highest system-valued features in early releases, because they have the highest potential implementation synergy with other features. This is based on the assumption that implementing features that a share high number of implementation components together would avoid haphazard implementation of related features, just as it would help component reuse and invariably lowers development effort.

DEFINITION 5.10 (SYSTEM VALUE OF A FEATURE)

Let f_i be a feature and $adj(\Phi_j)$ be the set of adjacent hyperedges to Φ_i. Then the system value of a feature f_i is defined as:

$$sv(i) = \sum_{j:\Phi_j \in adj(\Phi_i)} \theta(i, j) \qquad (5.3)$$

□

Algorithm 5.2 realizes the computation of sv(i) for all features. The condition $|\Omega(i,j)| > 0$ in the algorithm ensures that the two hyperedges representing features f_i and f_j must be adjacent in order for their intersection to count as part of the d_2.

Algorithm 5.2: System Value
Input: Strength of SD-coupling θ(i,j) and set of elements in adjacent hyperedges
Output: System-value sv(i) for all features.

1. **Begin**
2.   **For** i = 1 to n
3.   sv(i) = 0
4.   **For** j = 1 to n
5.   **If** ($|\Omega(i, j)| > 0$ **and** $i \neq j$) **Then** /* $\Phi_j \in adj(\Phi_i)$ */
6.   sv(i) = sv(i) + θ(i, j) /* Sum sv(i) over $d_2(\Phi_i)$ */
7.   **EndIf**
8.   **EndFor**
9.   **EndFor**
10. **Return** sv(i)
11. **End**

5.4 Feature Interrelatedness and Release Planning Implications

5.4.1 Overview

We consider a model that focuses the prioritization scheme on the values of features from both business and technical perspectives. Recall that the business perspective captures the views of the business stakeholders, while the technical perspective captures the implementation concerns. In order to address these two concerns at the same time, it is pertinent to consider tradeoffs between them, so as to find the best assignment of features into releases. It may not be possible to achieve the best result from both perspectives, because an increase in the value from one perspective could lead to a decrease in value from the other perspective. Handling this type of tradeoff analysis between two perspectives can be addressed by using bi-objective optimization models [117]. Before discussing the model, we first present the main constituents of the release planning model. The release planning model encompasses three key aspects: 1) the decision variables, 2) the constraints, and 3) the objectives of planning. We discuss all these constituents and the corresponding model in the sequel.

5.4.2 Release Planning Model

5.4.2.1 Decision Variables

Given a set of features $F = \{f_1, f_2, \ldots, f_n\}$. The goal of release planning is to assign the features to a finite number K of releases, while postponing features that cannot be accommodated. A release plan is characterized by a vector of binary decision variables x = (x(1), x(2), …, x(n)) such that,

$$x(i) = k \quad \text{if feature } f_i \text{ is assigned to release k} \in \text{K} \tag{5.4}$$

$$x(i) = K + 1 \quad \text{if feature } f_i \text{ is postponed} \tag{5.5}$$

5.4.2.2 Constraints

Constraints are the conditions that all features in a release plan must satisfy. These constraints could be related to resources, budget, interdependencies between features, or technical constraints. The resources required for the implementation of features refer to any input to the software production process. Suppose there are T different types of resources, then each feature f_i requires an amount $r(i,t)$ of resource $t \in T$, and there is a maximum amount of all resources $t \in T$ available for each release k. This available maximum per release is denoted $r_{max}(k,t)$. For a plan to be feasible, the resource usage for all features assigned to release k must satisfy:

$$\sum_{i:x(i)=k} r(i,t) \leq r_{max}(k,t) \ \forall \ k \in K \ and \ t \in T \tag{5.6}$$

Another dimension of constraints is the precedence between features. Two features f_i and f_j are said to be in precedence relation P (i.e. $(i, j) \in P$), if feature f_i must be released not later than feature f_j in that order. That is,

$$x(i) \leq x(j) \quad \forall \ (i, j) \in P \tag{5.7}$$

Also, the problem domain coupling (i.e. PD-coupling) specified by the project manager requires the features to be released jointly. The PD-coupling relation C (i.e. $(i, j) \in C$) is defined as:

$$x(i) = x(j) \quad \forall \ (i, j) \in C \tag{5.8}$$

5.4.2.3 Objectives of planning

Different factors contribute to the objectives of release planning. We consider two perspectives in defining the objectives of planning: 1) business perspective and 2) technical perspective.

1. Objective of Planning: The Business Perspective

In consonance with the views presented by Ruhe and Ngo-The [133], we compute the business value of feature f_i, denoted $bv(i)$, using an additive function. The additive function is defined such that, the total value of a feature is a weighted sum of the priorities assigned to the feature by all the stakeholders. The weight is based on the relative importance attached to each stakeholder s_h (where $1 \leq h \leq p$, recalling from Chapter 3 that there is a set Q of p stakeholders). Also, the stakeholders evaluate the features and assign priorities to each feature based on *value* of the feature. The value of a feature is assumed to be defined on a nine-point scale, for simplicity reasons[††]. That is, the value assigned by stakeholder s_h to feature f_i is defined such that, $v_{i,h} \in \{1,9\}$, where $v_{i,h} = 1$ means *lowest value* and $v_{i,h} = 9$ means *highest value*.

Based on these assumptions, the total business value of a feature f_i from the perspectives of all the stakeholders is computed as:

$$bv(i) = \sum_{h=1...p} \lambda_h \cdot v_{i,h} \qquad (5.9)$$

λ_h is the weight of importance attached to stakeholder s_h. Value-based priority (i.e. $v_{i,h}$) measures the expected value that the implementation of feature f_i will add to stakeholder s_h.

In order to define the objective function, we have to consider the release k to which the feature f_i is assigned, as the overall business value of feature f_i also depends on the release to which it is assigned. The concept that distinguishes the

---

[††] Note: The definition of priorities in our value function is not restricted to *value*. Other attributes of interest can be adopted in lieu of these (e.g. return on investment (ROI)). In addition, any convenient scale of measure can be adopted in assigning values to the chosen attributes (e.g. using Net Present Value (NPV) to assess ROI); and this also applies to the weighting scheme for stakeholders.

overall business value of feature f_i, based on the release k to which the feature is assigned, is the relative importance σ_k attached to release k, where $\sigma_k \in \{1,9\}$. This importance can also be chosen as $\sigma_k \in \{0,1\}$ such that $\sum_k \sigma_k = 1$. The relative importance ratio between consecutive releases describes how much more important it is to have a feature in the former release than in the latter. For example, weights 9, 3, and 1 (for three releases) indicate that it is always three times more important to have a feature in a former release than a latter (Release 1 versus Release 2, same for Release 2 versus Release 3). Consequently, we define an objective function $F_1(x)$ that captures the business perspective of release planning as:

$$F_1(x) = \sum_{k=1...K} \sum_{i:x(i)=k} \sigma_k \cdot bv(i) \qquad (5.10)$$

2. Objective of Planning: The Technical Perspective

It is more desirable to implement the highest system valued features early, because they possess the highest interrelatedness with the other features. Whenever feature f_i is assigned to a release k, the overall system-value $sv(i)$ of the feature is the overall priority in the corresponding release k, which is influenced by the importance σ_k attached to the release k. Based on this assumption, we define the objective function $F_2(x)$ that captures the technical perspective of release planning as:

$$F_2(x) = \sum_{k=1...K} \sum_{i:x(i)=k} \sigma_k \cdot sv(i) \qquad (5.11)$$

The function $F_2(x)$, as defined in Equation (5.11), is a first approximation. We call this an approximation because all the other SD-coupled features f_j that contribute to the system value of feature f_i may not necessarily be assigned to the same release as feature f_j. This is due primarily to a limited amount of available resources as well as other project constraints.

Nonetheless, given that our formulation of objective function $F_2(x)$ is based on a heuristic that strives to maximize the assignment of features with high interrelatedness as well as high strength of SD-coupling into the same release, this initial approximation is valid and it suffices. Once release plans are generated via the solutions to a formulated optimization model, we could recalculate the actual value of the objective function $F_2(x)$. The updated value is derived from the set of SD-coupled features that are assigned to the same release in a release plan. For example, suppose a feature f_i is SD-coupled to 9 other features, but on generating a release plan only 5 of these features are assigned to the same release as feature f_i, the initial system value $sv(i)$ for feature f_i would be based on its strength of SD-coupling with each of the 9 SD-coupled features, while the recalculated system value $sv(i)$ would be based on the strength of SD-coupling between f_i and each of the 5 SD-coupled features assigned to the same release.

In essence, the recalculated system values of the features are a more accurate description of the system values of features in a release plan. It should be noted that we cannot even know the actual value of $F_2(x)$, which is a function of the system values of features, until the plans are generated. Given the aforementioned observations, we wish to stress that using initial approximations in the objective function is not a drawback of the approach. Because the initial approximations represent the upper bound of the system values that we desire to achieve by formulating the release planning problem as a maximization problem.

5.4.3 Bi-Objective Release Planning Model

The goal of the bi-objective model is to support release planning decisions by optimizing the assignment of features in terms of both interrelatedness (in terms of potential synergy in implementation) and the business values (degree of stakeholder satisfaction) of the features. Since each of the two objective functions mean different things and their values are based on different scales (and units) of measure, we cannot integrate them into a single objective function upfront. Thus, we formulate the release planning problem as a bi-objective optimization problem as follows:

$$\text{Max}^* \quad \Upsilon = \left(F_1(x), F_2(x) \right) \tag{5.12}$$

Subject to

$$\sum\nolimits_{i:x(i)=k} r(i,t) \leq r_{\max}(k,t), \ \forall \ k \in K \ \text{and} \ t \in T \tag{5.13}$$

$$x(i) = x(j), \ \forall \ (i,j) \in C \tag{5.14}$$

$$x(i) \leq x(j), \ \forall \ (i,j) \in P \tag{5.15}$$

$$x(i) \in \{0,1\}, \quad \forall \ i = 1,...,n \tag{5.16}$$

where Equation (5.12) represents the two objective functions to be maximized. We have used Max* (instead of simply *Maximize*) to indicate that we require a vector optimization that seeks to maximize the two objective functions $F_1(x)$ and $F_2(x)$ simultaneously. Equations (5.13) – (5.15) are the constraints specified earlier, and (5.16) is an integer constraint indicating that a feature can either be assigned to a release or postponed. Thus, the given formulation of the release planning problem in (5.12) – (5.16) constitutes an integer linear programming problem (ILP) [163]. All the stated objectives and constraints are linear functions, and the decision variables are integers. A solution x to the formulated ILP is called a feasible solution if it satisfies all the constraints and variables bounds.

Having followed through the optimization model formulation, the model needs to be represented in the programmable format of a typical optimization problem, as discussed by Denzinger and Ruhe [41]. Suppose we represent the computed objective function for the business perspective simply as bv(i,k) (i.e., the business objective function score when feature f_i is assigned to release k), and that of the technical perspective as sv(i,k) (i.e., the implementation-based objective function score when feature f_i is assigned to release k). Let $x(i,k) \in \{0,1\}$ (i.e. binary decision variables, with $x(i,k) = 1$ if feature f_i is assigned to release k, and 0 otherwise). Then the formal optimization problem described by (5.12) – (5.15) can be re-written as:

Max*

$$\Upsilon = \left(\sum\nolimits_{k=1...K} \sum\nolimits_{i=1...n} bv(i,k) \cdot x(i,k), \ \sum\nolimits_{k=1...K} \sum\nolimits_{i=1...n} sv(i,k) \cdot x(i,k) \right) \qquad (5.17)$$

Subject to

$$\sum\nolimits_{i=1...n} r(i,t) \cdot x(i,k) \le r_{max}(k,t), \quad t \in T \,; \, k = 1...K \qquad (5.18)$$

$$x(i,k) = x(j,k), \qquad k = 1...K, \quad \forall \, (i,j) \in C \qquad (5.19)$$

$$\sum\nolimits_{k=1...K} (K+1-k)(x(i,k) - x(j,k)) \ge 0, \qquad \forall \, (i,j) \in P \qquad (5.20)$$

$$\sum\nolimits_{k=1...K} x(i,k) \le 1 \qquad \forall \, i \qquad (5.21)$$

$$x(i,k) \in \{0,1\} \qquad \forall \, i \text{ and } k \qquad (5.22)$$

Equation (5.21) ensures that in a release plan each feature must be assigned to only one release. Enforcing the coupling constraint is straight-forward, since the two coupled features can easily be integrated and temporarily assumed to be a single feature. For the precedence constraint, the easiest way to handle it in the model is to check for conformance to the precedence constraint after every release plan is generated. But this approach is naïve. A more efficient approach is to enforce the precedence constraint during the optimization process. Equation (5.20) is the model that handles this constraint in which feature f_i precedes feature f_j. The remaining parts of Equations (5.17) – (5.22) follow from the explanations given for Equations (5.12) – (5.16).

Once release plans are generated, we could evaluate the release plans using the SD-coupling satisfaction. To adopt SD-coupling in the evaluation of release plans, we have to develop a method to determine the level of satisfaction of SD-coupling in these release plans at a given threshold, say α. In order to measure the level of satisfaction of SD-coupling, we define a similarity measure that compares the set of SD-coupling satisfied in a release plan to the set of SD-coupling identified in the problem definition.

5.4.4 Measuring the Level of Satisfaction of SD-coupling in Release Plans

The notion of level of satisfaction of SD-coupling is reflected in the similarity between the set of SD-coupling identified in the problem and the set of SD-coupling fulfilled in a release plan. Our approach for determining the similarity is to represent the entire set of SD-coupling at the chosen threshold by a weighted graph $G = (F, E, w)$. The graph $G = (F, E, w)$ consists of $F = \{f_1, f_2, \ldots, f_n\}$ set of vertices (features), the set E of edges (SD-couplings), and the edge weights w (strength of SD-coupling). We have discussed an analogous representation in our earlier work in [114].

To measure the level of satisfaction of the SD-coupling, we compute the similarity between graph G of the original SD-coupling and graph G_x of SD-coupling satisfied in the release plan. According to the definition of SD-coupling, we define the edge weights of the SD-coupling problem graph G as:

$$w(i, j) = \theta(i, j) \quad \forall \ \Omega(i, j) \neq \emptyset \ and \ \theta(i, j) \geq \alpha \tag{5.23}$$

For the generated release plan, we determine the edge weights of its SD-coupling graph as:

$$w_x(i, j) = \begin{cases} \theta(i, j), & if \left(x(i) = x(j), \Omega(i, j) \neq 0, \ \theta(i, j) \geq \alpha \right) \\ 0 & otherwise \end{cases} \tag{5.24}$$

In Equation (5.24), the conditions $\theta(i, j) \geq \alpha$ and $\Omega(i, j) \neq 0$ show that there is SD-coupling between features f_i and f_j at the chosen threshold α, while $x(i) = x(j)$ implies that this SD-coupling is fulfilled in the release plan. If the SD-coupling is not fulfilled in the release plan, then we have a null edge with weight 0. Thus, the SD-coupling graph of the release plan x, which is given as $G_x = (F, E, w_x)$, is a replica of the original graph except that the edges where the SD-coupling is not satisfied are labeled with weight 0. Therefore, we define the level of satisfaction of SD-coupling in a release plan as follows.

DEFINITION 5.11 (LEVEL OF SATISFACTION OF SD-COUPLING)
We define the level to which release plan x satisfies the SD-couplings at threshold α, which is denoted μ_x^α $(0 \le \mu_x^\alpha \le 1)$, as follows:

$$\mu_x^\alpha = \frac{\displaystyle\sum_{\substack{(i,j) \in SD \\ \theta(i,j) \ge \alpha}} w_x(i, j)}{\displaystyle\sum_{\substack{(i,j) \in SD \\ \theta(i,j) \ge \alpha}} w(i, j)} \tag{5.25}$$

□

5.5 Solving the Bi-Objective Release Planning Model

In any optimization problem, there are always variable bounds restricting the values that the decision variables can take. These bounds, like integrality constraints (i.e. $x(i,k) \in \{0,1\}$) represented by (5.22), constitute the *decision variable space* or simply the *decision space*. In addition to this usual decision space, the objective functions in a bi-objective optimization also constitute a 2-dimensional space. This additional 2-dimensional space is known as the *objective space*, Υ. Thus, for every solution obtained in the decision space, there exists a corresponding point in the objective space. This point represents the objective function values $(F_1(x), F_2(x))$ for the obtained solution x. Recall from Section 5.4.2 that a solution x (i.e. release plan) is characterized by an n-dimensional vector of decision variables $x = (x(1), x(2), \ldots, x(n))$. This implies that, the mapping from the decision space to the objective space for a bi-objective optimization problem is a mapping between n-dimensional solution vector and a 2-dimensional objective vector. We illustrate this mapping between the decision space and the objective space in Figure 5.3.

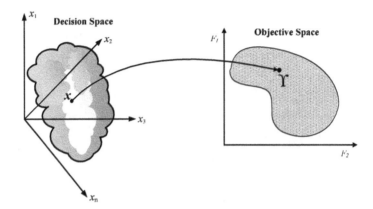

Figure 5.3: Illustration of the Decision Space and the Corresponding Objective Space

In a bi-objective optimization problem, the task is to determine a solution which optimizes the two objective functions, and also satisfies the constraints $x \in X$. There is always one optimal value for a single objective optimization problem, while a bi-objective optimization problem typically presents set of trade-off solutions. The set of solutions, which results from some optimal values, are said to be *Pareto-optimal* solutions if there are no other solutions that are superior to them when the two objectives are considered together [117]. These set of solutions are also referred to as *non-dominated* solutions.

DEFINITION 5.12 (PARETO-OPTIMALITY)

Given a bi-objective maximization problem $A(x)$, an n-tuple x^* is said to be a Pareto-optimal solution of the bi-objective maximization problem, if $x^* \in X$ and there does not exist any other $x \in X$ such that [101]:

    (i) $F_i(x) \geq F_i(x^*) \ \forall \ i \in \{1,2\}$ *and*

    (ii) $F_v(x) > F_v(x^*)$ *for at least one $v \in \{1,2\}$.* □

In simple terms, Pareto-optimal solutions are solutions in which no increase can be obtained in any of the objectives without causing a simultaneous decrease in the other objective (i.e. for a bi-objective maximization problem).

DEFINITION 5.13 (PARETO-OPTIMAL SET)

For a given bi-objective maximization problem A(x), the Pareto-optimal set is defined as:
$P = \{ x^* \in X \mid \nexists\ x \in X \ such\ that\ F(x) \geq F(x^*) \}.$ □

The solutions in the Pareto-optimal set must fall within the feasible region defined by the decision space and their corresponding objective values in the objective space (see Figure 5.3). The values in the objective space that correspond to the solutions in the Pareto-optimal set must also satisfy the two conditions (i) and (ii) in Definition 5.12.

DEFINITION 5.14 (PARETO FRONT)

For a given bi-objective maximization problem A(x) and Pareto-optimal set P, the Pareto front (PF) is defined as: $PF = \{ F(x) = (F_1(x), F_2(x)) \ such\ that\ x \in P \}.$ □

In simple terms, the set of all Pareto-optimal solutions is called the Pareto-optimal set, while the corresponding objective vectors are said to be on the Pareto front. In Figure 5.4, the plotted points A-H represent the performance of individual solutions in the objective space, where two objective functions $F_1(x)$ and $F_2(x)$ are to be maximized. The points A, B, C, and D in the objective space are the objective values that correspond to the solutions in the Pareto-optimal set. There exists no other point(s) in the objective space that outperforms the points A-D in the maximization of both objectives simultaneously. Therefore, the points A-D are non-dominated, and are said to be on the Pareto front. Points E, F, G, H are other possible objective values of solutions obtained in the feasible region, but each of them is dominated by at least one other solution in the Pareto-optimal set. Specifically, each Pareto-optimal solution dominates all solutions to its lower left.

120

For example, point C dominates points E-H, which implies that points E-H are not Pareto-optimal.

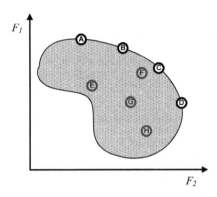

Figure 5.4: Illustration of Pareto front for a bi-objective maximization problem

The goal of any solution approach to a bi-objective optimization problem is to find several Pareto-optimal solutions, so as to uncover tradeoff information between the two objectives under consideration [117]. Since the improvement in one objective degrades the other objective, it is not possible to say which of the Pareto-optimal solutions is better than the other solutions. This implies that any of the Pareto-optimal solutions is as good as any of the other solutions. Once a set of solutions is obtained, a decision maker would be able to analyze the tradeoff in order to choose a final solution. Thus, Pareto-optimal solutions could serve as alternatives that support decision-making under uncertainty. In fact, the Pareto-optimal solutions obtained by solving the bi-objective optimization model described in Equations (5.17) – (5.22), correspond to alternative release plans.

There are several solution techniques available for solving bi-objective as well as general multi-objective optimization problems. Existing solution techniques include: the weighted method, the ε-Constraint method, goal programming, sequential optimization, and evolutionary algorithms. Detailed discussions of these methods can be found in

Collette and Siarry [33], Szidarovszky et al. [154], Coello et al. [32], and Deb [38]. Ehrgott and Gandibleux [46] also presents a detailed survey of existing methods for solving general multi-objective optimization problems. In this work, we adopt the method of objective-converted inequality constraints [102], or simply the ε-Constraint (epsilon-Constraint) method proposed by Haimes et al. [67].

5.5.1 Solution Method Based on ε-Constraint Characterization

The use of the ε-Constraint method in the literature has primarily focused on bi-objective optimization problems [108]. The ε-Constraint method requires the conversion of one of the objective functions into an inequality constraint, while the other objective function is taken as the primary objective to be optimized. Then, a bound is defined for the second objective, which is known as the ε-Constraint. By varying the bounds for each constrained objective, different Pareto-optimal solutions can be obtained for the resulting single-objective problem [90], [95]. In essence, the ε-Constraint method generates a Pareto-optimal set for a bi-objective optimization problem by solving a sequence of constrained single-objective optimization problems.

Suppose we denote our bi-objective optimization problem (BOP) (e.g. Equations (5.17) – (5.22)) as $A(x)$, a reformulation of the problem in terms of the ε-Constraint method which we denote as $A_u(\varepsilon)$, is described as follows:

$$max^* \quad F_u(x) \tag{5.26}$$
$$subject\ to\ F_v(x) \geq \varepsilon_v \quad \forall\ u,v \in \{1,2\}\ and\ u \neq v \tag{5.27}$$
$$x \in X \tag{5.28}$$

where X is the set of other constraints (i.e. apart from the constrained objective) that define the feasible region within which each generated solution must lie. The set of lower bounds $\varepsilon_v = \{\varepsilon_1, \varepsilon_2\}$ refers to the minimum values (i.e. for a maximization problem) that each constrained objective must attain. In other words, the ε-Constraint method basically transform the BOP, which is a vector optimization (i.e. due to the vector of 2 objectives) into a scalar optimization problem. In order to generate the Pareto-optimal set, the values of the lower bounds ε must be varied along the Pareto front for each objective, and a new optimization process is performed for each new set of the resulting lower bounds. To better explain how the constrained reformulation of the bi-objective optimization problem solves the original problem, we formulate the following Lemma:

LEMMA 5.1

Let $A(x) = max \{F_1(x), F_2(x) | x \in X\}$ *be a bi-objective optimization problem. A Pareto-optimal solution* x^* *of the problem* $A(x)$ *is equivalent to* $x^* = max^*\{F_u(x^*) | x^* \in X \cap X_{\varepsilon^*}^v\}$ *where* $X_{\varepsilon^*}^v \equiv F_v(x) \geq \varepsilon^*$, $u \neq v$, *and* ε^* *is chosen within the feasible region in the objective space. If for any given u, x^* solves* $A_u(\varepsilon^*)$, *then there exists* $\boldsymbol{\varepsilon}$ *such that x^* also solves* $A(\boldsymbol{\varepsilon})$. □

The proof for the above Lemma is supported by the following two results, which are based on Theorem 4.1 and Theorem 4.2 discussed in Chankong and Haimes [25]:

1. Let ε' be a vector of constraints for which $A_u(\varepsilon')$ is feasible, and let x' be the corresponding optimal solution of $A_u(\varepsilon')$. Then, x' is a Pareto-optimal solution of a bi-objective optimization problem if x' is a unique solution of $A_u(\varepsilon')$ for some $1 \leq u \leq 2$, or if x' solves $A_u(\varepsilon')$ for every $1 \leq u \leq 2$ (according to Theorem 4.1 and Theorem 4.2 in [25]). The implication of this result is that, some Pareto-optimal solutions can always be obtained by solving $A_u(\boldsymbol{\varepsilon})$ as long as we choose $\boldsymbol{\varepsilon}$ so that $A_u(\boldsymbol{\varepsilon})$ is feasible.

2. Conversely, for any given Pareto-optimal solution x^*, we can always find $\boldsymbol{\varepsilon}$ such that x^* solves $A_u(\boldsymbol{\varepsilon})$ for every $1 \leq u \leq 2$ (according to Theorem 4.1 in [25]).

The implication of this result is that, we can always obtain all Pareto-optimal solutions by solving the constraint problem $A_u(\varepsilon)$ for any chosen u.

Since we adopt and adapt Theorems 4.1 and Theorem 4.2 (see pp. 128-129, [25]), we restate the adapted versions as Theorem 5.1 and Theorem 5.2 respectively. Note that the theorems were discussed in the context of multi-objective optimization problem, but we restate the theorems for the specific case of our bi-objective optimization problem. For the proofs of these theorems, the reader should refer to [25].

THEOREM 5.1

x^* is a non-dominated solution of BOP if and only if x^* solves $A_u(\varepsilon^*)$ for every $u \in \{1, 2\}$, and for at least one ε^* chosen within the feasible region in the objective space. $\square$

THEOREM 5.2

If x^* solves $A_u(\varepsilon^*)$ for some u and if the solution is unique, then x^* is a non-dominated solution of BOP, for at least one ε^* chosen within the feasible region in the objective space. $\square$

5.5.2 Implementing the ε-Constraint Method for Release Planning

Implementation of the ε-Constraint method can be achieved in different ways [12], [101]. In order to implement the ε-Constraint method, we must partition the objective space into grids representing the bounds, ε. Then, we solve different single-objective problems that are constrained to each grid. The use of pre-defined partitioning of the objective space to vary the bounds ε is discussed in [67]. The idea is to iteratively change the bounds of the constraint by a pre-defined constant, say δ [12]. Although, defining the bounds for the ε-Constraint reduces the search space, which tends to leave out some portions of all possible Pareto-optimal solutions. It is noteworthy, however, that a complete enumeration of all the possible Pareto-optimal solutions is not in the least desired for the type of problem we address in this research, and by extension for most software engineering problems.

Our solution approach is a variation of the ε-Constraint, in which we do not pre-define the partitioning of the objective space until we have first reduced the search space for the Pareto-optimal solutions. Thus, we first locate the two extreme Pareto-optimal solutions, with each solution optimizing one of the objective functions. We achieve this by optimizing the first objective function, say F_1, without any constraint on the second objective, say F_2. This gives the maximum achievable value for F_1 (i.e. the upper bound). To ascertain that the F_1 value obtained is Pareto-optimal, we have to determine the maximum F_2 value that corresponds to the maximal value obtained for F_1. Therefore, we proceed by maximizing F_2 while the obtained F_1 value serves as a constraint. The resulting solution is Pareto-optimal when we consider the two objectives together. Again, we interchange the roles of F_1 and F_2 in order to obtain the second Pareto-optimal solution. The objective space that contains these two solutions is already a reduced search space, which we partition and explore to derive other Pareto solutions. The procedure we have just described also enables us to determine the upper and lower bounds for each objective.

Having identified the upper and lower bounds for the value of each objective, we would have reduced the search space. Suppose P_1 and P_2 correspond to the objective values of the first two Pareto-optimal solutions described above, then we explore the region enclosed by P_1 and P_2 for other Pareto solutions (see Figure 5.5). We achieve this by imposing additional inequality constraints that are offsets from P_1 and P_2 by certain distances from both directions of F_1 and F_2. These offsets, which are derived from partitioning the objective space, must be varied from the best value to the worst value for each objective (i.e. a search from the *ideal* to the *nadir* values of each objective function). In the case of F_1, for example, we start our search for other Pareto solutions from $\overline{F}_1(x_0)$

to $\underline{F_1}(x_1)$, while for F_2, we search from $\overline{F}_2(x_1)$ towards $\underline{F}_2(x_0)$. In Figure 5.5, we divide each constraint limit into 3 grids, giving the vector of constraint limits for F_1 as $\{\varepsilon_{11}, \varepsilon_{12}, \varepsilon_{13}\}$ and those for F_2 as $\{\varepsilon_{21}, \varepsilon_{21}, \varepsilon_{23}\}$.

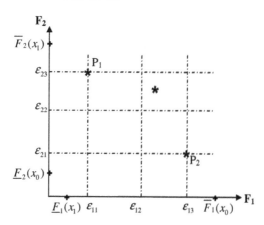

Figure 5.5: Representation of the ε-Constraint Method

The details of our implementation of the ε-Constraint method is described in Algorithm 5.4. The algorithm, like any other implementation of the ε-Constraint method, assumes that we have a solver for single-objective optimization. We need to first prepare our input data in the linear programming (LP) format for any single-objective optimizer to be able to solve the problem. We issue a call to the single-objective optimizer through *optimize(lpFile, π)*, where "lpFile" is the LP file and π is the set time limit specified for the optimizer to solve the constrained single-objective problem. We use the ILOG-CPLEX Optimizer [72] to solve the resulting single-objective optimization sub-problems via ILOG's branch-and-bound algorithm. For each run of the single-objective optimizer, we set the time limit π for which the ILOG-CPLEX should run. After the set time limit expires, the ILOG-CPLEX would return an optimal result for the constrained single-objective problem or an approximation of the optimal. Algorithm 5.4 also uses Algorithm 5.3 as a utility algorithm to test the Pareto-optimality of all the solutions obtained.

In Algorithm 5.4, we determine the bounds for the two objectives by successively running single-objective optimization problem on each of the objectives in turn, and without constraining the second objective in each case. This bounds computation as well as the generation of the initial set of Pareto-optimal solutions is handled by Lines 4–17 of the algorithm. Before any call is issued to ILOG, we need to rewrite the LP file again to specify which of the two objectives to be optimized, and which one to serve as the constrained objective. The ε value of the constrained objective must reflect the updated results from previous optimization.

In the remaining part of the algorithm, we partition the objective space into grids, based on the range of the objective function values, and also on the number of Pareto-optimal solutions desired by the user. The number of solutions in our case corresponds to the number of release plans desired. For illustration purposes, the algorithm shows F_1 as the primary objective to be optimized while F_2 serves as the constraint. This explains our partitioning of the F_2 axis in Line 21 to define the δ offset, which ensures that the constraint points ε to be used on F_2 are equally spaced in their projection over the F_1 axis. The roles of F_1 and F_2 can be interchanged, as we have during our implementation. Interchanging the roles imply that we rerun Lines 24-34 by treating F_2 as the primary objective and F_1 as the constraint. Also note that we have a procedure to handle Line 4-10, Line 11-17, and Line 26-32, instead of repeating them as shown in Algorithm 5.4.

Algorithm 5.3: TestParetoOptimality(x, P)
Input: Solution x and Pareto-optimal set P
Output: Set P of Pareto-optimal solutions
1. **Begin**
2.   **If** $\nexists\, x^* \in P$ such that $x^* \succ x$ **Then** /* x is non-dominated wrt P */
3. $P = P - \{x^* \in P \mid x \succ x^*\}$ /* Remove any solution dominated by x */
4. $P = P \cup \{x\}$ /* Update Pareto-optimal set */
5.   **End If**
6. **End**

Algorithm 5.4: Bi-objective ε-Constraint for Release Planning
Input: Pre-processed text file (input.txt) containing the input data
Output: Set P of Pareto-optimal solutions
1. **Begin**
2. $P = \varnothing$
3. $inputData = readInputFile(input.txt)$
4. **Repeat**
5. $lpFile = writeLP(inputData, F_1)$
6. $A_0 = F_1(optimize(lpFile, \pi))$
7. $lpFile = writeLP(inputData, F_2, A_0)$
8. $x_0 = optimize(lpFile, \pi)$ /* To ensure optimality of result from Line 6*/
9. $P = TestParetoOptimality(x_0, P)$ /* Obtain 1st Pareto-optimal solution*/
10. **Until** x_0 is non-dominated in P
11. **Repeat**
12. $lpFile = writeLP(inputData, F_2)$
13. $B_0 = F_2(optimize(lpFile, \pi))$
14. $lpFile = writeLP(inputData, F_1, B_0)$
15. $x_1 = optimize(lpFile, \pi)$ /* To ensure optimality of result from Line 13*/
16. $P = TestParetoOptimality(x_1, P)$ /* Obtain 2nd Pareto-optimal solution*/
17. **Until** x_1 is non-dominated in P
18. **If** ($numSol \% 2 \neq 0$) **Then** $numSol = numSol + 1$
19. /* Let F_1 be objective to be optimized, and F_2 the ε-Constraint objective*/
20. $\bar{F}_2 = F_2(x_1); \underline{F}_2 = F_2(x_0)$ /* For upper and lower bounds of F_2*/
21. $\delta = 2 * (\bar{F}_2 - \underline{F}_2)/(numSol)$ /* Partition the constrained axis, say F_2 */
22. count = 3 /* There are 2 solutions already, seek the remaining */
23. $\varepsilon = \bar{F}_2$
24. **While** $count < numSol$ **Do**
25. $\varepsilon = \varepsilon - \delta$ /* Move from best to worst value of F_2 */
26. **Repeat**
27. $lpFile = writeLP(inputData, F_1, \varepsilon)$
28. $y = optimize(lpFile, \pi)$
29. $lpFile = writeLP(inputData, F_2, F_1(y))$
30. $x_{count} = optimize(lpFile, \pi)$
31. $P = TestParetoOptimality(x_{count}, P)$
32. **Until** x_{count} is non-dominated in P
33. count = count+1
34. **End While**
35. **Return** P
36. **End**

5.6 CASE STUDY: Release Planning for ReleasePlanner® System

5.6.1 Context

To investigate the applicability of the proposed release planning approach, we present a case study that is based on the real-world data collected from the ReleasePlanner system [127]. ReleasePlanner® is a web-based decision support system for release planning and prioritization. It is a commercial tool offered by Expert Decisions Inc (see http://www.expertdecisions.com). Among the companies who have performed trial or professional projects using the tool include: Corel iGrafx, Siemens Corporate Technology, Trema Laboratories, Nortel Networks, Solid Technology, City of Calgary, Autotech, and Ericsson Canada.

The data we collected on the ReleasePlanner include the new set of features required to be added in the forthcoming releases, the priorities of the features based on the values assigned to them by the stakeholders, and the resources required for implementing the features. There are N=33 features in the project, K=2 releases to be planned ahead, P=3 stakeholders and T=5 types of effort-based resources: analysts, developers, quality assurance, user interface designers, and researchers. For all the resource types, the total amount required to implement all the features exceed the available capacity. All the three stakeholders s_1, s_2, and s_3 evaluated the features using a value-based priority scheme on a scale of 1-9, as discussed earlier. Table 5.1 contains details of these data.

Table 5.1: Business Value Data for the ReleasePlanner System

	Features	Business Values			Precedence & Coupling Constraints		Resource Consumption (person-days)				
ID	Features	S1	S2	S3	Precedes	Coupled To	Developer	Quality Assurance	User Interface	Research	System Designer
1	Comparative analysis manual versus RP solutions	2	4	3		3	10	4	5	5	10
2	Record of history of sets of alternative solutions	1	1	4			10	5	10	8	10
3	Conformance measure for requirements across alterantive solutions	2	8	4		1	1	1	2	0	1
4	Comparison between solutions: within one set and across sets	3	4				10	5	15	5	10
5	MS excel advanced compatibility	5	2	1	32	16	20	10	10	7	15
6	MS Project compatibility	1	4	3			10	3	8	5	10
7	Analysis of compatibility requirements with existing RM tools (DOORS, Requisite Pro)	1	6	8			0	0	0	5	5
8	Generation of solutions based on selected criteria (Stakeholder in isolation, criteria in isolation, trade-off)	3	3	8			10	5	7	5	8
9	Planning across projects	3	6	5			15	5	15	30	10
10	Re-planning capabilities		5	3			20	10	20	30	10
11	Allowing splitting of features over two releases	3	9	4		12	15	10	10	10	10
12	Accomodation of different skill sets	1	4	1		11	12	8	8	12	6
13	Fuzzy boundaries	1	0				5	5	3	5	3
14	Value-risk trade-off analysis	6	0	3			8	4	6	10	5
15	Multiple windows accessible	2	0			19	1	1	1	0	1
16	Integrated Excel sheet with effort data, voting and generated alternatives	5	6	2		5	5	2	1	2	1
17	Dashboard to show user actual study of Project Planning	3	6	2	9	-	15	3	5	6	8
18	Professional UI re-development	7	7	6			0	0	0	0	0
19	Extending reporting component	3	6	4		15, 22	15	5	10	5	8
20	Explanation Component	3	4	3			20	10	15	80	30
21	Visualization of Output	4	5	2			30	15	10	20	15
22	Context sensitive explanation of terms	7	0	7		19	5	3	5	5	5
23	Further development of the validator to give on demand help	2	0	2			20	5	20	10	15
24	Fine tuning optimization algorithms (back tracking strategies, heuristics)	9		7			0	0	0	0	0
25	Elimination of open source code	1	0	9			0	0	0	0	0
26	Caching mechanisms	1	0	3			0	0	0	0	0
27	Stakeholder allowed to enter request for requirements	4	0	1			5	2	5	2	10
28	Stakeholder to enter resource estimates	1	4	5			5	2	4	1	10
29	Multiple stakeholder weights based on groups of reqs. they are voting on	3	8	2			10	3	5	3	5
30	Improved stakeholder conformance (percentages of the idea solution model)	3	4	5			5	2	5	2	5
31	Individual stakeholder voting feedback	6	5	3			8	2	5	2	7
32	Competitor stakeholder voting	3	4	2			10	3	5	1	10
33	Stakeholder Voting analysis extension	6	1	4			7	3	5	5	5
	Total Amount of Resources Required						307	136	220	281	248
	Available Capacity: Release 1						100	40	70	60	80
	Available Capacity: Release 2						100	40	70	60	80

For this case study, the 3 stakeholders were assigned the same importance value, which in this case was weight 5 to each one of them. The two release milestones were also assigned importance values 9 and 7 for Release 1 and Release 2, respectively. Table 5.1 also contains data on problem domain coupling and precedence constraints, under "Coupled To" and "Precedes" columns. In the "Precedes" column, an entry in each cell indicates that the feature in that row must come before the feature in the "Precedes" column in the release plan. Similar interpretation applies to the "Coupled To" column. These coupling and precedence data were identified by the development team.

The development team also identified 8 high level components that would be impacted when adding the features. The impact data is shown in Table 5.2, where each feature has corresponding set of impacted components. An entry "x" in a cell of Table 5.2 indicates that the component in the column is impacted by the feature in the corresponding row.

5.6.2 SD-coupling and System Value Computation

Applying the SD-coupling algorithm to the data in Table 5.2, we compute the SD-coupling between every pair of features. Since we need to determine whether SD-coupling exists between all possible pairs of features, the SD-coupling matrix easily grows large. The 33 features would require 528 comparisons to establish the SD-coupling matrix. For this reason, the table of the strength of SD-coupling, which is derived from the SD-coupling matrix, cannot be replicated here. Table 5.3 contains a snapshot of the table of SD-coupling when the strength of coupling $\alpha = 1.0$. In Table 5.3, we have a total of 16 pairs of features that are SD-coupled at $\alpha = 1.0$. The result in the table also shows that 17 features are involved in this SD-coupling dependency (which constitutes 51.5% of the total number of features).

Table 5.2: Features and their Set of Impacted Components

ID	Feature Description	C1 Reporting	C2 Validator	C3 IP Component	C4 Java Brokers	C5 Import/Export Component	C6 Stakeholder Voting Analysis	C7 DB Connectivity Class	C8 Alternative Analysis Wizard	Change set
				Impacted components						Change set
1	Comparative analysis manual versus RP solutions	X		X	X	X		X	X	{c1, c3, c4, c5, c7, c8}
2	Record of history of sets of alternative solutions	X			X	X		X	X	{c1, c4, c5, c7,c8}
3	Conformance measure for requirements across alterantive solutions	X			X			X	X	{c1, c4, c7, c8}
4	Comparison between solutions: within one set and across sets	X			X			X	X	{c1, c4, c7, c8}
5	MS excel advanced compatibility				X	X		X		{c4, c5, c7}
6	MS Project compatibility				X	X		X		{c4, c5, c7}
7	Analysis of compatibility requirements with existing RM tools (DOORS, Requisite Pro)				X	X		X		{c4, c5, c7}
8	Generation of solutions based on selected criteria (Stakeholder in isolation, criteria in isolation, trade-off)	X		X	X			X		{c1, c3, c4, c7}
9	Planning across projects	X	X	X	X		X	X	X	{c1, c2, c3, c4, c6, c7, c8}
10	Re-planning capabilities	X							X	{c1, c8}
11	Allowing splitting of features over two releases	X	X	X	X			X	X	{c1, c2, c3, c4, c7, c8}
12	Accomodation of different skill sets	X	X	X	X	X	X	X	X	{c1, c2, c3, c4, c5, c6, c7, c8}
13	Fuzzy boundaries	X			X			X	X	{c1, c4, c7, c8}
14	Value-risk trade-off analysis	X						X	X	{c1, c7, c8}
15	Multiple windows accessible							X		{c7}
16	Integrated Excel sheet with effort data, voting and generated alternatives					X		X		{c5, c7}
17	Dashboard to show user actual study of Project Planning				X			X		{c4, c7}
18	Professional UI re-development	X					X		X	{c1, c6, c8}
19	Extending reporting component	X						X		{c1, c7}
20	Explanation Component							X		{c7}
21	Visualization of Output	X					X	X	X	{c1, c6, c7, c8}
22	Context sensitive explanation of terms							X		{c7}
23	Further development of the validator to give on demand help		X	X	X			X		{c2, c3, c4, c7}
24	Fine tuning optimization algorithms (back tracking strategies, heuristics)			X	X					{c3, c4}
25	Elimination of open source code			X						{c3}
26	Caching mechanisms			X	X					{c3, c4}
27	Stakeholder allowed to enter request for requirements	X						X		{c1, c7}
28	Stakeholder to enter resource estimates	X						X		{c1, c7}
29	Multiple stakeholder weights based on groups of reqs. they are voting on	X				X	X	X		{c1, c5, c6, c7}
30	Improved stakeholder conformance (percentages of the idea solution model)	X		X	X			X	X	{c1, c3, c4, c7, c8}
31	Individual stakeholder voting feedback	X					X	X		{c1, c6, c7}
32	Competitor stakeholder voting	X					X	X		{c1, c6, c7}
33	Stakeholder Voting analysis extension	X					X	X		{c1, c6, c7}

In fact, none of the SD-couplings identified at α=1.0 was initially identified as a problem domain coupling (i.e. PD-coupling) by the development team during the case study. However, there is no restriction that both PD-coupling and SD-coupling must be mutually exclusive. There are possibilities that some of the PD-couplings could correspond to SD-couplings, and vice versa. We did not have this correspondence in the data collected from this study.

Table 5.3: SD-coupling Between the Features at α = 1.0

Pair of features (i, j)	$|\Phi_i|$	$|\Phi_j|$	Adjacency Sets $\Omega(i,j)$	$|\Omega(i,j)|$	Coupling Strength $\theta(i,j)$
(3,4)	4	4	{c1, c4, c7, c8}	4	1.000
(3,13)	4	4	{c1, c4, c7, c8}	4	1.000
(4,13)	4	4	{c1, c4, c7, c8}	4	1.000
(5,6)	3	3	{c4, c5, c7}	3	1.000
(5,7)	3	3	{c4, c5, c7}	3	1.000
(6,7)	3	3	{c4, c5, c7}	3	1.000
(15,20)	1	1	{c7}	1	1.000
(15,22)	1	1	{c7}	1	1.000
(19,27)	2	2	{c1, c7}	2	1.000
(19,28)	2	2	{c1, c7}	2	1.000
(20,22)	1	1	{c7}	1	1.000
(24,26)	2	2	{c3, c4}	2	1.000
(27,28)	2	2	{c1, c7}	2	1.000
(31,32)	3	3	{c1, c6, c7}	3	1.000
(31,33)	3	3	{c1, c6, c7}	3	1.000
(32,33)	3	3	{c1, c6, c7}	3	1.000

At a lower threshold α=0.90, there were more sets of features involved in the SD-coupling. A total of 28 SD-couplings involving 24 features (i.e. 72.7% of the total features) were identified at threshold α=0.90. Figure 5.6 shows the total number of SD-coupling identified at different α thresholds.

In Figure 5.6, the number of SD-couplings between the features decreases with increasing α threshold. The interpretation for this is straightforward. The more stringent the α threshold, the less likely we would be able to find pairs of features that would be SD-coupled at that threshold. This is even more likely to be the case if the impact analysis is conducted at a more fine-grained level (e.g. method or class level). The decision regarding what α threshold to adopt depends on the granularity of the impact analysis data collected.

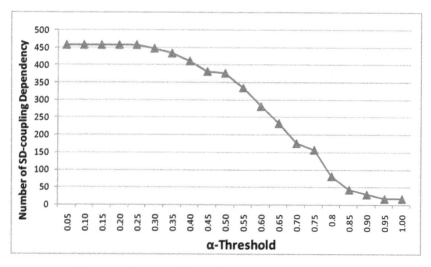

Figure 5.6: Number of SD-coupling at Different α Thresholds

We compute the initial system value for each feature using Algorithm 5.2; the result appears in Table 5.4. The table also shows the number of other features to which each feature in the row is SD-coupled (i.e. derived from the 2nd order degree (d_2) of the hyperedge representing each feature). Recall that the heuristic behind the objective function representing the technical perspective aims on generating release plans that assign high system valued features to early releases. The data in Table 5.4 offers insights into the reasoning behind this heuristic. We can deduce from Table 5.4 that, the more the number of features to which a feature f_i is SD-coupled, and the higher the strength of these SD-couplings, the higher the resulting system value will be for feature f_i.

Table 5.4: Initial Approximation of System Values

ID# of features	2nd order degree $(d_2(i))$	sv(i)
1	32	22.191
2	31	21.156
3	31	21.208
4	31	21.208
5	29	16.621
6	29	16.621
7	29	16.621
8	32	20.90
9	32	21.593
10	20	12.169
11	32	21.078
12	32	22.32
13	31	21.208
14	29	19.294
15	27	18.294
16	27	14.413
17	29	17.919
18	20	11.719
19	29	19.627
20	27	18.294
21	29	18.762
22	27	18.294
23	30	16.036
24	17	9.778
25	9	5.650
26	17	9.778
27	29	19.627
28	29	19.627
29	29	17.671
30	32	21.885
31	29	17.926
32	29	17.926
33	29	17.926

The result given in Table 5.4 also shows that it is not enough for a feature to be SD-coupled to so many other features in order to have high system value; the strength of the SD-couplings contributes significantly. For example, feature f_{23} is SD-coupled to 30 other features and has a system-value of 16.036, while feature f_{19} that is coupled to a lesser number of other features (i.e. 29 features in this case) has a higher system-value of 19.627. Similarly, we have features f_{16} and f_{20} that are both SD-coupled to 27 features, but have system values 14.413 and 18.294, respectively. The explanation for this derives from the effects of the strength of SD-coupling, which is more important than just the number of features involved in SD-coupling.

Figure 5.7 plots system value against total number of features involved in the SD-coupling for feature. We can see from Figure 5.7 that system value does not only depend on the number of features involved in the SD-coupling. Otherwise, we would have had a steady monotonically increasing curve in Figure 5.7. The drops at various points (e.g. with 27 features, 30 features) show the hidden effects of strength of SD-coupling on system values. It would be easier to see the effects of strength of SD-coupling on system value, if we show the strength of coupling for all the features to which a particular feature f_i is SD-coupled. But such details are not necessary, given that we have earlier discussed the algorithm for computing system values.

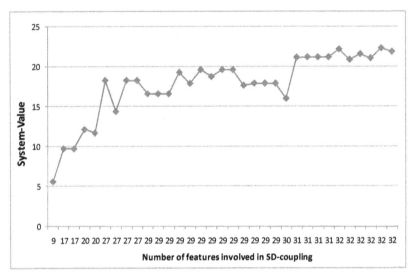

Figure 5.7: System-value in Relation to the Number of Features Involved in SD-coupling

5.6.3 Release Plan Generation

To generate a release plan, we implement a C# program that uses the callable libraries of the ILOG-CPLEX Optimizer [72] to solve single-objective sub-problems of the bi-objective optimization problem. The C# code implements the ε-Constraint method via Algorithm 5.3. For every run of the experiment, we set the time limit for the single-objective optimizer (i.e. ILOG-CPLEX) to 30 seconds in order to balance the quality of solutions generated with performance of the algorithm in terms of computational cost.

On applying this solution to the case study data, 3 release plan alternatives which correspond to 3 Pareto-optimal solutions were generated. Figure 5.8 shows the values of the objective functions F_1 and F_2 that correspond to each Pareto-optimal solution. These solutions are indicated by the points A, B, and C, where the values in parentheses represent the objective values of functions F_1 and F_2.

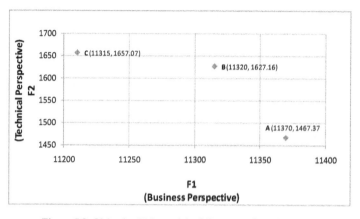

Figure 5.8: Objective Values of the 3 Pareto-optimal Solutions

In Figure 5.8, the release plan whose objective values are represented by the point A is more biased towards the business perspective (F_1), while the plan whose objective values are given by the point C is biased towards the technical perspective (F_2). The plan whose objective values are given by the point B is a tradeoff that is not biased towards either of the perspectives. However, if the two objectives are considered together we cannot claim that any of the solutions (A, B, & C) is better than another solution in the set. Because all the release plans are derived from Pareto-optimal solutions.

Table 5.5 is the structure of the three release plans whose objective corresponding to the Pareto-front shown in Figure 5.8. In Table 5.5, the numbers (i.e. 1, 2) in the row of each plan represent the releases to which the corresponding feature in the column is assigned, while number 3 represents the postponed features. Release plan A assigned a total of 26 features into either of the two releases, while release plans B and C assigned 27 features each. All the release plan alternatives in Table 5.5 are structurally different in terms of which release to which each feature in the release plan is assigned.

Table 5.5: Alternative Release Plans

	f_1	f_2	f_3	f_4	f_5	f_6	f_7	f_8	f_9	f_{10}	f_{11}	f_{12}	f_{13}	f_{14}	f_{15}	f_{16}	f_{17}	f_{18}	f_{19}	f_{20}	f_{21}	f_{22}	f_{23}	f_{24}	f_{25}	f_{26}	f_{27}	f_{28}	f_{29}	f_{30}	f_{31}	f_{32}	f_{33}
Alternative A	1	3	1	3	2	2	1	1	1	3	2	2	3	2	1	2	1	1	1	3	3	1	3	1	1	1	2	2	1	1	1	2	1
Alternative B	1	3	1	3	2	2	1	2	1	3	2	2	1	1	1	2	1	1	1	3	3	1	3	1	1	1	2	2	1	1	1	2	1
Alternative C	1	3	1	1	2	3	1	1	2	3	2	2	1	1	1	2	2	1	1	3	3	1	3	1	1	1	2	2	1	1	1	2	1

Despite the release plans corresponding to different Pareto-optimal solutions, they show similarities in some of their assignment of features to releases. For example, alternative release plans A and B have only 5 feature assignments in which the two release plans do not agree (i.e. f_6, f_9, f_{13}, f_{14}, f_{17}) in the releases that the features should be assigned. Also, if we consider all the 3 alternative release plans, there are only 7 feature assignments in which the plans do not agree on which release a feature should be assigned (including the postponed features). The implication of these results is that the decision maker has a much smaller space to explore for comparison of solutions. The decision maker might accept the fact that all the features assigned to the same release in the 3 alternatives should be fixed into the assigned release. For the result given in Table 5.5, the decision maker can restrict the evaluation of release plans to those 7 features that are assigned differently in the 3 alternatives.

In addition to the release plan alternatives, we also compute the values of the objective function $F_2(x)$ in each release alternative. The goal is to validate the heuristics employed in maximizing the assignment of features with higher system values into early releases. Figure 5.9 shows the results of this evaluation for the 3 alternative release plans given in Table 5.5. As shown in Figure 5.9, the objective function value for $F_2(x)$ is consistently higher for the features assigned to "Release 1" than is the case for "Release 2". This implies that the features with higher interrelatedness are assigned to an earlier release, thereby validating the planning heuristic.

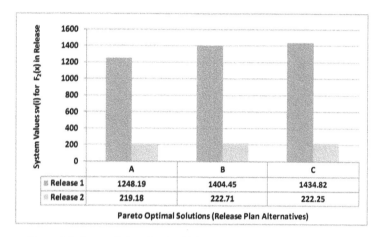

	A	B	C
▓ Release 1	1248.19	1404.45	1434.82
▓ Release 2	219.18	222.71	222.25

Pareto Optimal Solutions (Release Plan Alternatives)

Figure 5.9: System Values for the Objective Function F2 in Each Release

5.6.4 Recalculating the System Values in the Release Plans

As we have stated in Section 5.4.2.3, the initial approximations for the system values of features are used in the maximization of $F_2(x)$. Since all the SD-couplings would not necessarily be satisfied in the release plans, the recalculated system values are expected to be lower in each release plan. Because, for every feature f_i that is assigned to one of the two releases, the postponed features that are SD-coupled to the feature f_i would not contribute to the recalculated system values for f_i. Figure 5.10 shows the recalculated system values for each feature in the alternative (i.e. whether the feature is assigned or not), in comparison to the initial approximation. This figure indicates that the features in all the alternative release plans have lower system values than their initial approximations. The details of all the recalculated data appear in Table 5.6.

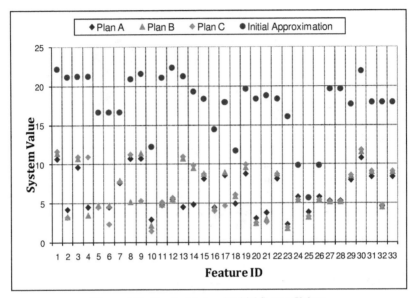

Figure 5.10: Recalculated and Initial System Values

Table 5.6 contains system values and the number of SD-coupled features that contribute to the recalculated system values. Note that for every postponed feature f_i in each alternative plan, the recalculated system value of the feature is based on the other features that are SD-coupled with f_i and which are also postponed.

5.6.5 Correlation Coefficients between the Recalculated System Values and the Initial Approximations

To gain further insights into the relationship between the initial approximations and the recalculated system values for the features in each alternative, we compute the *correlation coefficient*[‡‡] using the data in Table 5.6. Correlation coefficient value ranges from −1 to 1. A value of 1 shows that the relationship between the two variables is perfect and positive. A correlation coefficient value of −1 shows that the relationship between the two variables is perfect and negative (i.e. one variable decreases as the other increases); a value of 0 shows that there is no linear relationship between the variables.

Table 5.6: Recalculated System Values and the Number of SD-coupling in Each Plan

	Recalculated System Values				Number of SD-coupled Features			
ID#	Plan A	Plan B	Plan C	Initial Approximation	Plan A	Plan B	Plan C	Initial Approximation
1	10.649	11.399	11.624	22.191	16	17	17	32
2	4.225	3.325	3.225	21.156	6	5	5	31
3	9.601	10.726	10.94	21.208	15	16	16	31
4	4.525	3.525	10.94	21.208	6	5	16	31
5	4.521	4.771	4.497	16.621	8	8	8	29
6	4.521	4.771	2.342	16.621	8	8	4	29
7	7.592	7.925	7.782	16.621	14	15	15	29
8	10.685	5.207	11.232	20.9	16	8	17	32
9	10.695	11.409	5.307	21.593	16	17	8	32
10	2.95	2.2	1.45	12.169	4	3	2	20
11	4.792	4.875	5.138	21.078	8	8	8	32
12	5.502	5.564	5.689	22.32	8	8	8	32
13	4.525	10.726	10.94	21.208	6	16	16	31
14	4.854	9.515	9.842	19.294	8	14	14	29
15	8.13	8.797	8.726	18.294	12	13	13	27
16	4.458	4.416	4.029	14.413	8	8	8	27
17	8.552	8.969	4.685	17.919	14	15	8	29
18	4.956	5.914	6.075	11.719	9	10	11	20
19	8.76	9.593	9.95	19.627	13	14	14	29
20	3.1	2.475	2.517	18.294	5	4	4	27
21	3.8	3.05	2.592	18.762	6	5	5	29
22	8.13	8.797	8.726	18.294	12	13	13	27
23	2.325	1.825	1.908	16.036	5	4	4	30
24	5.802	5.427	5.409	9.778	9	9	9	17
25	3.879	3.254	3.308	5.65	6	5	5	9
26	5.802	5.427	5.409	9.778	9	9	9	17
27	5.292	5.209	5.185	19.627	8	8	8	29
28	5.292	5.209	5.185	19.627	8	8	8	29
29	7.955	8.538	8.574	17.671	13	14	14	29
30	10.756	11.556	11.799	21.885	16	17	17	32
31	8.372	9.039	9.074	17.926	13	14	14	29
32	4.604	4.52	4.735	17.926	8	8	8	29
33	8.372	9.039	9.074	17.926	13	14	14	29

[‡‡] Correlation coefficient measures the strength and direction of a linear relationship between two variables. It is a measure of the tendency of the variables to increase or decrease together.

Figure 5.11 shows the correlation coefficients between the recalculated system values in each release plan alternative and the initial approximations. From the results in Figure 5.11, we observe that the recalculated system values in each plan have positive correlations with the initial approximations. The implication of this result is that for many of the features, high recalculated system values co-occur with high initial approximation of the system values, and vice versa. A perfect correlation can only exist when the correlation coefficient is 1.0, but this is not expected to be the case here, since only the initial approximation of the system values could have perfect correlation with itself. Any correlation greater than zero is taken as positive correlation; and the closer to 1 the correlation coefficient is, the higher the positive correlation. Thus, positive correlations that we observe here are already a good result that is consistent with our planning heuristics.

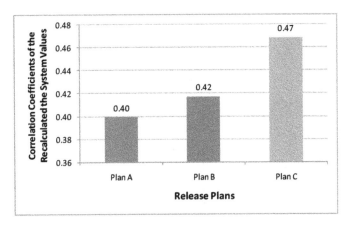

Figure 5.11: Correlation Coefficients of the Recalculated System Values

The second observation is that, the recalculated system values of the features in Plan C have the highest positive correlation with the initial approximation (i.e. correlation coefficient 0.47). On the other hand, the recalculated system values of Plan A have the lowest positive correlation (i.e. 0.40). This observation is particularly important. Recall from our discussion of the objective values results shown in Figure 5.8 that Plan C is biased towards the technical-oriented objective function, while Plan A is biased towards the business-oriented objective function. Thus, with alternative plan C having the highest positive correlation with the initial approximations of the systems values, the result validates our proposed planning heuristic for the objective function $F_2(x)$, at least for the case study under consideration. Since this objective function aims to assign features with higher system values together in the same release, then it is expected to exhibit the highest correlation with the initial approximations, if our planning heuristics would be considered valid. The explanation for Plan A having the least positive correlation coefficient follows accordingly.

5.6.6 Evaluating Release Plans using Satisfaction of SD-Coupling

Since the structures of the release plan alternatives are different and the objective values are also different, it is important to have a way to evaluate the alternative release plans. We discuss this aspect in details in the next chapter, in which we discuss the decision support technique for release planning. In the mean time, we evaluate the alternative release plans generated here, using the level of satisfaction of SD-coupling (see Section 5.4.4).

In the first instance, we chose threshold $\alpha=1.0$ to evaluate the level of satisfaction of SD-coupling in the alternative plans. Using the similarity metric defined in Equation (5.25), we compute the level of satisfaction of the SD-coupling at threshold $\alpha=1.0$ for each alternative. The level of satisfaction for plan A is $\mu_A^1=0.3125$. That is, a total of 31.3% of the required set of SD-couplings is satisfied by this release plan. Performing the same computation for Plans B and C, the level of satisfaction of the SD-coupling are $\mu_B^1=37.5\%$ and $\mu_c^1=43.8\%$, respectively. Besides the fact that the levels of satisfaction of SD-coupling are different for the different alternative plans, each alternative plan also satisfies different SD-couplings (compare Table 5.3 at $\alpha=1.0$ and their satisfaction in

Table 5.5). In the absence of any additional information, the level of satisfaction of SD-coupling could be used to choose among the alternatives. At threshold α=1.0, alternative C is the best release plan alternative.

Again, we evaluated the release plans at thresholds α=0.95, 0.9, 0.85, and 0.8, the levels of satisfaction of the SD-coupling by the different alternatives are shown in Figure 5.12. At these new thresholds, the alternative C also remains the best plan in terms of SD-coupling satisfaction. And this is expected to be the case.

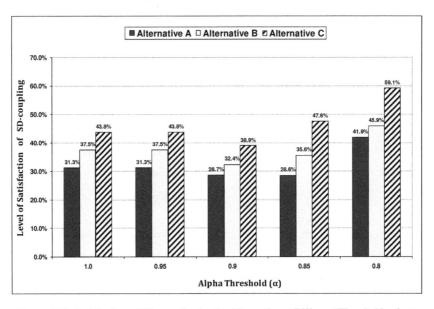

Figure 5.12: Satisfaction of SD-coupling by the Alternative at Different Thresholds of α

It is noteworthy that Plan C that has the highest level of satisfaction of SD-coupling also corresponds to the Pareto-optimal solution that is biased towards the technical perspective. This correspondence also validates our algorithm for computing the system value, because the system value aims to assign as many SD-coupled features to the same release as possible.

5.6.7 Discussions

The SD-coupling dependency results we have discussed for this case study need to be interpreted with caution. The impact analysis data was collected at a coarse-grained components level rather than at a more fine-grained level (e.g. classes or files). Impact analysis conducted at components level could easily lead to several interrelated features. This is not considered a drawback of our approach, because scalability is guaranteed for any granularity of impact analysis data used. The more fine-grained the impact analysis data, the better we can justify the existence of SD-coupling between interrelated features.

The alternative release plans generated via Pareto-optimal solutions provide better support for decision-making than providing just a single solution, because we cannot claim that a formal model completely captures all the decision parameters for such a human-centric decision problem. However, the additional information required to select between alternative plans must align with the project goals. Such information may be related to the experience of the decision-maker, market forces, or other project constraints that are missing in the formal model. In this chapter, we have discussed one approach to aid this selection from alternatives by using the level of satisfaction of SD-coupling. We shed more light on this aspect of decision support for release planning in the next chapter.

5.7 Related Work

Interdependency between features (or requirements) has been studied from different perspectives [35], [168]. Report from interviews conducted in Swedish software industries by Dahlstedt et al. [34] and Karlsson et al. [78], indicate that development companies cluster requirements based on which of them should be implemented together. This clustering decision often depends on whether the requirements in a cluster affect the same part of the system, and it could be based on whether it would be cost efficient to implement them together, or based on whether the same developer should implement the requirements [35]. In a recent study, Zhang et al. [168] observed that one fundamental problem remains that of determining the nature of influence that requirements interdependency exerts on the development of software products. These studies further highlight the importance of the work discussed in this chapter, in which we extract feature coupling due to the interrelatedness of features.

Carlshamre et al. [24], to the best of our knowledge, is the only reported work that studied interdependency from the perspective of release planning. Carlshamre and his colleagues classified interdependencies as being functionality-related or value-related. Using the classification scheme discussed in this chapter, both types would still fall within the realm of functionality-related interdependency in the problem domain. In comparison to our work, they have not discussed interdependency in the solution domain, and have also not proposed any technique to incorporate the interdependencies into release planning decision.

In comparison to the existing work on feature interaction, we have studied interdependency between features in relation to the set of impacted components that would be modified to implement the features in the existing system. Since we investigate this interdependency with the aim of identifying interrelatedness of features based on overlaps in the components implementing them, we refer to the resulting interdependency as feature coupling in the solution domain (or simply SD-coupling). And we also refer to those discovered in the problem domain as problem domain coupling (PD-coupling). Also, in contrast to the existing feature (or requirements) interdependency (or interaction) detection techniques that focus on functionalities or behavioral aspects, we focus on the results from change impact analysis to determine the interdependency between features.

There are existing works that explored the mapping of features to the code segments or components that implement the features in the existing system (e.g. Wong et al. [164],

Wilde and Casey [161], Wilde and Scully [162], Giroux and Robillard [59]). All these works are different from ours, because they focus on existing features that have already been implemented, rather than features that are yet to be added. On the other hand, we examined coupling between features that are yet to be implemented in order to sequence their implementation in the release plans, using the SD-coupling information. As a result, we may be able to avoid the unplanned dependency (*see* Giroux and Robillard [59]) that could result from haphazard implementation of features.

5.8 Summary

In this chapter, we discussed a technique for computing the SD-coupling between features and the implications of SD-coupling for release planning. Release Planning is just one of the several application areas for the SD-coupling computation approach discussed here. The information derived from the strength of coupling between features would help developers scan through features assigned to a release in order to take advantage of their interrelatedness. We have also discussed the feasibility and applicability of the proposed approach in release planning via a case study conducted using a real-world data.

In summary, the work discussed in this chapter supports release planning decisions by:

1. Providing a technique for detecting and quantifying the interrelatedness of features based on the overlaps in their implementation in the existing system.
2. Providing a technique for incorporating the detected feature coupling information into release planning decisions.
3. Formulating the release planning problem as a bi-objective optimization problem that seeks to maximize both business concerns and technical concerns.
4. Proposing a solution approach that generates alternative release plans to address decision-making under uncertainty.

5. Performing a case study to show the applicability of the proposed technique. Early results show good correlation between release plans generated and the level of satisfaction of SD-coupling.

CHAPTER SIX

DECISION SUPPORT TECHNIQUE FOR RELEASE PLANNING OF SOFTWARE SYSTEMS

Uncertainty is not a result of ignorance or the partiality of human knowledge, but is a characteristic of the world itself.
- Mark C. Taylor

6.1 Introduction

In this chapter, we present a decision support technique, SoRPES, for release planning of software systems. The formal models implemented in the decision support technique integrate concepts discussed in Chapters 4 and 5. This chapter also presents an approach to address uncertainties from the release planning perspective. The decision support technique is an instantiation of the framework discussed in Chapter 3.

6.2 Constituents of the Formal Model in SoRPES

SoRPES is partly based on a bi-objective optimization model for planning the next releases of existing software systems. The constituents of the model include the following: 1) the handling of business concerns using priorities of features specified by the stakeholders, 2) the potential synergy in the implementation of features as a result of their interrelatedness, and 3) the technical constraints of implementing features in the existing system.

We have discussed the first two constituents of the model in Chapter 5. Before discussing the integration of these three aspects into a unified optimization model, we first present an approach to measure the technical constraints of implementing the features in the existing system. We assess the technical constraints of implementing each feature as a function of the modifiability of the impacted components of the existing software architecture and the extent of modification required in these components.

6.3 Technical Constraints

The technical constraint of adding a feature to an existing system is a function of the restrictions that the components of the system place on the implementation of the feature. This technical constraint is determined by the level of dispersion of the components that the feature impacts, the ease of modification (EoM) of these components in order to add the feature, and the extent of modification (XoM) required to add the feature.

DEFINITION 6.1 (EASE OF MODIFICATION, $EoM(c_m)$)

Given a component c_m of an existing system S, the ease of modification of the component c_m, denoted $EoM(c_m)$, measures the ability to add new features or changes to the component quickly. □

DEFINITION 6.2 (EXTENT OF MODIFICATION, $XoM(c_m, f_i)$)

Given a component c_m of an existing system S and a feature f_i, the extent of modification $XoM(c_m, f_i)$ is a measure of the extent of changes required in a component c_m that would be modified in order to add feature f_i. □

We illustrate the two concepts (i.e. EoM and XoM) in Figure 6.1. Suppose we have a system S that is made up of six components, $C = \{c_1, c_2, c_3, c_4, c_5, c_6\}$. For illustration purposes, the set of impacted components $\Phi_i \subset C$ for the implementation of a given feature f_i consists of four components $\Phi_i = \{c_1, c_2, c_4, c_6\}$. In Figure 6.1, the different shading levels of the components c_m refer to the different levels of their $EoM(c_m)$. The darker the shading, the more difficult it is to modify the component. The hatched area within each component describes the $XoM(c_m, f_i)$ (i.e. the notation for XoM because the measure is feature- and component-specific). The larger the hatched area, the higher is the approximated extent of modification. For example, the $\text{XoM}(c_3,f_i)=0$ and $\text{XoM}(c_2,f_i) > \text{XoM}(c_6,f_i)$.

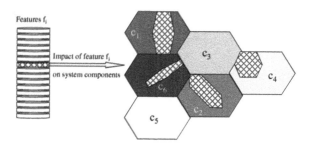

Figure 6.1: Impact of Implementing Feature f_i in the Components c_m

The level of dispersion of the impacted components is determined via feature-driven impact analysis, as discussed in Chapter 5, the EoM computation is performed at components level using the EBEAM technique discussed in Chapter 4, and the XoM is based on the approximate estimation of the extent of changes that would be made to each component by the developers.

We discuss the technical constraints model next. We begin by instantiating the EBEAM technique for component-level modifiability assessment.

6.3.1 Evaluating the EoM of Components using EBEAM

To use EBEAM for evaluating software components, we need to characterize modifiability in terms of components, rather than in terms of the whole architecture. In Chapter 4, we focused these characteristics on basic design principles in order to evaluate architectures. The applicability of these characteristics depends on the level of granularity at which components are defined (see Definition 5.1 in Chapter 5 for granularity of components). For example, a characteristic like "Appropriate use of design patterns and architectural styles" applies to architectural designs of a system, but not for components defined at a more fine-grained level. On the other hand, some of the design characteristics mentioned in Chapter 4 could still apply to components.

Recall from our discussion in Chapter 4 that modifiability can be influenced by different factors, which may not necessarily be related to design goodness. Regardless of the factors used, the relative nature of knowledge elicitation process in EBEAM ensures that the factors (or characteristics) used to evaluate EoM do not influence results. It is sufficient for the designers or developers performing the evaluation to have a common understanding of what the factors mean. Because all the components would be relatively evaluated using the same set of factors.

These factors, which we have also adopted in an earlier pilot study reported in [141], include: 1) size, 2) complexity, 3) understandability, 4) health, 5) criticality, and 6) number of functionalities. In discussing each factor, we cite the prior research supporting their inclusion in the list. We make it a duty to emphasize here that these factors are not assumed to be necessarily orthogonal – for example, complexity may impact understandability of a component. In addition, we cannot lay claim to their completeness, despite several empirical studies that abound in the literature, which investigate the effects of these factors on modifiability. We discuss each factor next.

6.3.1.1 Size of Component

Components of a software system exhibit varying sizes, depending on the functionalities they implement. When adding features to components with large sizes, it is harder to keep track of all details and interactions in mind, and vice-versa for components with smaller sizes.

6.3.1.2 Complexity of Components

The complexity of a component is determined by the structure of the code that implements the component and its interactions with other components. As the coupling value of a component increases, for example, so does the number of other components that need to be modified whenever a change affects one of them. Lehman's laws of software evolution [96] states that, software complexity tends to increase over time while the quality of the product will tend to decrease. According to Lehman *et al.* [98], increasing complexity results from greater inter-element connectivity.

6.3.1.3 Understandability of Components

Understandability of a component refers to the ease with which developers can develop a grasp of the component. This is the ability to determine what a component does and how it works. Empirical studies show that this factor is influenced by the expertise of whoever is making the changes [47] [64], the growth rate of the component overtime [96], how long the component has been part of the system [47], and quality of documentation available [64]. All this information put together could guide developers in understanding a component. Component understanding is said to consume a significant proportion of maintenance effort and resources [64], which further justifies its inclusion as part of the factors contributing to EoM.

6.3.1.4 Health of Components

The health of a component is a measure of its fault-proneness. If components are unhealthy, they will be fault-prone, and changing any small part of the code can be very risky and time consuming. Empirical studies [60] [47] show that correlations exist between the health (i.e., ability to use or reuse existing code base [37]) of program code, the quality of the resulting product, and the functionality that can be added to the system.

6.3.1.5 Criticality of Component

Some parts of a system are critical while others are not, and normal operations could continue without the non-critical parts. Some components add only minor functionality, or functionality that is rarely used. Clearly, deficiencies in these kinds of components, although unpleasant, may not be service impacting. The criticality of a component must be taken into consideration when evaluating EoM, as extra effort and resources may be needed to ensure that critical components achieve their goals.

6.3.1.6 Number of Functionalities Implemented

The number of functionalities a component implements could contribute to the ease of modifying the component. Modifying components that implement several functionalities in order to add features would be more arduous. Apart from adding new features, extra care must be taken to ensure that all the existing functionalities are not adversely affected. This extra attention makes those components more difficult to modify than those that implement single functionality.

Having identified the factors for evaluating the EoM of components, the computation of the $EoM(c_m)$ is a straight-forward application of the EBEAM technique described in Chapter 4. The $EoM(c_m)$ could also be assessed using any other applicable method. Although, not discussed as part of this book, we have proposed another method that uses Bayesian Belief Networks (BBN) for the same purpose in [140]. However, the amount of real world probability data required from the technical team to complete the BBN-based evaluation of components limits its real-world applicability.

6.3.2 Determining the Extent of Modification of Components

We can measure the $XoM\left(c_m, f_i\right)$ as a percentage of the expected code modification relative to the original size of the component. This is expected to be an approximation, and would suffice for estimation at the early stages during which release planning decisions are made. In [141], we have carried out such assessments using opinions of developers/designers who are familiar with the existing system, and would be modifying the components. Measuring XoM could also be done at higher granularity than the code level – for example, it could be measured as percentage of objects or class modifications.

6.3.3 Calculating the Technical Constraints of Implementing Features

The technical constraints of implementing feature f_i in the existing components requires the aggregation of the $EoM(c_m)$ and $XoM(c_m, f_i)$ for all set of components $c_m \in \Phi_i$ that would be modified to add feature f_i. We define the following aggregation formula for the technical constraints $tc(i)$.

$$tc(i) = \sum_{m=1\ldots M} \delta_{im} \cdot \left(1 - EoM\left(c_m\right)\right) + \sum_{m=1\ldots M} \delta_{im} \cdot XoM\left(c_m, f_i\right) \qquad (6.1)$$

where,

$$\delta_{im} = \begin{cases} 1 & \text{if } c_m \in \Phi_i \\ 0 & \text{otherwise} \end{cases}$$

and $0 \leq EoM\left(c_m\right) \leq 1$, $0 \leq XoM\left(c_m, f_i\right) \leq 1$.

The metric in Equation (6.1) represents the formal model for computing the technical constraints of implementing a feature in the existing system. The metric makes it possible to differentiate between features that involve difficult and complex changes to the existing system and those involving simple and small changes.

We used $1 - EoM\left(c_m\right)$ in Equation (6.1) because EBEAM computes EoM, but technical constraints could be assumed to reflect the risk associated with implementing each feature, and it is expected to increase with increasing difficulty of modification as well as with increasing XoM. With a risk-averse decision maker, the goal is always to obtain maximum values possible from the objective functions while minimizing the risk level.

The entire process for computing technical constraints is shown in Figure 6.2. As shown in Figure 6.2, EBEAM is adopted for evaluating the EoM of the components of existing systems. Each feature in the feature repository goes through feature-driven impact analysis on the existing system to determine the set of components to be modified and the XoM required to add the feature. The process ends with the computation of the technical constraints for each feature.

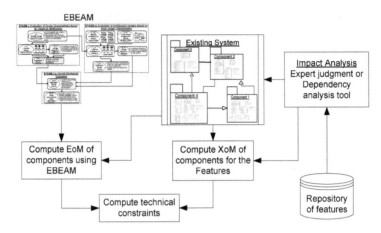

Figure 6.2: Technical Constraints of Implementing Features

6.4 SoRPES Optimization Model

The optimization models for SoRPES integrate technical constraints into the bi-objective optimization model discussed in Chapter 5. The goal of this integration is to bring together, in a unified model, constituents of the two perspectives that influence release planning decision making. Recall that the business concerns have an associated objective function and business-related constraints, while the technical concerns also have an associated objective function (defined on interrelatedness of features) and technical constraints.

The resulting bi-objective optimization model for release planning, which is an extension of Equations (5.17)–(5.22), becomes:

$$\text{Max}^*$$

$$\Upsilon = \left(\sum_{k=1...K} \sum_{i=1...n} v(i,k) \cdot x(i,k), \ \sum_{k=1...K} \sum_{i=1...n} sv(i,k) \cdot x(i,k) \right) \quad (6.2)$$

Subject to

$$\sum_{i=1...n} r(i,t) \cdot x(i,k) \le r_{\max}(k,t), \quad t \in T; \quad k = 1...K \tag{6.3}$$

$$x(i,k) = x(j,k), \quad k = 1...K, \quad \forall\, (i,j) \in C \tag{6.4}$$

$$\sum_{k=1...K} (K+1-k)(x(i,k)-x(j,k)) \ge 0, \quad \forall\, (i,j) \in P \tag{6.5}$$

$$\sum_{k=1...K} tc(i) \cdot x(i,k) \le \beta_k \quad \forall\, i \tag{6.6}$$

$$\sum_{k=1...K} x(i,k) \le 1 \quad \forall\, i \tag{6.7}$$

$$x(i,k) \in \{0,1\} \quad \forall\, i \text{ and } k \tag{6.8}$$

In the new bi-objective optimization model given by Equations (6.2)–(6.8), the left hand side of Equation (6.6) is the technical constraints, while the right hand side represents the thresholds β_k that must not be exceeded in each release.

Asking the development team to specify values for threshold β_k would be difficult. To alleviate this problem, we propose an approach that solves a single-objective optimization sub-problem. This sub-problem is based on an objective function defined on the technical constraints, which is subject to other release planning constraints. The single-objective optimization sub-problem maximizes the technical constraints $tc(i)$ to obtain τ_k, thereby allowing us to explore a subset of the solution space that is capped by the maximal values τ_k. The single-objective optimization sub-problem is formulated as follows:

Max

$$\tau_k = \sum_{k=1...K} \sum_{i=1...n} tc(i) \cdot x(i,k) \tag{6.9}$$

Subject to

$$\sum_{i=1...n} r(i,t) \cdot x(i,k) \le r_{\max}(k,t), \quad t \in T; \; k = 1...K \tag{6.10}$$

$$x(i,k) = x(j,k), \quad k = 1...K, \quad \forall\, (i,j) \in C \tag{6.11}$$

$$\sum_{k=1...K} (K+1-k)(x(i,k)-x(j,k)) \ge 0, \quad \forall\, (i,j) \in P \tag{6.12}$$

$$\sum_{k=1\ldots K} x(i,k) \leq 1 \qquad \forall\; i \tag{6.13}$$

$$x(i,k) \in \{0,1\} \qquad \forall\; i \; and \; k \tag{6.14}$$

After obtaining the maximal values τ_k, then we define the threshold β_k as follows.

$$\beta_k = \rho \cdot \tau_k \tag{6.15}$$

The ρ in (6.15) is the percentage of solution space to be explored. The lower the value of ρ, the more risk-averse the decision maker is assumed to be, since the less risk the decision maker would be willing to accommodate. For example, if $\rho = 80\%$, it implies that the threshold is set to accept any release plan generated within 80% of the maximum technical constraints.

The solution approach for the bi-objective optimization problem for SoRPES, which is described in Equations (6.2)–(6.8), is our implementation of the ε-Constraint algorithm (i.e. Algorithm 5.4) already discussed in Chapter 5.

6.5 The SoRPES Decision Support

6.5.1 Overview

We presented the decision-centric framework for software release planning in Chapter 3. Apart from the formal models discussed for SoRPES above, we now instantiate SoRPES as a decision support technique via a concrete implementation of the framework. The instantiation of the framework is based on the hybrid decision support approach proposed by Ruhe [131], and discussed in the context of release planning by Ruhe and Ngo-The [133], and Ruhe and Saliu [134]. This approach to decision support argues in favor of augmenting the benefits of computational intelligence with the knowledge of human experts, and it gives a guide on how to achieve this.

6.5.2 A Hybrid Approach to Decision Support for Release Planning

A formalized description of the release planning problem, as given by the optimization models in Equations (6.2)–(6.8) and Equations (6.9)–(6.15), and the corresponding solution to the models, is not expected to completely address all aspects of the problem. Some aspects of the decision could be influenced by previous experiences of the human decision maker; these experiences may not be amenable to formalized descriptions.

We present a hybrid approach to decision support for release planning that offers an iterative and continuous process. This process allows the decision maker to evaluate the solution generated and possibly redefining the problem parameters, if necessary. This process, which allows for planning and re-planning, is modeled after the hybrid approach to evolutionary problem solving proposed in [131]. The high-level structure of the hybrid implementation of SoRPES is shown in Figure 6.3. This structure involves the performance of a variety of tasks during three phases of the planning process: 1) modeling, 2) exploration, and 3) consolidation. We discuss these phases next.

6.5.2.1 Phase 1: Modeling

The top of the triangle in Figure 6.3, which is known as the modeling phase, addresses the problem conceptualization. It focuses on the formal description of the dynamic real world to make it suitable for computational-intelligence-based solution techniques. In this modeling phase, we construct the formal model that integrates several factors that influence release planning decisions. It encompasses all the activities that led to the formulation of the bi-objective optimization model discussed in Section 6.4.

Apart from objectives of planning, the modeling phase also encompasses the definition of the various constraints that restricts the number of features that can be implemented and which also restrict the sequencing of the features into different releases. We have discussed these release planning constraints in Chapter 5 and in Section 6.3 of this chapter. We have also integrated these constraints into the formal model in Section 6.4.

160

The generation of the initial set of release plans is based on the results from the optimization models formulated in the modeling phase.

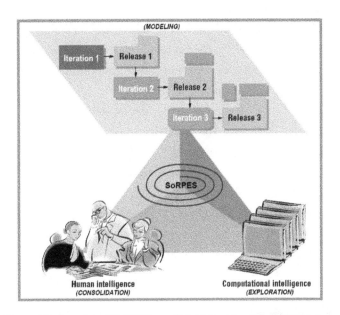

Figure 6.3: Overview of SoRPES as a Hybrid Decision Support Technique

6.5.2.2 Phase 2: Exploration

In this phase, the computational part of the SoRPES decision support generates the release plans based on the formal models described in Section 6.4. Because of the model's sophistication, we need efficient solution techniques that could explore the solution space and generate sets of solution alternatives. We have implemented an ε-Constraint algorithm that searches for the Pareto-optimal solutions to the bi-objective optimization problem.

6.5.2.3 Phase 3: Consolidation

In the consolidation phase, the decision maker (such as the project manager) evaluates the solution alternatives generated using the computational algorithm. If necessary, (s)he can modify parameters of the problem or make some context-specific decisions (e.g. pre-assigning some features to specific releases). Several iterations are possible until a desirable solution alternative is obtained. During each iteration, the decision maker gains more insight into the problem because (s)he has sample solution alternatives to evaluate. In performing what-if analysis, the decision maker can base re-planning decisions on questions such as:

- What if some of the stakeholder weights change?
- What if some of the resource capacities are increased (or decreased)?
- What if stakeholders modify the priorities of features?
- What if we reduce or increase the level of satisfaction of SD-coupling desired in a release plan, and so on?

6.6 Instantiation of the SoRPES Framework

Figure 6.4 details the SoRPES decision support technique. It provides detailed implementation for the relevant process elements identified in the framework discussed in Chapter 3. The focus is more on the software systems that have pre-existing designs in place. Next, we discuss SoRPES decision support based on the 3 phases of the hybrid decision support approach – modeling, exploration, and consolidation.

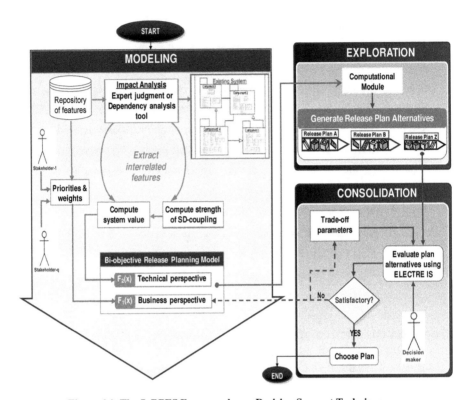

Figure 6.4: The SoRPES Framework as a Decision Support Technique

During the *modeling phase*, impact analysis is conducted to identify components that would be modified to add features in the repository to the existing system. Using the results from impact analysis, we extract interrelated features, compute strength of SD-coupling and system values for the features. Then, we formulate the objective function representing the technical perspective. These two perspectives have been formally modeled as a bi-objective optimization problem described by Equations (6.2)–(6.8). The parts of SoRPES that are not explicitly represented in the diagram are the constraints (e.g. resources, capacities, and technical constraints). Resource required and the available resource capacities are specified by the project manager in conjunction with the development team. The constraints already constitute part of the bi-objective optimization model; explicitly representing them in Figure 6.4 would only serve to make the figure unnecessarily complex.

In the *exploration phase*, the ε-Constraint algorithm discussed in Chapter 5 is implemented as part of the computational module that generates release plan alternatives.

In the *consolidation phase*, the solution alternatives generated during the exploration phase are evaluated, using the factors that cannot be explicitly incorporated into the formal model. The factors, which we generally classify under the trade-off parameters in Figure 6.4, can originate from organizational factors, people issues, or technology-related considerations [172]. SoRPES provides mechanisms to allow human experts to bring their intuition and experience into the decision making process. In the event that a specific alternative satisfies the decision maker, the release plan is chosen for implementation. On the other hand, if none of the release plan alternatives satisfy the decision maker, (s)he can either redefine the trade-off parameters and repeat the evaluation process, or redefine some problem parameters (e.g. relative importance of the stakeholders) and regenerate a new set of alternative solutions.

The dotted arrows in the figure indicate the path to the parameters that the decision maker can interactively modify during the decision making process. The human decision maker's interaction and redefinition of the problem instances align with the iterative approach to providing decision support for release planning. This is motivated by the evolutionary view of decision problems in multi-criteria decision aid (MCDA) [128]. In the next section, we discuss the preference analysis scheme that is adopted as part of the exploration process in SoRPES.

6.7 Preference Analysis in SoRPES

In terms of optimality, none of the release plan alternatives obtained via Pareto-optimal solutions can be said to be better than the other. Meanwhile, decision makers are able to express their preferences for various solution alternatives. One of the basic functions of decision support is to provide ways for a decision maker to specify his/her preferences. It is, however, possible to employ any suitable multi-criteria decision analysis (MCDA) approach to assist the decision maker in evaluating the trade-offs between various alternatives. MCDA is a process that helps in making decisions with regards to choosing, ranking or sorting alternatives [53]. MCDA has as its basic constituents: 1) a set of alternatives, 2) at least the presence of two criteria, and 3) the presence of at least one decision maker. Some MCDA approaches like the multi-attribute utility theory (MAUT) [88] and outranking methods (e.g. ELECTRE-IS [130]) present useful activities to aid the decision maker in the selection of one release plan from the alternatives. The ELECTRE-IS that we adopt in this phase of SoRPES is a member of the family of the MCDA approach called ELECTRE [130]. We succinctly introduce ELECTRE IS next.

6.7.1 Analyzing Preferences using ELECTRE IS

ELECTRE IS (electre one esse) [53] is a method for supporting the problem of selecting one alternative solution from a given finite set of alternatives, especially in situations where we are dealing with imperfect knowledge (see Chapter 4 in [53]). The ability of ELECTRE IS to handle uncertainty in building preferences is a rationale for adopting it in SoRPES. ELECTRE IS is useful in situations where we have heterogeneity among the evaluation criteria, which could render the aggregation of all the criteria in a common scale meaningless [130].

Modeling of preferences in ELECTRE IS (and other member of the ELECTRE family) is achieved by using the binary outranking relations, R, in which the meaning of R(a,b) is that "*alternative a is as good as alternative b*". In the definition of the relation R, it is possible to have two alternatives *a* and *b* that are incomparable. The incomparability relation is used for describing situations in which the decision maker cannot compare the two alternatives. To establish an order relation for each criterion, the ELECTRE IS does not require accurate estimates. Rather, enough information to show ordering among the solutions would suffice. For example, it is enough to be able to show that alternative *a* is riskier than alternative *b*.

In the evaluation of alternatives using ELECTRE IS, each individual order relation R(a,b) derived from a criterion *j* is assigned a weight w_j. This weight represents the relative importance of the criterion in the overall comparison where the criterion favors an outranking. The weights neither depend on the scales used nor the range of the scales [130]. Using the weights of the relation, ELECTRE IS aggregates these relations to achieve a final outranking relation. From this final outranking relation, one alternative can be identified as not outranked by any other alternative. In order to validate the assertion R(a,b), the following two conditions on concordance/non-discordance must be satisfied [130]:

DEFINITION 6.3 (CONCORDANCE)
For an outranking R(a,b) to be validated, a sufficient majority of criteria should be in favor of this assertion. □

DEFINITION 6.4 (NON-DISCORDANCE)
When the concordance condition holds, none of the criteria in the minority should oppose too strongly to the assertion R(a,b). □

Applying ELECTRE IS involves two main procedures: 1) construction of one or several outranking relation(s), followed by 2) an exploitation procedure. The goal of constructing one or several outranking relation(s) is to be able to compare each pair of alternatives in a comprehensive manner. The exploitation procedure is used to structure the recommendations from the results achieved from the first phase [53],[130].

According to the ELECTRE IS [130] method, the overall outranking relation R(a,b) is defined to represent the degree to which each of the criteria supports the statement "*a outranks b*" (the degree is known as the concordance level), as follows:

$$R(a,b) = \frac{\sum_{j \in C(a,b)} w_j}{\sum_j w_j}$$

(6.16)

where C(a,b) = {j: alternative *a* outranks alternative *b* from the perspective of criterion j}. This implies that R(a,b) is the same as the ratio of the total weight of all the criteria that agree on "*a outranks b*" to the total weight of all the criteria. By the definition of R(a,b), it is straight-forward to deduce that $0 \le R(a,b) \le 1$. The closer the concordance level R(a,b) is to 1, the more confidence we have in accepting the fact that "*a outranks b*". the application of Equation (6.16) to the alternatives, and for all criteria, generates the whole outranking relation.

After constructing the entire outranking relation, which is a fuzzy relation, a threshold η can be set for the concordance level, in order to obtain the crisp outranking relation $R_\eta(a,b)$ at the chosen threshold. This threshold is also known as the discrimination threshold that helps in constructing a preference structure in the form of a graph [53]. The crisp outranking relation is defined as:

$$R_\eta(a,b) = 1 \quad \text{if and only if} \quad R_\eta(a,b) \ge \eta$$

(6.17)

Further details on ELECTRE IS can be found in Figueria et al. [53] and Roy [130].

6.7.2 Evaluation Criteria (Trade-off Parameters) for SoRPES Alternatives

Each release plan alternative can be evaluated against a set of individual criteria. The project manager, who would possibly double as the decision maker, could come up with at least one or more criteria for evaluating alternative plans. Most often, it is difficult to combine these criteria into an objective function, especially under the assumption of non-compensatory aggregation. The non-compensatory aggregation procedure is one of the strengths of ELECTRES IS, in which case it is not acceptable to compensate for the loss on a given criterion by a gain on another criterion. The ELECTRE IS fits well within the decision support technique we present for the release planning problem.

For illustration purposes only, we show how release plan alternatives can be evaluated using the ELECTRE IS by defining the following three criteria.

1.   Level of satisfaction of SD-coupling in a release plan
2.   Structural blend of features across releases.
3.   Attractiveness of release plan

We have discussed the *level of satisfaction of SD-coupling* and its computation in Chapter 5. The measure of level of satisfaction of SD-coupling is based on a ratio scale. We discuss the other two criteria next.

DEFINITION 6.4 (STRUCTURAL BLEND OF FEATURES IN A PLAN)

The structural blend of features in a release plan refers to the diversity of the assigned features across different groups, without the concentration of all assigned features in one group. □

In simple terms, the structural blend of features in a release plan seeks for a balance in the assignment of features to releases, such that each group of features has a good enough representation in the release plan. For example, the set of features shown in Table 7.2 are grouped into 6 different groups. Evaluation of structural blend would involve checking through a plan to determine the extent to which each group is represented in the plan.

To measure this, the decision maker could check through a release plan to see the relative number of features from each group that has been assigned to one of the releases in a release plan. Based on this personal assessment, s(he) could assign a value to each alternative as s(he) deems fit. A simple ordinal scale measurement, which preserves ordering among the alternatives, would suffice.

DEFINITION 6.5 (ATTRACTIVENESS OF PLAN)
The attractiveness of a release plan refers to the appeal that the plan makes to the project manager or decision maker. □

Several factors could contribute to a decision maker finding a particular solution attractive. It could possibly be that s(he) sees a reflection of his expectations more in one alternative than in another alternative. It could also be due to prior experience or knowledge of successful projects with similar features in the past, whose order of implementation is closer to one of the alternatives than another. It is clear from this description that such criterion cannot be incorporated into a model, as it must reflect the judgment of the decision maker during the evaluation task. An ordinal scale measure that ranks the alternatives would also be sufficient for assessing this criterion.

Once again, the above three criteria are simply for illustrating ELECTRE IS in the context of SoRPES. A completely different set of criteria can be employed during the evaluation.

6.7.3 Usage Scenario of ELECTRE IS in SoRPES – An Example

To illustrate the application of ELECTRE IS in SoRPES, we consider the 3 release plan alternatives (A, B, and C) contained in Table 5.5 (refer to the case study result in Chapter

5). The level of satisfaction of SD-coupling (at threshold $\alpha = 1$) in the alternatives (A, B, C) have been calculated as $\mu_A = 0.3125$, $\mu_B = 0.3750$, and $\mu_C = 0.4380$, respectively. We assume that the project manager uses an ordinal five point scale measure 1(worst) to 5(best) to assess the *structural blend* and *attractiveness* in each alternative, as shown in Table 6.1. Let the weight w_j of the criteria *SD-coupling satisfaction*, *structural blend*, and *attractiveness* be given as 2.5, 1.5, and 4.0 respectively. Recall that the range and scale of the weights are immaterial, as long as ordering is preserved. Result of the evaluation of each release plan alternative, based on each criterion, is shown in Table 6.1. The weight of each criterion is also given in parenthesis in the table.

Table 6.1: Evaluation of Release Plan Alternatives using ELECTRE IS

Release plan alternatives	SD-coupling satisfaction (2.5)	Structural blend (1.5)	Attractiveness (4.0)
A	0.3125	5	4
B	0.3750	1	2
C	0.4380	2	3

From Table 6.1, we can deduce that the criteria *structural blend* and *attractiveness* agree with the assertion that "alternative A outranks alternative B", while only criteria *SD-coupling satisfaction* disagree with this assertion by showing the exact opposite. Using the relation defined in Equation (6.16), we have R(A,B) = (1.5+4.0)/8.0 = 0.6875, while R(B,A) = (2.5)/8.0 = 0.3125. Similarly, the assertion "alternative C outranks alternative B" is supported by all 3 criteria. In this case, the relation R(C,B) = (2.5+1.5+4.0)/8.0 = 1.0. Again, there is no criteria that is against the assertion R(C,B), which implies that we should have confidence in accepting the assertion "C outranks B".

The complete set of the outranking relation is shown in Table 6.2. Note that we did not perform any arithmetic operations on the actual values assigned to each alternative from the perspective of each criterion. All arithmetic operations performed to generate the result in Table 6.2 are based on the weights of the criteria, depending on which assertion the criteria support. This confirms that the use of different scales is immaterial.

Table 6.2: Outranking Relation R for Alternatives A, B, and C

	A	B	C
A	1.0	0.6875	0.6875
B	0.3125	1.0	0.0
C	0.3125	1.0	1.0

Let $\eta = 0.5$ be the chosen threshold, for example, the corresponding graph of the outranking relation $R_{0.5}$ is given in Figure 6.5. At the chosen threshold, alternative A is the best solution (it outranks all other alternatives), while alternative B is the worst alternative (it is outranked by all other alternatives). In this case, it is easy to choose alternative A as the best solution. Recall that if we had considered only the SD-coupling satisfaction, as discussed in Chapter 5, alternative C would have been chosen as the best solution. This does not necessarily mean that A remains the best solution for all possible values of thresholds η. The graph of the outranking relation may change to support another alternative, if the threshold changes.

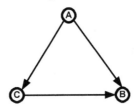

Figure 6.5: Outranking Relation $R_{0.5}$

6.8 Prototype Implementation for SoRPES

This section discusses our implementation of SoRPES and demonstrates the feasibility of providing a full-fledged decision support tool. We describe the architectural overview of the proposed support environment and status of our implementation of a research prototype.

6.8.1 Architecture of the Support Environment

Figure 6.6 is the proposed architecture of the SoRPES support environment. It shows the conceptual structure of the components that make up the architecture and the dataflow between the components. The support environment consists of the following:

- *Presentation layer:* this layer contains the interface through which the user interacts with the system – it accepts input from and presents results to the users. As of the moment, and considering that this is a research prototype, we have yet to implement a user-friendly graphical user interface.
- *Business logic:* this layer, which is the core of the support environment, implements the various models and algorithms discussed earlier.
- *Data layer:* contains all the data required in the support environment.

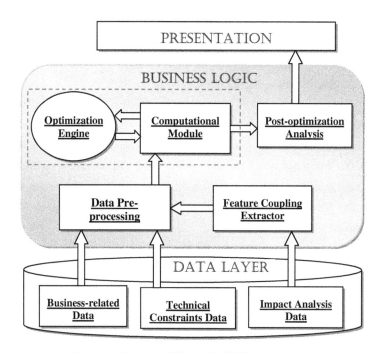

Figure 6.6: Conceptual View of SoRPES Implementation

6.8.2 Implementing the Different Components

We briefly discuss our implementation of the various components in the current prototype. The layered separation of the architecture allows for implementation flexibility. This includes the language of implementation and the integration of the different components to realize the prototype. Since we have not implemented a graphical user interface, we do not discuss this component of the architecture further in this section. We expatiate on the data layer and the business logic.

6.8.2.1 The Data Layer

The data layer is meant to maintain all the data required in the models and algorithms discussed for SoRPES. The data from business perspective are collected using a standard MS Excel template. This same template is currently used by the ReleasePlanner system [127]. In the alternative, and as we actually did for our empirical studies, we used ReleasePlanner to collect these data because of the user interface it provides, and then we export the data to the standard MS Excel template. Table C.1 – Table C.4 in Appendix C show sample data collection using the MS Excel template.

The technical constraints data are also collected in an MS excel template. Recall that technical constraints is derived from Equation (6.1). As part of the technical constraints computation, the evaluation of the components using EBEAM relies on MS Excel mathematical functions to aggregate the judgments made by experts. The impact analysis data is a text file containing the list of impacted components by each feature. All these data are passed to the business logic layer.

At the moment, the use of text files and MS Excel file formats for data collection suffices for our purposes. In developing a complete decision support system in the future, a database engine would be necessary.

6.8.2.2 The Business Logic Layer

Apart from the optimization engine, the business logic layer contains 4 key components that implement different algorithms and models discussed earlier. These components are: 1) Feature coupling extractor, 2) Data pre-processing, 3) Computational module, and 4) Post-optimization analysis.

1. Feature coupling extractor

   The feature coupling extractor implements both Algorithm 5.1 (Section 5.3.4) and Algorithm 5.2 (Section 5.3.6) discussed in Chapter 5. We have implemented this part in Java. It takes the impact analysis data as input and generates all the SD-couplings, the strength of SD-couplings, and the system values for all features.

2. Data pre-processing

   This component pre-processes and integrates all the planning data into a single text file that would be passed to the computational module. The implementation of this integration is done in Java.

3. Computational module

   The computational module is the heart of SoRPES. This is where the actual implementation of the ε-Constraint algorithm and generation of plans are handled. This module implements the single-objective optimization model for determining the technical constraints threshold given by Equations (6.9)–(6.15), the bi-objective release planning model formulated in Equations (6.2)–(6.8) and solved via the ε-Constraint algorithm discussed in Algorithm 5.3 and Algorithm 5.4 (see Section 5.5.2). As discussed in Chapter 5, our implementation of the ε-Constraint algorithm uses the ILOG-CPLEX Optimizer [72] as the single-objective optimizer to solve several single-objective optimization sub-problems. Thus, there are several calls between the Computational Module and ILOG-CPLEX Optimizer, depending on how many single-objective optimization sub-problems to be solved.

Even for a small size problem, many calls are made, depending on the number of iterations it takes to locate each Pareto-optimal solution.

The input to the Computational Module is the pre-processed data from the Data Pre-processing component. The entire activities in the Computational Module have been implemented using Microsoft Visual C#.NET. Since the ILOG cannot process the raw data in the text file, the C#.NET code initially converts the text file to a linear program (LP) format for the first optimization run. During every other instance of our search for Pareto-optimal solutions, the code rewrites variants of the LP file. The results from ILOG are contained in an MST (Windows SDK Setup Transform Script) file. For all the Pareto-optimal solutions, we process the MST file to rewrite the results (i.e. release plan alternatives and their objective values) in an easily understandable text file format or MS Excel format.

4. Post-optimization analysis

All the activities in the post-optimization analysis are based on the results generated from the computational module, and they are aimed at supporting release plan evaluation during the consolidation phase of SoRPES. We implement this component in Java. The Java code takes the text file generated by the computational module as input and supports various analyses of release plan alternatives. For example, it supports the test for the satisfaction of SD-coupling by implementing Equation 5.25 (Section 5.4.4), it supports the test for the level of diversification in the release plan alternatives, the recalculation of system values, and so on. If the decision maker needs to modify the parameters of the original problem during consolidation, s(he) would have to make these changes in the original MS Excel file.

6.8.3 Challenges in Building a Full-Fledged Support Environment

To speed up the development time and facilitate validation of the underlying optimization models and algorithms, which essentially are the important theoretical basis of the research, we have adopted an optimization engine called ILOG-CPLEX Optimizer [72]. It should be noted that it has not been one of the objectives of this book to build a readily deployable decision support tool for release planning (this constitutes part of the long term goal, though). We set out to investigate, design, develop, and validate the theoretical foundation for such complete tool support. This theoretical basis has been outlined in SoRPES. The current implementation of all the core aspects, except the user interface and complete integration of all the components, has been done to support our empirical validation studies that investigate both applicability and feasibility of the SoRPES technique. We discuss these validation studies in Chapter 7.

Our current implementation of the SoRPES support environment is still a research prototype, which implies that usability is a major issue at this point. A full-fledged support tool for SoRPES would constitute part of the future work, as discussed later in Chapter 8. In fact, several parts of the current implementation still require human intervention.

In order to collect release planning data, for example, we offer a standard template using MS Excel. Alternatively, we allow the users to use the ReleasePlanner system to specify all the business-related data, and then export this to the standard MS Excel template.

The ReleasePlanner system implements a single-objective optimization engine and a fully functional graphical user interface to support users. We are looking at the possibility of extending the ReleasePlanner by implementing SoRPES as a plug-in in the future. This would depend on the results obtained from further empirical validation of SoRPES.

6.9 Related Work

Greer [61] took an initial shot at considering risk in release planning. In Greer's case, an assumption is made that the developers should be able to give the risk values for the feature without contextual basis. In contrast to their work, we defined the technical constraints of implementing a feature as a function of the diversity of the impacted components of the existing system, the ease of modification of these impacted components, and the extent of modification required in these components to add a feature. Since risk could mean different things to different developers assigning values for risk, we have developed a more robust approach to meaningfully evaluate technical constraints. The technical constraints capture most of the parameters that could be said to constitute technical risk of implementing a feature. On the release planning side, the closest to the work discussed in this chapter, from the business perspective, is the EVOLVE* developed by Ruhe and Ngo-The [133].

A more recent work by Zhang et al. [169] attempt to formulate the release planning problem as a bi-objective optimization problem. Zhang and colleagues focused exclusively on optimizing only value and cost, but ignores other release planning parameters and constraints. Our work is fundamentally different and more sophisticated, because we took a holistic view of the release planning problem. In this view, our bi-objective model achieves the following: 1) it incorporates both business and technical concerns in release planning, 2) it allows several types of resources (not only cost), 3) it handles coupling and precedence relations between features, 4) it enables the planning of several releases ahead, 5) it incorporates a procedure for handling technical constraints, and above all 6) it provides a decision support-based solution.

6.10 Summary

In this chapter, we discussed an instantiation of the SoRPES framework by providing a concrete implementation. We presented the SoRPES decision support technique. Since release planning is a decision problem that is plagued with uncertainties, it needs to be formulated and addressed as such. The approach we have taken in developing the SoRPES decision support is also aimed at addressing these uncertainties. The work by Ngo-The and Ruhe [113] suggests uncertainties management for software engineering problems via the provision of alternative solutions. The decision support technique discussed in this chapter generates alternative solutions for decision maker(s) to evaluate, and also include a methodology to guide the decision makers in selecting among the alternatives.

In summary, the work discussed in this chapter contributes to software engineering by providing:

1. Methodology for assessing the technical constraints associated with adding features to the existing systems.
2. Formalized description of the release planning problem accompanied with a robust solution methodology based on bi-objective optimization. We also support the generation of alternative release plans that are Pareto-optimal in a mathematical programming sense.
3. Trade-off analysis scheme that guides the human experts in the evaluation of solution alternatives and selection of the most appropriate alternative. For this purpose, we have adopted the MCDA method known as ELECTRE IS.
4. Implementation architecture of the SoRPES technique. We have implemented the core components of the architecture as a proof of the feasibility of building such a support environment.

CHAPTER SEVEN

EMPIRICAL VALIDATION

A theory has only the alternative of being right or wrong. A model
has a third possibility: it may be right but irrelevant.
- Jagdish Mehra

7.1 Introduction

This chapter presents an empirical validation of the proposed decision support technique from the *feasibility*, *relevance*, *scalability* and *consistency* perspectives. We discuss two empirical studies through which we answered series of validation questions. As part of the studies, we compare SoRPES to another release planning decisions support tool known as ReleasePlanner. The comparison is based on the following criteria: quality of solution, satisfaction of SD-coupling, structural diversity of release plans, and runtime.

In order to investigate *feasibility*, we look at the practicality of using SoRPES to generate release plans, given the relevant planning data. We investigate *relevance* by comparing the results obtained from SoRPES to the results from an existing industrial scale release planning software, the ReleasePlanner system. We discuss *scalability* issues by applying SoRPES to problems of different sizes. In investigating *consistency*, we compared the results from SoRPES to the results from ReleasePlanner on different datasets from different environments. To follow through the empirical studies, we defined some validation questions that center on *feasibility*, *relevance*, *scalability*, and *consistency* issues.

The first empirical validation study is aimed at addressing the *feasibility* and *relevance* questions, which we have further refined into the following questions:

    Q1.   Given the planning data, how does SoRPES generate release plan alternatives?

Q2. How does the inclusion of technical constraints affect the quality of release plans?

Q3. How does the SoPRES technique compare to ReleasePlanner?

Q3.1 How does it compare in terms of quality of solutions generated?

Q3.2 How does it compare in terms of the satisfaction of SD-coupling in release plans?

Q3.3 How does it compare in terms of structural diversity of release plans?

Q3.4 How does it compare in terms of runtime to generate solution?

The second empirical validation study addresses scalability (see [17] for in-depth discussion of what constitutes scalability) and consistency issues. We have also refined these two broad issues into the following questions:

Q1. Does SoRPES guarantee scalability?

Q1.1 How does SoRPES deal with large numbers of features, stakeholders, resource types, and releases?

Q1.2 How does SoRPES deal with incomplete data?

Q2. How consistent are the results obtained from SoRPES?

7.2 Empirical Study I – Feasibility and Relevance of SoRPES

7.2.1 Context

In this empirical study, we used the dataset discussed in Chapter 5. The entire data collection and study setup remains as described in Chapter 5. A summary of the project characteristics is given in Table 7.1. The vote coverage at 100% shown in Table 7.1 indicates that all the stakeholders specified their value-based priorities for all features. The vote coverage could be less than 100% if some stakeholders have no interest in some features and do not specify values for those features.

Table 7.1: Snapshot of the Project Characteristics for Empirical Study I

No. of Features	No. of Stakeholders	No. of Resources	No. of Releases	Technical Constraints	Vote Coverage

33	3	5	2	1	100%

In addition to the data provided in Table 5.1 and Table 5.2 (*see* Chapter 5), three members of the development team participated in the evaluation of the components of the ReleasePlanner system using EBEAM. During the study, we held a mini-workshop to present EBEAM to members of the development team who would be involved in the assessment of EoM and XoM. After the presentation, we asked the participants to individually perform their assessments. Then, we computed the technical constraints for the features using the aggregated results from their assessments of EoM and XoM. The data representing technical constraints, the system values derived from the impact analysis data given in Table 5.2, and data from the business concerns given in Table 5.1 were used for the release planning experiments discussed here.

7.2.2 Computing Technical Constraints

To accommodate different views, members of the development team that participated in the study were asked to make independent assessments of the EoM. Weights of relative importance were assigned to the development team members (we will refer to them as expert-A, expert-B, and expert-C) that participated in the study. The weights, based on familiarity of the development team members with the components, were provided as follows: Expert-A (0.5), Expert-B (0.3) and Expert-C (0.2).

The results from the two stages of EBEAM are given in Table B.1. and Table B.2. respectively (*see* Appendix 2). Please note that we have not presented details of the intermediate results of the assessments, as the procedures for arriving at the results have been discussed in Chapter 4. Table B.1. contains the results of the evaluation of modifiability characteristics. From the evaluation results in the table, all the three experts did not completely agree on the effects of the characteristics on modifiability. A unified opinion, as contained in the aggregated results column, favors the fact that *size of components* has the least effect on modifiability, while understandability of components has the highest effect. Table B.2. presents the results of the expert's evaluation of the components with respect to each modifiability characteristic. Using the EBEAM aggregation scheme, the consolidated result showing the EoM for each component is given in the last row of Table B.2.

The extent of modification required to add each feature to the impacted components was assessed as a percentage of code modification required. The results are given in Table 7.2. For example, feature f_1 requires 20% modification in the Reporting component, but would not affect the Validator component, because there are no changes required in the Validator component. Using Equation (6.1), we aggregate the XoM and EoM results to obtain the technical constraints $tc(i)$, which is also given in Table 7.2.

Table 7.2: Features and their Groupings, the EoM, XoM and Technical Constraints

Features Grouping	ID	Features	Reporting 0.120	Validator 0.098	IP Component 0.174	Java Brokers 0.121	Import/Export 0.169	Stakeholder Voting 0.129	DB Connectivity 0.089	Alternative Analysis 0.102	XoM(c_m,f_i)	1-EoM(c_m)	tc(i)
						Size of modification of the component in the column required by implementing the feature in the rows (%)						
Comparative analysis of solutions	1	Comparative analysis manual versus RP solutions	20		10	10	10		10	150	2.10	5.225	7.325
	2	Record of history of sets of alternative solutions	20			25	10		30	75	1.60	4.399	5.999
	3	Conformance measure for requirements across alterantive solutions	20			15			10	25	0.70	3.568	4.268
	4	Comparison between solutions: within one set and across sets	20			15			40	200	2.75	3.568	6.318
Compatibility	5	MS excel advanced compatibility				20	200		20		2.40	2.621	5.021
	6	MS Project compatibility				20	200		20		2.40	2.621	5.021
	7	Analysis of compatibility requirements with existing RM tools (DOORS, Requisite Pro)				20	200		20		2.40	2.621	5.021
Extended modeling capabilities	8	Generation of solutions based on selected criteria (Stakeholder in isolation, criteria in isolation, trade-off)	10		15	15			10		0.50	3.496	3.996
	9	Planning across projects	20	30	5	15		20	25	10	1.25	6.167	7.417
	10	Re-planning capabilities	20							50	0.70	1.778	2.478
	11	Allowing splitting of features over two releases	10	20	5	5			30	50	1.20	5.296	6.496
	12	Accomodation of different skill sets	20	20	20	20	20	10	20	30	1.60	6.998	8.598
	13	Fuzzy boundaries	20			10			10	25	0.65	3.568	4.218
	14	Value-risk trade-off analysis	20						5	10	0.35	2.689	3.039
Usability	15	Multiple windows accessible							10		0.10	0.911	1.011
	16	Integrated Excel sheet with effort data, voting and generated alternatives					200		15		2.15	1.742	3.892
	17	Dashboard to show user actual study of Project Planning					60		30		0.90	1.790	2.690
	18	Professional UI re-development	10					10		10	0.30	2.649	2.949
	19	Extending reporting component	30						10		0.40	1.791	2.191
	20	Explanation Component	0						10		0.10	0.911	1.011
	21	Visualization of Output	50					20	10	20	1.00	3.560	4.560
	22	Context sensitive explanation of terms							10		0.10	0.911	1.011
	23	Further development of the validator to give on demand help		20	10	20			10		0.60	3.518	4.118
Improvements backup algorithms	24	Fine tuning optimization algorithms (back tracking strategies, heuristics)			20	5					0.25	1.705	1.955
	25	Elimination of open source code			500						5.00	0.826	5.826
	26	Caching mechanisms			20	10					0.30	1.705	2.005
Stakeholder related extensions	27	Stakeholder allowed to enter request for requirements	5						5		0.10	1.791	1.891
	28	Stakeholder to enter resource estimates	5						5		0.10	1.791	1.891
	29	Multiple stakeholder weights based on groups of reqs. they are voting on	5				5	20	10		0.40	3.493	3.893
	30	Improved stakeholder conformance (percentages of the idea solution model)	10		10	10			5	20	0.55	4.394	4.944
	31	Individual stakeholder voting feedback	5					10	5		0.20	2.662	2.862
	32	Competitor stakeholder voting	10					15	5		0.30	2.662	2.962
	33	Stakeholder Voting analysis extension	20					100	10		1.30	2.662	3.962

7.2.3 Answering the Feasibility Questions

7.2.3.1 The Release Plans from Pareto-optimal Solutions

The study question that we address in this section is as follows.

> Q1.   Given the planning data, how does SoRPES generate release plan
> alternatives?

To generate release plans, we first determine the maximal values τ_k of the technical constraints $tc(i)$ for each release, and then we use a percentage of the obtained maximal to set the threshold β_k in the bi-objective release planning model.

Using the technical constraints data given in Table 7.2 and the data defining the remaining release planning constraints given in Table 5.1, we run the single-objective optimization model (i.e. Equations (6.9)–(6.15)) to obtain the maximal values for τ_k in each release.   These maximal values for the two releases are $\tau_1 = 64.192$ and $\tau_2 = 50.688$, respectively. For a sample run of the experiment, we chose the threshold β_k at 80% of this maximal values to obtain $\beta_1 = 51.5356$ and $\beta_2 = 40.5504$ for the two releases respectively. We chose the 80% threshold simply for experimental purposes. The percentage of the maximal value adopted can vary. Later in this section, we discuss the effects of the chosen percentages on results.

Based on the data in Table 5.1 and Table 7.2, and also the technical constraints thresholds obtained above, we generate 5 release plan alternatives. Table 7.3 shows the release plan alternatives, and Figure 7.1 shows the corresponding objective values of the Pareto-optimal solutions that produced the release plans. The values of objective function F_2 in Figure 7.1 are obtained from the recalculated system values for the features. We have discussed the procedure for recalculating the system values for each assigned feature in Chapter 5; we would not reproduce the recalculated system values for all features here.

Table 7.3: Structure of the 5 Alternative Release Plans

	f₁	f₂	f₃	f₄	f₅	f₆	f₇	f₈	f₉	f₁₀	f₁₁	f₁₂	f₁₃	f₁₄	f₁₅	f₁₆	f₁₇	f₁₈	f₁₉	f₂₀	f₂₁	f₂₂	f₂₃	f₂₄	f₂₅	f₂₆	f₂₇	f₂₈	f₂₉	f₃₀	f₃₁	f₃₂	f₃₃
A	2	3	2	3	1	2	1	1	2	3	3	3	3	2	1	1	1	1	1	3	2	1	3	1	1	1	2	1	1	1	1	2	2
B	1	3	1	3	2	2	1	1	2	2	3	3	3	1	1	2	1	1	1	3	3	1	3	1	2	1	2	1	2	1	1	2	1
C	1	3	1	3	2	2	2	1	2	3	3	3	2	1	1	2	1	1	1	3	2	1	3	1	3	1	2	1	1	1	1	2	1
D	1	2	1	3	2	2	2	1	2	3	3	3	1	2	1	2	1	1	1	3	3	1	3	1	3	1	2	1	1	1	1	2	1
E	1	2	1	2	2	2	2	1	3	3	3	3	1	1	1	2	2	1	1	3	3	1	3	1	3	1	1	1	1	1	2	2	1

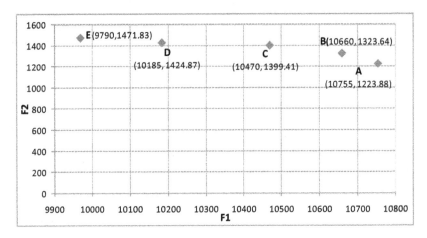

Figure 7.1: Objective Values of the 5 Alternative Release Plans

From the results in Table 7.3 and Figure 7.1, the solution that corresponds to alternative A is the best solution when we consider "only" the business perspective of release planning, while the solution corresponding to alternative E is the best solution from the technical perspective. If we consider the two objective functions together, then both alternatives A and E are of equal strength, and neither of the two alternatives would be assumed to be better than the other. Thus, these two alternatives are of equal status as the other 3 alternative release plans (i.e. B, C, D). We discuss these results further in this chapter while answering the remaining set of the empirical study questions.

7.2.3.2 Effects of the Technical Constraints

In this section, we discuss the effects of technical constraints and the chosen thresholds on the quality of release plans. The goal is to address the study question Q2.

Q2.   How does the inclusion of technical constraints affect the quality of release plans?

We address question Q2 from the following two perspectives:

1. The effects of the chosen thresholds of the technical constraints on solutions obtained

2. The effects of using the actual maximal value τ_k to define the threshold β_k.

1.   Effects of technical constraints at different thresholds

Recall that the technical constraints thresholds β_k are derived from a percentage ρ of the maximal technical constraint value τ_k. We investigate the effects of these chosen percentages on the Pareto-optimal solutions generated. To investigate these effects, we perform 3 runs of the experiment at different percentages of ρ, which are $\rho = 80\%$, 90%, and 100% respectively.

In each run, we generate 4 alternative release plans that correspond to 4 Pareto-optimal solutions. It should be noted that, it is sufficient to generate more than one solution alternative at each threshold, simply for comparison purposes. This would enable us to show which set of solutions dominates which other set(s) of solutions at different percentage ρ.

The objective values of the Pareto-optimal solutions obtained via these experiments are given in Figure 7.2. Since the release plans corresponding to these objective values are not necessarily relevant to the point we wish to highlight in this result, we do not present

186

them here. In Figure 7.2, all the Pareto-optimal solutions generated at thresholds with higher percentages of the technical constraints dominate all the other Pareto-optimal solutions obtained at lower percentages. This result is more or less expected, because the higher the percentage of the technical constraints solution space we explore, the higher the possibility of discovering Pareto-optimal solutions that dominate the solutions obtained within a more restricted solution space, and vice versa.

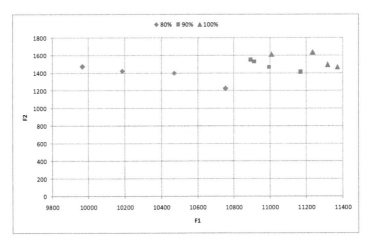

Figure 7.2: Objective Values of the Pareto-optimal Solutions at Different Technical Constraints Percentage ρ of the Threshold β_k

2. Effects of using the maximal value τ_k to define the threshold β_k

We present the results from another experiment to compare the results obtained without considering the technical constraints in the bi-objective optimization model (i.e. using the bi-objective optimization model discussed in Chapter 5) with results obtained by including technical constraints at $\rho = 100\%$ (i.e. using the bi-objective optimization model discussed in Chapter 6). Ordinarily, we would assume that the two results should be the same, since considering technical constraints at $\rho = 100\%$ is like saying that, we are not considering the technical constraints, because the entire solution space should be available at $\rho = 100\%$. The point of this experiment is to verify this assertion.

Figure 7.3 shows the results of the two sets of Pareto-optimal solutions obtained using the two scenarios described above. The objective values represented by the points A, B, C, and D in Figure 7.3 correspond to the solution alternatives obtained without considering the technical constraints $tc(i)$ at all, while those represented by the points E, F, G, and H correspond to the solution alternatives obtained when we consider the technical constraints using the maximal values of τ_k (i.e. at $\rho = 100\%$) as the threshold for β_k.

The results show that, except for one single case (i.e. point B in Figure 7.3), the set of Pareto-optimal solutions obtained without considering the technical constraints dominate at least one other solution in the set of solutions obtained if we consider the technical constraints at $\rho = 100\%$. None of the solutions obtained at $\rho = 100\%$ dominates any of the solutions obtained without considering technical constraints.

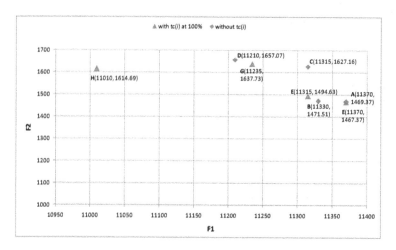

Figure 7.3: Objective Values of the Solutions without $tc(i)$ **and with** $tc(i)$ **at** $\rho = 100\%$

The significance of the result shown in Figure 7.3 leads us to ask the following: *why did we not obtain the same results for both cases shown in Figure 7.3?* Ordinarily, at $\rho = 100\%$ the entire solution space of the maximal values τ_k of the technical constraints should be available for exploration. Thus, we expect the solution space at $\rho = 100\%$ of τ_k to be the same as the solution space available without considering $tc(i)$. But this is not the case in reality. Because the maximal values τ_k obtained are just the maximal values of the technical constraints, which is subject to the feasible region already defined by the other release planning constraints. Recall that we have formulated these other release planning constraints as part of the single-objective optimization model for determining τ_k in Equations (6.9)–(6.15). The significance of the results lies in the validity of the heuristic we have employed in determining the value τ_k.

Without the optimization model for determining τ_k in Equations (6.9)–(6.15), summing the $tc(i)$ values over all the features given in Table 7.2 would have given the maximal value τ_k as "130.839" for the two releases. Meanwhile, the actual maximal value τ_k when we factor the other release planning constraints into the model (*see* Equations (6.9) –(6.15)) is "114.88". This discrepancy is because the ordinary sum of the $tc(i)$ values ignores the other release planning constraints, which already defines the initial feasible region. By including the other release planning constraints in Equations (6.9)–(6.15), it further reduces the feasible region that can be explored even at $\rho = 100\%$ of the τ_k. But this reduced space is the actual feasible region within which we can obtain feasible solutions.

7.2.4 Answering the Questions on Relevance – ReleasePlanner as a Baseline

In this section, we address the following questions:

Q3.   How does the SoPRES technique compare to ReleasePlanner?

We addressed this broad question in this section. Specifically the concrete results for comparison are addressed in the following three sub-questions.

Q3.1   *How does it compare in terms of quality of solutions generated?*
We address this question about the quality of solutions in Section 7.2.4.3.

Q3.2   *How does it compare in terms of satisfaction of SD-coupling in release plans?*
In terms of the level of satisfaction of SD-coupling, we compare the release plan alternatives generated using both techniques, and we discuss the results in Section 7.2.4.4.

Q3.3   *How does it compare in terms of structural diversity of release plans?*
Section 7.2.4.5 addresses the question on the structural diversity of the release plan alternatives generated by the two techniques considered.

Q3.4   *How does it compare in terms of runtime?*
Section 7.2.4.6 addresses the question on runtime to generate solutions.

7.2.4.1 Context

In order to validate the results obtained from SoRPES for release planning, we selected an existing release planning technique called the EVOLVE* [133] which is implemented in the ReleasePlanner software. The choice of the ReleasePlanner as a baseline to validate our result is informed by the result of our survey of the literature in Chapter 2. Of all the release planning techniques available in the literature, the EVOLVE* implemented by ReleasePlanner is the closest to our approach from the business perspective. Although, like every other techniques available, the EVOLVE* does not address the technical concerns of software release planning. The model implemented in ReleasePlanner is based on a single-objective optimization model which is similar to the objective function $F_1(x)$ in our bi-objective model. To the best of our knowledge, ReleasePlanner is about the only industrial scale decision support tool for software release planning that could plan multiple releases. Since the EVOLVE* is implemented in the ReleasePlanner tool, we would henceforth refer to ReleasePlanner and EVOLVE* interchangeably to mean the same thing.

For our comparison to be valid, and to also avoid bias, it is important to present the same data to both SoRPES and ReleasePlanner, at least in the areas where they share similar model characteristics. In terms of release planning constraints, both SoRPES and ReleasePlanner handle the same set of constraints, except for the technical constraints added to the optimization models in SoRPES.

Although, ReleasePlanner does not handle technical constraints, but it supports the definition of the risk of implementing features as a resource type. The assessment of risk in ReleasePlanner is based on estimates given by the project manager (or any other technical team member designated for that purpose) who also determines the risk capacity that is admissible in each release. We argue that the handling of risk as a resource type is not an effective way to handle it during release planning. We would revisit this issue during our discussion of results. To present both SoRPES and ReleasePlanner with the same data, we adopt the values of the technical constraints $tc(i)$ shown in Table 7.2 as well as the thresholds β_k determined using SoRPES to represent both the technical constraints values and the capacities respectively.

During the experiments, we set the threshold for technical constraints at $\rho = 80\%$ of the maximal values of τ_k obtained earlier (i.e. $\tau_1 = 64.192$ and $\tau_2 = 50.688$). This gives the threshold β_k at 80% of this maximal values as $\beta_1 = 51.5356$ and $\beta_2 = 40.5504$, respectively.

7.2.4.2 Generated Release Plan Alternatives using SoRPES and ReleasePlanner

The structure of 5 alternative release plans generated by ReleasePlanner is given in Table 7.4. Table 7.4 also contains values of the objective function F(x) corresponding to release plans. Table 7.5 contains the results from SoRPES using the same data as the ReleasePlanner, with the exception of system values that constitute the objective function $F_2(x)$ in SoRPES. Table 7.5 also contains values of the objective functions $F_1(x)$ and $F_2(x)$ that correspond to the release plans. It should be noted that the release plans in Table 7.5 are presented here for convenience purposes, as it is the same result discussed in Table 7.3.

Table 7.4: Structure of the 5 Alternative Release Plans Generated by ReleasePlanner

	f₁	f₂	f₃	f₄	f₅	f₆	f₇	f₈	f₉	f₁₀	f₁₁	f₁₂	f₁₃	f₁₄	f₁₅	f₁₆	f₁₇	f₁₈	f₁₉	f₂₀	f₂₁	f₂₂	f₂₃	f₂₄	f₂₅	f₂₆	f₂₇	f₂₈	f₂₉	f₃₀	f₃₁	f₃₂	f₃₃	F
A1	1	3	1	3	2	2	1	2	2	1	3	3	3	1	1	2	1	1	1	3	2	1	3	1	2	1	2	1	1	1	2	3	1	10570
B2	1	3	1	3	1	2	1	1	2	3	3	3	3	2	2	1	1	1	2	3	2	2	3	1	2	3	2	2	1	2	1	2	1	10215
C3	2	3	2	3	2	2	1	1	3	2	3	3	1	1	2	1	1	1	3	3	1	3	1	3	1	2	1	2	1	1	1	2	1	10155
D4	2	3	2	3	1	2	1	1	3	2	3	3	2	1	1	1	3	1	1	1	3	2	1	3	1	2	1	2	2	1	1	2	1	10135
E5	1	2	1	3	3	2	1	1	2	1	3	3	3	2	1	3	2	1	1	3	2	1	3	1	2	2	2	2	1	1	1	3	1	10075

Table 7.5: Structure of the 5 Alternative Release Plans Generated by SoRPES

	f₁	f₂	f₃	f₄	f₅	f₆	f₇	f₈	f₉	f₁₀	f₁₁	f₁₂	f₁₃	f₁₄	f₁₅	f₁₆	f₁₇	f₁₈	f₁₉	f₂₀	f₂₁	f₂₂	f₂₃	f₂₄	f₂₅	f₂₆	f₂₇	f₂₈	f₂₉	f₃₀	f₃₁	f₃₂	f₃₃	F₁	F₂
A	2	3	2	3	1	2	1	1	2	3	3	3	3	2	1	1	1	1	1	3	2	1	3	1	1	1	2	1	1	1	1	2	2	10755	1223.88
B	1	3	1	3	2	2	1	1	2	2	3	3	3	1	1	2	1	1	1	3	3	1	3	1	2	1	2	1	2	1	1	2	1	10660	1323.64
C	1	3	1	3	2	2	2	1	2	3	3	3	2	1	1	2	1	1	1	3	2	1	3	1	3	1	2	1	1	1	1	2	1	10470	1399.41
D	1	2	1	3	2	2	2	1	2	3	3	3	1	2	1	2	1	1	1	3	3	1	3	1	3	1	2	1	1	1	1	2	1	10185	1424.87
E	1	2	1	2	2	2	2	1	3	3	3	3	3	1	1	1	2	2	1	1	3	3	1	3	1	3	1	1	1	1	2	2	1	9790	1471.83

The structures of the release plans are different both within each table as well as across the two tables (*see* Table 7.4 and Table 7.5). The basis of our comparison of results is not on the structural differences between the plans, but the quality of solutions. We determine the quality of the solutions using the optimal values of the objective functions.

7.2.4.3 Comparing the Quality of Solutions

Ordinarily, it would be assumed that we cannot have fair comparison between the results from SoRPES and those from ReleasePlanner. Because SoRPES focuses on optimizing 2 objective functions simultaneously and also strives to achieve Pareto-optimal solutions when the two objective functions are taken together, while the ReleasePlanner optimizes only a single objective function. Given this situation, ReleasePlanner has more flexibility in the solution space it can explore, and would be expected to generate better quality solutions.

To compare the two solutions, we chose the values of the objective function $F_1(x)$ from the Pareto-optimal solutions generated by SoRPES and the values of the objective function $F(x)$ from the solutions generated by ReleasePlanner. These $F_1(x)$ values are chosen after optimizing the two objectives to obtain Pareto-optimal solutions (see Figure 7.1 for the values of both $F_1(x)$ and $F_2(x)$). Figure 7.4 shows the results comparing objective values $F_1(x)$ from SoRPES to the objective values $F(x)$ from ReleasePlanner, for the 5 release plan alternatives in Table 7.4 and Table 7.5.

In all but 1 of the 5 alternative solutions generated, the results generated by SoRPES outperform the results generated by ReleasePlanner, despite SoRPES not focusing exclusively on $F_1(x)$. In essence, SoRPES can generate solutions that are as good as (or even better than) ReleasePlanner in terms of quality of solution, while also optimizing the assignment of features with high interrelatedness in the same release. For clarity sake, we state that the results from SoRPES benefit from the power of ILOG optimization engine, which we have used as the single-objective optimizer. We discuss this issue further while comparing runtime of the solutions later in Section 7.2.4.6.

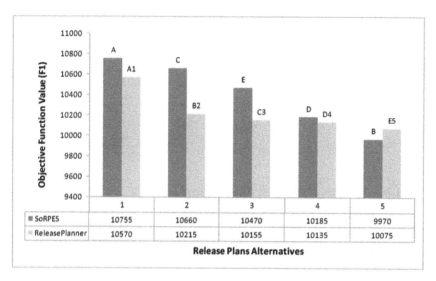

Figure 7.4: Comparing the Values of F₁(x) Obtained by SoRPES and ReleasePlanner

7.2.4.4 Comparing Level of Satisfaction of SD-coupling in the Release Plans

Table 7.6 presents the results of the computation of level of satisfaction of SD-coupling in the release plan alternatives generated by SoRPES and ReleasePlanner. The first two columns of the table represent the list of SD-coupled features and the strength of coupling between the features respectively. An entry "1" in a column shows that the SD-coupling listed in that row is satisfied by the release plan alternative in the column. The entry "1" represent the α threshold at which the SD-couplings are derived (refer to Chapter 5 for discussions on α threshold).

As shown in Table 7.6, the level of satisfaction of SD-coupling in the 5 release plan alternatives generated using SoRPES (i.e. alternative A, B, C, D, E) at threshold $\alpha=1$ are given as $\mu_A^1 = 31.3\%$, $\mu_B^1 = 31.3\%$, $\mu_C^1 = 43.8\%$, $\mu_D^1 = 50.0\%$, and $\mu_E^1 = 62.5\%$ respectively. This implies that, the release plan alternative A satisfies only 31.3% of the total number of SD-coupling identified at $\alpha=1$, while alternative E satisfies 62.5% of the total number of SD-coupling identified at the same threshold. Similar interpretation holds for all the other computed level of satisfaction of SD-coupling. In terms of SD-coupling satisfaction, alternative E is the best of all the solutions. The alternative E corresponds to the Pareto-optimal solution generated when the focus of the search is biased towards the technical perspective as captured in objective function $F_2(x)$. This again is a validation of the heuristics employed both in the definition of system values of features and the objective function $F_2(x)$ that uses system values to assign features to releases.

Table 7.6: Comparing the Level of Satisfaction of SD-coupling in the Release Plans Generated using SoRPES and ReleasePlanner

SD-coupling	Strength	SD-coupling Satisfaction in the Plans Generated by SoRPES					SD-coupling Satisfaction in Plans Generated by ReleasePlanner				
	$\theta(i,j)$	A	B	C	D	E	A1	B2	C3	D4	E5
(3,4)	1										
(3,13)	1				1	1				1	
(4,13)	1										
(5,6)	1		1	1	1	1	1		1		
(5,7)	1	1		1	1	1		1		1	
(6,7)	1			1	1	1					
(15,20)	1						1				
(15,22)	1	1	1	1	1	1		1	1	1	1
(19,27)	1					1	1	1			
(19,28)	1	1	1	1	1	1		1	1		
(20,22)	1						1				
(24,26)	1	1	1	1	1	1			1	1	
(27,28)	1					1		1		1	1
(31,32)	1					1					
(31,33)	1		1	1	1			1	1	1	1
(32,33)	1	1									
Sum	16	5	5	7	8	10	4	6	5	6	3
μ^1		31.3%	31.3%	43.8%	50.0%	62.5%	25.0%	37.5%	31.3%	37.5%	18.8%

With the exception of release plan alternatives A and B from SoRPES, the levels of satisfaction of SD-coupling in the release plans generated by ReleasePlanner are lower than those generated by SoRPES. The case of alternative A having lower level of satisfaction of SD-coupling is not surprising. This is the alternative generated when the focus of optimization is on the objective function $F_1(x)$ that represents the business perspective. Recall from our implementation of the ε-Constraint algorithm (Algorithm 5.3 and Algorithm 5.4) in Chapter 5 that Alternative A corresponds to one of the first 2 solutions obtained before defining the feasible region to explore for all the other Pareto-optimal solutions. The second of these two solutions is Alternative E mentioned above.

In general, SoRPES obtained solutions with higher level of satisfaction of SD-coupling than any of the solutions obtained from ReleasePlanner.

7.2.4.5 Comparing Structural Diversity of the Release Plans

In this section we compare the structural diversity of the release plans generated by the two techniques. Structural diversity refers to the degree to which two release plans are different in terms of the different releases to which each feature is assigned. If two release plan alternatives are essentially the same in terms of structure, then there is no point considering them as alternatives. The notion of structural diversity of release plan alternatives is discussed by Ngo-The and Ruhe [113].

To characterize the extent of diversity that exists between release plan alternatives, it suffices to measure their structural similarity/differences. As a simple measure of structural similarity between the plans, we adopt a measure of Hamming distance, which is defined as follows:

DEFINITION 6.3 (HAMMING DISTANCE)

The Hamming distance $H(a,b)$ between two strings of the same length is the number of places or positions in the two strings a and b in which the two strings defer in characters. □

Succinctly put, the Hamming distance measures the extent of dissimilarity between two strings of the same length. Since every feature in a release plan is either assigned to a release or postponed, all the release plan alternatives are guaranteed to be of the same length (i.e. the length is the total number of features). Therefore, it is straightforward to observe that the Hamming distance between two release plans is the number of features that the two plans assigns to different releases. As observed in [113], once a measure of distance between a pair of solution alternatives exists, the diversification of the entire set of alternatives can be defined as a sum of all the distances between the alternatives in the set of release plans.

To measure the Hamming distance between all pairs of release plan alternatives, suppose we have a set of γ alternative release plans, we require ${}^{\gamma}C_2$ (i.e. different ways to select 2 items from set γ) operations to compare and obtain the Hamming distances between all possible pair of alternatives. Table 7.7 shows the results of the Hamming distance measure. A sum of the Hamming distances over the entire set of release plan alternatives for each technique shows that the set of alternatives from ReleasePlanner are more structural diversified than those from SoRPES. With the sum of the Hamming distances over all alternatives given as 113 for ReleasePlanner and 87 for SoRPES, the alternatives from ReleasePlanner are about 29.89% more diversified. It should be noted that SoRPES does not have any structural diversification algorithms implemented.

Table 7.7: Comparing Structural Diversity of the Release Plans

SoRPES		ReleasePlanner	
Pair of Plans	H(a,b)	Pair of Plans	H(a,b)
(A,B)	10	(A1,B2)	13
(A,C)	9	(A1,C3)	9
(A,D)	10	(A1,D4)	12
(A,E)	16	(A1,E5)	9
(B,C)	6	(B2,C3)	15
(B,D)	7	(B2,D4)	12
(B,E)	11	(B2,E5)	11
(C,D)	4	(C3,D4)	6
(C,E)	8	(C3,E5)	14
(D,E)	6	(D4,E5)	12
	87		113

7.2.4.6 Comparing the Time To Generate Solutions

To generate release plans using SoRPES, we set the time limit for each constrained single-objective optimization to run on the ILOG Optimizer for a maximum of 20 seconds. To obtain one Pareto-optimal solution for an instance of the problem, our algorithm issues several calls to ILOG until our tests for optimality confirms the solution generated to be Pareto-optimal (the number of iterations cannot be determined beforehand). We have discussed these as part of our implementation strategy in Chapter 6. The time limit we set to 20 seconds is meant to handle each of these calls. This does not necessarily imply that ILOG would take 20 seconds to obtain a solution for every instance of the constrained single-objective problem, as the solution times are much lesser and are typically in milliseconds.

To generate the 5 alternative solutions discussed earlier in this study, the total runtime on completion of the optimization was 00:00:04.968750 (hh:mm:ss.msec). That is, it took 4 seconds and 9687500 milliseconds for SoRPES to generate the 5 alternative release plans. This runtime is not exclusive to the calls issued to ILOG, but it also includes the time for processing the data and preparing the data in linear programming (LP) format for ILOG. The time also includes the process of partitioning the objective space and exploring this space for all the 5 Pareto-optimal solutions as well as the time to write and display solutions. We repeated these experiments several times, and the execution time continually falls between 4+ seconds to 5+ seconds, but never took up to 6 seconds.

To calculate the execution time discussed above, we retrieve the current system time at the beginning of each run of the experiment and also retrieve the system time on termination. The experiments were conducted on a Pentium 4, 2.80 GHz CPU and 1GB RAM. We ensured that, there were no other resource-intensive processes running on the computer during the experiments.

The ReleasePlanner system gives a user the choice to generate solutions in 5 seconds, 10 seconds and 5 minutes. To allow for a fair comparison, we chose the 5 seconds option to generate the release plan alternatives discussed above. Thus, the two techniques are comparable in terms of execution time.

7.2.4.7 Summary Discussion of Empirical Study I

Using the ILOG as the underlying single-objective optimizer, SoRPES was able to generate release plans that are slightly better in quality and also having similar runtime as ReleasePlanner. Our implementation of the ε-Constraint algorithm benefits from this powerful optimization engine, but the strategy we have employed in implementing the bi-ε-Constraint algorithm ensures SoRPES strikes a good balance between the two objectives. This makes it possible to obtain comparable solution quality to those from ReleasePlanner.

The major conclusion we draw from the results of this study is that, despite the results from SoRPES outperforming those from ReleasePlanner in terms of the quality of solution, SoRPES has an added advantage of accommodating higher percentage of SD-coupled features in release plans. Thus, the fact that we focus on the two planning perspectives simultaneously, the heuristics employed in our implementation generate release plans of equal or higher quality than ReleasePlanner. ReleasePlanner generated solution alternatives that are more structurally diversified than the alternatives from SoRPES. Unlike ReleasePlanner, however, SoRPES has not implemented any diversification algorithms.

Our formulation of the release planning problem as a bi-objective optimization problem and the implementation of the ε-Constraint algorithm to generate Pareto-optimal solutions offer additional benefits. These benefits derive from the fact that, our solution approach in SoRPES guarantees that we can obtain two initial solutions, either of which at one extreme is optimal from the business perspective (similar to ReleasePlanner), while at the other extreme is optimal from the technical perspective that considers interrelatedness of features. Between these two extremes, we offer solutions that are compromises from the two perspectives.

7.3 Empirical Study II – Scalability and Consistency of SoRPES

7.3.1 Context

Most of the data used in this study were collected from one of our industrial partners. The industrial partner, which we simply refer to as "The Company", develops online games for the web, personal computers, and mobile phones. The company also produces a set of back-office tools that are used for monitoring and reporting on games played and for collection of royalties. The project on which the data was collected consists of features to be added to the existing system in chunks of future releases. We characterize the data next. Some specific detail data is hidden to protect intellectual property of the company.

7.3.2 Data Description

7.3.2.1 Overview

A summary of the project data is given in Table 7.8. The planning for the project is to be done for the next 5 releases (i.e. quarterly releases), and the corresponding relative importance of the next 5 releases are given as 9, 7, 5, 3, and 1 respectively. With a total of 190 features, 33 stakeholders, 15 resource types and 5 releases to plan ahead, the project is a fairly large one. The vote coverage reflects the subset of features that have priorities assigned to them by a subset of the stakeholders. The vote coverage for the dataset under consideration is 27.5%, which implies that not all the stakeholders assigned priorities to the features. The reason for this could be that, most of the stakeholders are interested in different subsets of the features. The dataset already contains values for technical risk, which is defined as a resource type. Because of the technical risk, we do not have to consider evaluating the technical constraints for the features. Recall from our discussion on technical constraints in Chapter 6 that it is to some extent synonymous with the technical risk of implementing features in the existing system.

Table 7.8: Snapshot of the Problem Characteristics for Empirical Study 2

No. of Features	No. of Stakeholders	No. of Resources	No. of Releases	Vote Coverage
190	33	15	5	27.5%

It should be noted that the company already has the dataset described above in place and not specifically collected or specified for the purpose of this study. The description of the entire dataset is given in Appendix C (see Table C.1 – Table C.5). We have removed the detail descriptions of the features and groupings of features to protect intellectual property of the company. We have done the same thing for the descriptions of stakeholders. At the same time, the entire dataset provided in Appendix C still makes it possible for the study described in this section to be replicated.

7.3.2.2 Coping with Incompleteness of the Dataset

The vote coverage of 27.5% already indicates that we have largely incomplete data in terms of priorities of features on the one hand. On the other hand, during our meetings with the company, they admitted that their feature-driven impact analysis is mostly done ad hoc and it resides in the heads of their developers. Thus, a documented list of the components of the system that would be impacted by the features does not currently exist. The company admitted that, the non-existence of documented impact analysis could be a direct effect of their maturity level. The project manager suggested that we could possibly extract the impact data by having their developers make an initial list of impacted components, while we use the technical risk estimation (TRE) tool (see Walker et al. [158]) to predict the remaining set of impacted components. We both saw this to be a very plausible route to take, but unfortunately the company does not have enough resources (i.e. developers) to commit to that at the moment.

To be able to proceed with the empirical study and provide answers to the questions raised in Section 7.1, we make the following observations. First, the incomplete data in terms of priorities of features is not a hindrance. We can safely assume that a feature that a specific stakeholder does not assign priority to is of no significant value to the stakeholder in question, and we can assign a value zero to the feature concerned. Second, we can generate synthetic impact analysis data for each feature in a systematic manner. As long as the synthetic data does not make assumptions about the nature of SD-coupling relationships expected between the features. Since we are only interested in answering the *scalability* and *consistency* questions in this study, generating such synthetic data would suffice.

7.3.2.3 Generating Synthetic Impact Analysis Data for the Study

To generate synthetic impact analysis data for all features, we randomly generate a pool of components from which impacted subsets could be randomly drawn for each feature. Since we do not pre-determine the results, it implies that all the features would not have the same number of components in their set of impacted components. For example, the implementation of a given feature may require 10 components to be modified, while another feature may require modification to 25 components. These numbers are all randomly generated. Once these numbers are determined, we randomly pick the set of impacted components for each feature from the original pool. Algorithm 7.1 describes this procedure.

After obtaining all the sets of impacted components for all features, we compute the SD-coupling, strength of SD-coupling, and system values for all features. We have not provided the final impact analysis data and the list of SD-couplings between the features, but the system-values are given in Appendix C. The reason for excluding them is that the actual set of impact analysis data are only used for computing SD-coupling and system-values. For the 190 features, we could have a total of $^{190}C_2$ number of SD-coupling between all pairs of features, which gives a total of 17, 955 SD-couplings rows in the feature coupling matrix. The data is too large to be reproduced here.

Algorithm 7.1: Generating Artificial Impact Dataset
Input: A set $F = \{f_1, f_2, \ldots, f_n\}$ of features
Output: Collections ξ of the sets of impacted components for all the features

1. **Begin**
2.   Generate a pool C of m components /*e.g. m = 200 classes or files */
3. $C = \{c_1, c_2, \ldots, c_m\}$
4. $\xi = \varnothing$
5.   **For** i = 1 to n
6.   Let r = any random number between 5 and 20   /* r represents the number impacted components by the feature f_i */
7. $\Phi_i = \{c_1, c_2, \ldots, c_r\}$ /* randomly pick any r components from the pool C without repetitions allowed in the set Φ_i*/
8. $\xi = \xi + \Phi_i$
9.   **EndFor**
10.   **Return** ξ
11. **End**

7.3.3 Generating Release Plans

In order to generate release plans using the data described above, we do not need to make any changes to the underlying model, regardless of the size of the problem. For example, we have 190 x 5 = 950 decision variables upon which integrality constraints must be imposed in order to obtain values for the objective functions. Similarly, 190 x 15 = 2850 variables in terms of the resources. The mere size of the problem does not preclude the feasibility of obtaining Pareto-optimal solutions. It could take a little longer to explore and search the feasible region for solutions, however. A single instance of the constrained single-objective optimization could have the corresponding linear programming (LP) file run to about 100 pages. We set the time limit for every call to ILOG at 20 seconds, as discussed for Empirical Study I.

Using the dataset described above, the total time taken to generate 5 release plan alternatives was <u>00:05:39.5646732</u> (hh:mm:ss.msec). That is, it took 5 minutes, 39 seconds and 5646732 milliseconds to generate the 5 release plans. This runtime is all inclusive, as discussed earlier for Empirical Study I. This study was also carried out on the same system – Pentium 4, 2.80 GHz CPU, and 1GB RAM.

7.3.4 Answering the Scalability and Consistency Questions

For convenience, we restate the questions addressed in this empirical study as follows:

Q1.   *Does SoRPES guarantee scalability?*

    Q1.1   *How does SoRPES deal with large number of features, stakeholders, resource types, and releases?*

    Q1.2   *How does SoRPES deal with incomplete data?*

Q2.   *How consistent are the results obtained from SoRPES?*

7.3.4.1 Answering the Scalability Questions (Completeness and Size)

Figure 7.5 shows the objective values of the five alternative release plans generated, while Table C.6 (see Appendix C) contains the structure of the alternative release plans. The 5 release plan alternatives are labeled SP1, ..., SP5. In terms of the *size* scalability, we did not experience any problems in generating the solutions. Although, it could take longer to obtain results, than it would be the case for problems of smaller sizes. This is reflected in time taken to generate solution, which falls in the range of 5-6 minutes on the average. Given the integrality constraints imposed on the decision variables, the space of the feasible solutions greatly reduces as the problem grows in size. But this is in fact the reality and not necessarily a drawback of the underlying optimization model or the solution approach. During the experiments, there were situations where ILOG's search resulted in infeasible solutions for certain instances of the problem. In the event that further searches result in infeasible solution, we backtrack to the previous optimal solution obtained before the infeasible solution.

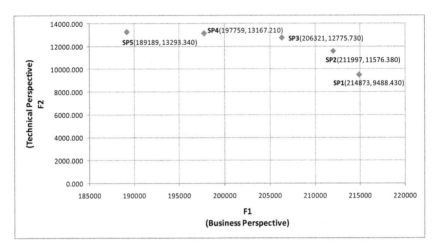

Figure 7.5: Objective Values of the 5 Release Plans for the 190 Features

In terms of incompleteness in the dataset, we have shown by generating the sets of solutions that SoRPES would still be able to generate solutions based on the available data. For example, only 27.5% coverage on priority voting for features was available. There is a certain type of incomplete data that would be difficult for any technique to handle, though. For example, if the resource capacities are not given by the project managers (or other designated role), there would be no way to determine whether the results are optimal, since all the features would practically make it through and be assigned to different releases. At the other end of incompleteness are the data that cannot be integrated into the formal model, which could be addressed by the decision maker during the evaluation of plans.

Although, our discussions here are based on the data we have used in the study, it is safe to conclude that this could easily extend to datasets of varying sizes. The very essence of the formal optimization model is to be able to handle the cognitive complexity associated with large and complex datasets. But the effort required in collecting the input data for large project sizes may limit the applicability of the technique.

7.3.4.2 Answering the Consistency Question

During Empirical Study I, we compared results obtained from SoRPES with those from ReleasePlanner, using selected criteria. To investigate whether there is consistency in the pattern of results obtained from SoRPES in Study I, we once again compare the results from SoRPES to those generated by ReleasePlanner on the new dataset discussed in this study.

Apart from the impact analysis data that is required for computing system values for features, all data used for the experiments with SoRPES were also given to ReleasePlanner. To enable fair comparison, we ran ReleasePlanner for 5 minutes on the dataset. The 5 alternative release plans generated by ReleasePlanner are given in Table C.7 (*see* Appendix C). The 5 release plan alternatives are labeled RP1,..., RP5.

We compare the structural diversification of the release plan alternatives generated by both SoRPES and ReleasePlanner. The result appears in Table 7.9. It is surprising, however, that the results from SoRPES are by far more structurally diversified than those from ReleasePlanner. With the Hamming distances of the set of alternatives generated by SoRPES adding up to 641, while those by ReleasePlanner is 152, the alternative plans by SoRPES are about 321.7% more diversified. Although, this is a positive result for SoRPES, but we take the result to be atypical, as no specific conclusions can be drawn. Because, SoRPES does not have any diversification algorithm implemented. The only plausible explanation for this is that, using the ILOG optimizer, SoRPES can always obtain the optimal value for $F_1(x)$ just as ReleasePlanner could. Once this optimal value is obtained for $F_1(x)$, the ε-Constraint algorithm we have implemented for SoRPES then constraints $F_1(x)$ on this optimal value and searches for the best value for $F_2(x)$ that corresponds to this value of $F_1(x)$. For this reason, there could be several solutions of $F_2(x)$ that correspond to the optimal value of $F_1(x)$, thus increasing the chances of obtaining solutions that could be structurally different than the initial solution.

Table 7.9: Structural Diversity of the Release Plans

SoRPES		ReleasePlanner	
Pair of Plans	H(a,b)	Pair of Plans	H(a,b)
(SP1,SP2)	56	(RP1,RP2)	13
(SP1,SP3)	75	(RP1,RP3)	13
(SP1,SP4)	97	(RP1,RP4)	17
(SP1,SP5)	105	(RP1,RP5)	18
(SP2,SP3)	38	(RP2,RP3)	5
(SP2,SP4)	65	(RP2,RP4)	20
(SP2,SP5)	77	(RP2,RP5)	21
(SP3,SP4)	46	(RP3,RP4)	21
(SP3,SP5)	60	(RP3,RP5)	21
(SP4,SP5)	22	(RP4,RP5)	3
	641		**152**

As part of the consistency evaluation, we assess the level of satisfaction of SD-coupling in the release plans generated by SoRPES and ReleasePlanner at different α thresholds (see Chapter 5 for discussions on this threshold). Recall from Chapter 5 that the number of SD-coupled features that has to be satisfied increases with decreasing α threshold. Table 7.10 shows the results of the SD-coupling satisfaction. At threshold $\alpha = 1.0$, for example, it is only alternative 5 (i.e. SP5) by SoRPES that has higher level of satisfaction of SD-coupling at 46.15% than the alternatives generated by ReleasePlanner. The highest level of SD-coupling satisfaction in the alternatives generated by ReleasePlanner at threshold $\alpha = 1.0$ is 30.77%. Meanwhile, ReleasePlanner has higher level of satisfaction of SD-coupling at this threshold for the other alternative solutions. This trend continues up to threshold $\alpha = 0.8$.

As the value of threshold α (e.g. at $\alpha = 0.7$ and at 0.5) reduces, which requires that more SD-coupling between features should be satisfied, the alternatives from SoRPES start showing more consistency in achieving higher level of satisfaction of SD-coupling. In general, throughout all the thresholds selected for the experiments, SoRPES consistently has at least one solution for which the level of satisfaction of SD-coupling is higher than all the alternatives from ReleasePlanner. Specifically, the release plan alternative 5 by SoRPES consistently performs better than ReleasePlanner at all the thresholds considered. This is the alternative that has the highest objective value of $F_2(x)$ (see Figure 7.5), and it is expected to exhibit the highest level of SD-coupling satisfaction. Thus, for any set of alternative solutions generated by SoRPES, it is guaranteed that at least one of the solutions in a set of alternative solutions would consistently have higher level of satisfaction of SD-coupling than any of the solutions from ReleasePlanner (see the shaded region in Table 7.10)

Meanwhile, at thresholds $\alpha = 1.0$ and $\alpha = 0.8$, ReleasePlanner have more alternatives with higher level of satisfaction of SD-coupling than the alternative from SoRPES. As observed for SoRPES achieving higher structural diversity than ReleasePlanner in Table 7.9, the good performance by ReleasePlanner in terms of SD-coupling satisfaction is atypical, since it does not formally make provisions for handling SD-coupling. Recall from Chapter 5 that the objective function $F_2(x)$ is focused on maximizing the assignment of SD-coupled features.

Table 7.10: Level of Satisfaction of SD-coupling at Different Thresholds

| | $\mu^{1.0}$ | | $\mu^{0.8}$ | | $\mu^{0.7}$ | | $\mu^{0.5}$ | |
	SoRPES	Release Planner	SoRPES	Release Planner	SoRPES	Release Planner	SoRPES	Release Planner
Alternative 1	7.69%	30.77%	10.24%	22.35%	12.52%	15.24%	13.07%	11.92%
Alternative 2	15.38%	30.77%	15.83%	22.35%	16.15%	12.51%	13.42%	11.67%
Alternative 3	7.69%	30.77%	14.72%	22.35%	16.53%	12.51%	14.21%	11.44%
Alternative 4	15.38%	30.77%	20.30%	22.35%	14.13%	14.60%	14.29%	10.53%
Alternative 5	46.15%	30.77%	31.47%	22.35%	19.35%	13.91%	14.32%	10.34%

7.4 Threats to Validity

7.4.1 Empirical Study I

The dataset used for Empirical Study I is a relatively small dataset, but the dataset is complete in every sense. The feedback cycle is missing here because we collected this data long before the development of the SoRPES technique was completed. All the 4 participants that performed stakeholders voting, software components evaluation, and feature-driven impact analysis are no longer with the development team. Thus, there is no way to verify whether the release plans generated are pragmatically good solutions in terms of capturing the business and technical concerns, as opposed to solutions that are only good under the assumptions of the heuristics implemented in the technique.

In addition, we probably were able to get the complete data in this sense because our research laboratory and the ReleasePlanner team are under the same headship. Thus, it may be the case that participants from the ReleasePlanner team were highly cooperative because they felt obliged to dig out this dataset, just for political reasons. We cannot independently verify the soundness of the dataset itself.

The findings from this empirical study are specific to the case study data we have used and cannot be generalized as representing the entire spectrum of software projects. Several other empirical studies would have to be conducted over several projects, different environments, and would have to be done over time, in order to confirm the findings.

7.4.2 Empirical Study II

The industrial dataset used in this second study is incomplete, although representative. Since we have generated synthetic impact analysis data rather than using an actual data, the best we can conclude from the results is that the study was conducted as a proof-of-concept validation of the technique. And this is where our comparison with the results from ReleasePlanner makes sense.

Once again, the feedback cycle on the meaningfulness of the release plans cannot be ascertained. First, because the company has not provided the impact analysis data, and would not be able to judge the soundness of results based on the impact data, which has not been extracted from their system. However, the fact that the dataset from the business perspectives came directly from the company lends a flavor of reality to the study. Second, the project planning is still on-going, and several features could still be added or deleted from the feature repository. For example, more stakeholders are still expected to give priority values over the next couple of months. Thus, it is not feasible to have the feedback cycle for a project that has not yet been completed.

7.5 Summary

In this Chapter, we have presented two empirical validation studies evaluating SoRPES. Through the studies, we addressed questions regarding the *feasibility*, *relevance*, *scalability* and *consistency* of SoRPES. In these regards, we have shown that SoRPES is feasible and can be applied to plan releases of any software development project, as long as the necessary data can be made available. The inability to provide such data is not a limitation of SoRPES itself, but probably the maturity level of the organizations involved. For example, the company representatives that I dealt with acknowledged the importance of having the impact analysis data and the potential benefit they can see in our ideas to extract feature coupling using impact analysis data, as well as the tremendous help that would accrue from assigning such interrelated features to the same release. Unfortunately, such data reside in the heads of their developers.

Through the studies, we have been able to show that the only possible concern with scalability is that, the time taken to generate results from data of larger sizes would be expected to increase with increasing data size. But this is expected for any other technique for that matter. In terms of consistency, we have obtained promising results from both studies. Since the quality of solutions generated by SoRPES are comparable to those generated by ReleasePlanner, in spite of the second objective that we sought to simultaneously maximize from the technical perspective, it is safe to conclude that SoRPES can be taken as a worthy improvement on ReleasePlanner.

The empirical studies discussed here can be taken as initial proof-of-concept validation exercise necessary to verify the feasibility of the technique and its underlying assumptions. In validating the results, we have compared our results to those generated by ReleasePlanner, and the findings are promising. We have shown that the inclusion of the technical perspective does not considerably degrade the attainable objective values from both perspectives.

CHAPTER EIGHT

CONCLUSIONS AND FUTURE WORK

The outcome of any serious research can only be to make two
questions grow where only one grew before.
- Thorstein Veblen

8.1 Introduction

According to Basili [10], *"{A software engineering} researcher needs laboratories; they only exist where practitioners build software systems. The practitioner needs to understand how to build better systems; the researcher can provide the models to make this happen."* In most cases, however, software companies are reluctant to provide software engineering researchers access to their data, if they even maintain them. At the onset of this research, we made several persistent efforts to leverage our ideas on developing models for release planning (especially with existing system-awareness) with the everyday experiences of practitioners in the software industry, as well as their historical data that could be relevant to release planning decisions. Some of the companies that I have had the privilege to visit, or chat with a representative during the various stages of this research include Nortel Networks, Trema Laboratory Inc, and Chartwell Technology. One important feedback from these chats remains clear, there is a consensus about the fact that bringing the interrelatedness of features into release planning decisions remains a fundamental and practical industrial problem. Whether the companies collect the relevant data, or are ready to give access to such remains another question. However, our interactions with the practitioners from companies mentioned above helped in shaping our ideas in developing the theoretical basis of the release planning technique and models discussed in this book.

This chapter presents a summary of the key contributions, findings, limitations, and suggested future directions that could improve this research work.

8.2 Book Summary

Software features originate from the customers, but it is the developers that implement them. The former relates to the business concerns while the later relate to the technical concerns of a software project. Most works on software release planning in the literature have only focused on the values of features to the stakeholders as the main planning objective. These works have largely ignored the intrinsic difficulty associated with adding features to an existing system. We have developed a framework for software release planning that integrates these two concerns. We have demonstrated one use of the framework via the SoRPES technique.

The first contribution of this work is a decision-centric framework for software release planning. As a prerequisite to evaluating the level of difficulty associated with the implementation of software features in the components of the existing architecture, we developed an expert-based technique for assessing the modifiability of software architectural designs. We have also developed models and algorithms for detecting the coupling that exists between features due to the synergy in their implementation. In addition, we developed a technique to assess the technical constraints associated with the implementation of the features in the existing system. Finally, we integrate all these aspects into a decision support technique that implements an instance of the framework, and performed empirical validation studies to show the applicability of the technique.

8.3 Contributions and Findings

The main goal of this research is to: *provide a release planning decision framework that addresses both business and technical concerns*. We have further broken this objective into the following six research objectives:

- **Objective 1:** *Develop a decision-centric framework that addresses both business and technical concerns of release planning.*

- **Objective 2:** *Investigate the constraints that the design decisions in an existing system exert on the implementation of new or changed features.*

- **Objective 3:** *Develop a technique to detect and quantify the interrelatedness of features.*

- **Objective 4:** *Provide a theoretical foundation for modeling the release planning problem in a way that can underlie the design of a decision support system.*

- **Objective 5:** *Design a decision support technique that supports release planning decision making.*

- **Objective 6:** *Evaluate the decision support technique in order to determine its applicability.*

In addressing these objectives, we have made a number of contributions to the field of software engineering, which we summarize in the sequel.

8.3.1 Decision-Centric Framework for Release Planning

We have introduced a decision-centric framework for release planning that addresses both business and technical concerns. The proposed framework is flexible and the implementation of the individual process elements is customizable to different organizations and project contexts. The framework provides an environment that allows for the integration of business concerns with the technical concerns in order to define feasible release plans.

8.3.2 Evaluation of Architectural Design for Modifiability

We proposed an expert-judgment technique known as EBEAM (Expert-Based Evaluation of Architectures for Modifiability) for evaluating the modifiability of software architectural designs. The design and development of EBEAM involves an exploratory study to investigate the characteristics that influence the modifiability of software architectural designs. We develop EBEAM as an evaluation method that can transform the judgment of experts into measurable quantities. In order to aggregate the judgment of experts, EBEAM also presents a new weighting scheme for assigning importance to experts. We report a case study that uses EBEAM to evaluate the architectural designs of the prototype system for NASA flight assistance known as TSAFE (Tactical Separation Assisted Flight Environment). To validate the results obtained from EBEAM, we defined a set of design metrics, evaluated the modifiability of the architectural designs of TSAFE using these metrics, and compared the results. Both EBEAM and the metrics show correlation in their results.

8.3.3 Quantifying Feature Interrelatedness

We have proposed a technique to quantify the interrelatedness of features using impact analysis data. This interrelatedness is based on the overlaps between the components that would implement the features in the existing system. We believe that, by taking advantage of this interrelatedness during implementation, it would help the developers to reduce the cognitive complexity associated with understanding the implementation of features.

8.3.4 Bi-Objective Release Planning Model

We have formulated the release planning problem as a bi-objective optimization problem that would take advantage of the interrelatedness of features as one objective. This first objective leads to features that share maximal implementation-related dependency being assigned to the same release. The second objective of the model aims to assign features to releases in a way that maximizes the priorities attached to the features by the stakeholders. The results obtained via proof-of-concept case studies showed the applicability of the proposed approach. These results also showed good correlation between the release plans generated and their level of satisfaction of coupling between the features.

8.3.5 Decision Support for Release Planning

We have developed a decision support technique known as SoRPES (Software Release Planning with Existing System-awareness). SoRPES extends the bi-objective release planning model to include the technical constraints associated with implementing features in the existing system. The technical constraints aims to treat features that involve difficult and complex changes to the existing system differently from those involving simple and small changes. By generating portfolio of alternative solutions, the SoRPES also provides the decision maker with the privilege to evaluate the alternatives using prior experience and knowledge that cannot be formally modeled.

8.3.6 Empirical Validation

We have conducted empirical validation of SoRPES technique that showed the potential of SoRPES to generate results that are as good as (or even better than) a similar technique that is based on single objective optimization, both in terms of quality of solutions and satisfaction of feature coupling. The empirical validation also investigated the applicability of the SoRPES technique.

8.3.7 Prototype Tool

We have provided a proof-of-concept implementation of the key components of the SoRPES technique. This initial prototype can serve as a basis for the development of a full-fledged decision support tool.

Table 8.1 presents a summary of the research objectives we outlined above and the contribution(s) that address(es) each of the objectives.

Table 8.1: Matching the Contributions to Research Sub-objectives

Research Objectives	Contributions Matching the Objectives
Objective 1	Section 8.3.1
Objective 2	Section 8.3.2
Objective 3	Section 8.3.3
Objective 4	Section 8.3.4
Objective 5	Sections 8.3.5 and 8.3.7
Objective 6	Section 8.3.6

8.4 Limitations

In previous chapters, we have discussed the limitations of the work presented in those chapters. In this section, we focus on the limitations of the SoRPES technique.

8.4.1 Using the EBEAM to Evaluate Software Components

While the EBEAM is suitable for evaluating architectural designs, our experience during the empirical studies in which we generated synthetic impact analysis data revealed the limitations of EBEAM for a fine-grained component evaluation. It is easier to apply if the components are defined at a very high granularity level, such as those we dealt with in the case study discussed in Chapter 5. The more fine-grained the components are defined, the more the number of comparison that needs to be performed. Consequently, the harder and more tedious it becomes to evaluate the modifiability of components.

In addition, the metric suite for assessing the technical constraints of adding new or changed features to the existing system uses the results from the above component evaluation. It aggregates these results with the level of dispersion of the components to be modified and the extent of modifications required. But the type of changes required in the components to add the features does not constitute part of the metric suite. This is a limitation, since the change type is expected to influence the constraints imposed by the pre-existing design. We have started to address this limitation in a new assessment scheme that uses Bayesian Networks (*see* Saliu & Ruhe [140]).

8.4.2 Cost of Adoption

Most of the techniques discussed in this book are semi-automatic as they try to balance the challenges of dealing with complexities of software project development and their human-centric nature. Thus, substantial input is required from the developers, project managers, and other stakeholders. Being such a heavy weight technique, it raises questions of practicality. Substantial effort is required to supply all the input data and this effort must be weighed against the potential benefits. The decision to adopt SoRPES would depend on a cost/benefit analysis within the adopting organization.

8.4.3 Availability and Accuracy of Data

SoRPES requires a lot of input data. Some of this data could be difficult to get, especially if it is not the practice to maintain such data in an organization. If, for instance, the impact analysis data is unavailable, then there is no means to handle the implementation-related objective function in the SoRPES model. In this case, the model reduces to single-objective optimization model that is similar to the underlying model implemented in ReleasePlanner. It is likely that development companies with a higher process maturity would find the technique more practical than companies with lower process maturity. Because the companies with a high-level process maturity would probably have processes in place to collect the necessary data. We delve more into this correlation between process maturity and the applicability of SoRPES in our future work section.

In the same vein, the results of the computed strength of coupling and the system values for the features may not reflect reality, if the impact analysis data are faulty. And this would be propagated to the quality of the release plans generated. Apart from the impact analysis data, it is important to have value propositions from stakeholders, and resource estimations from the development team. The process of deriving all these can be tedious.

If some or all of these data are not available, the technique would only be able to generate solutions that are as good as the input data.

8.4.4 Evaluating the Goodness of Solutions

The empirical validation studies we have conducted could only serve to test the quality of solutions (i.e. release plans) generated by SoRPES based on the input data and parameters of the optimization models. We cannot make claims about the goodness of the solutions in terms of whether the chosen release plan alternative would actually be adhered to during implementation. Feature change during development, political and business interests could take precedence over the scheduled release plans. Only a longitudinal study could verify the reliability of the release plans generated by SoRPES.

8.4.5 Tool Support

The current implementation is not immediately adoptable in the industry without *a priori* preprocessing of the input data. Unlike ReleasePlanner that is a full-fledged decision support tool, the current research prototype for SoRPES serves only as a proof-of-concept implementation of the decision support technique. The acceptance of such techniques by the practitioners would require well-designed interfaces that make the collection of data and analysis of resulting release plans easier.

8.5 Future Work

This book has answered several questions, yet it generates many more. This section lists suggestions for possible extensions of the research work presented.

8.5.1 Architecture Evaluation using EBEAM

In developing the EBEAM, we performed an exploratory study to elicit the design characteristics that influence modifiability of software architectural designs. We assert that the list generated is not exhaustive, because some other factors (which may not necessarily be design characteristics related) also have impact on modifiability of architectural designs. For example, the modifiability of architectural designs can be influenced by the following other factors: 1) the characteristics of the development team and the development environment, 2) the characteristics of the features (or change requests) to be implemented in the architectural design, and 3) the number of changes required in order to implement and incorporate the features into the existing architecture. The next steps for extending EBEAM involve building on the existing model and incorporating the other factors into the existing scheme.

It would also be worthwhile to investigate an extension that considers the combination of both expert judgment and objective metrics in a unified evaluation framework. A unified model of this sort appears challenging because of the scale issues, units, and range of values on which metrics are defined, but it deserves further investigation.

8.5.2 Feature Coupling and Release Planning Implications

The feature coupling detection method we have discussed in this book is based on the assumption that, implementing features that share common implementation components together would reduce cognitive effort during implementation. This is expected to result in development effort savings. We have not been able to verify this claim independently. Future work is necessary to empirically validate this assumption via several industrial case studies.

Instead of the current effort estimation on per feature basis, it would be important to investigate cluster estimation of development efforts for group of features using their feature coupling information. Results from such research can be used to analytically validate the assumptions that assigning interrelated features to the same release leads to effort savings. In addition, the results from cluster estimation of efforts could be used to evaluate alternative release plans, in order to determine which of the alternatives achieves the highest effort savings, and why. This can be achieved through the extraction of the cluster of features that are involved in SD-coupling in the alternative release plans, and development effort re-estimated based on each cluster.

8.5.3 Correlation between Release Planning and Process Maturity

Obviously, most of the data we require for the decision support technique developed for release planning is expected to be available in matured organizations. During one of my visits to Chartwell Technology, a project manager had this to say: *"...your ideas about extracting implementation synergy between features from impact analysis data, and its subsequent use in release planning decisions to encourage the implementation of related features together in the same release, is a fundamental and practical industrial problem that we face every day. But impact analysis is a human exercise in our organization, which is never documented. I think companies at CMM Level 4 and above would definitely be an ideal target for such data and they would find this work extremely useful..."* I was not overly surprised when I heard this, because the technique we have developed is a heavy weight technique that might likely require higher level process maturity to achieve the real benefits. This aspect in and of itself require further studies to investigate whether higher level process maturity would lead to higher benefits derived from the ideas, models, and techniques discussed in this book. Clark [28] conducted a similar study in the context of the alignment between software development effort and process maturity.

8.5.4 Building a Complete Support Environment for SoRPES

We have implemented the key components of a prototype tool to support the release planning technique presented in this research. In order for the technique to gain widespread acceptance among practitioners, a full-fledged decision support that integrates all aspects of the technique would be needed. One immediate possibility is to extend the existing commercial tool, ReleasePlanner, with SoRPES extension.

8.5.5 Comprehensive Empirical Validation Studies

Most of the empirical studies we have conducted in this research can only be seen as initial attempts to show the feasibility and applicability of the different ideas, models, and techniques developed in this work. Like most software engineering research related to software process and product management, long-term comprehensive empirical studies would have to be conducted on a variety of projects to establish the viability of the theories developed in this work. Replicating the empirical studies for the technique presented in this book in several industrial settings would enable us to determine the generality of the results. To be able to draw such conclusions, the empirical validation studies must take the form of longitudinal studies that span several projects, environments, and would need to be carried out over several releases of the software systems. The work we have presented provides the foundation for such studies in the context of release planning that considers existing systems. The outcome of such studies can lead to critical insights that can be used to enhance the SoRPES technique and its associated models.

8.6 Closing Remarks

The problem of software release planning is important and difficult. It is made difficult because apart from the resources needed to accomplish the development tasks, there are two major important development considerations. First, it is extremely important to consider details of customers' needs. Second, it makes sense technically to develop some kinds of interrelated features together. We have investigated and presented a clear and precise approach to address both sets of concerns at once. We have developed a decision support technique for release planning known as SoRPES. By virtue of the underlying formal modeling of the problem, SoRPES is clear about what it assumes and what problems it addresses and solves. And by virtue of its incorporating the knowledge and experience of human experts, it understands and deals with the limitations of the formalized description of the problem.

This work shows that software release planning needs to address both business and technical concerns. We have also shown that impact analysis data contains a wealth of information that could help project managers make better release planning decisions. Although, impact analysis in some organizations (like one of those we have visited) is a human exercise, the results reside in the heads of the developers, and are never documented. We hope this work would encourage software practitioners to consider a more systematic collection of impact analysis data given its relevance to release planning decision making.

In closing, despite advancing release planning research in this book, there exists several unanswered research questions. Future research in release planning should use the ideas and materials presented in this book as building blocks for further theory and experimentation in release planning. This work and its future applications essentially depend on results from further empirical studies. It also depends on actual experiences with the performance of the models and the decision support technique in different industrial settings. We believe we have set the stage for evolving our knowledge of release planning via the research cycle of *modeling, experimenting, learning* and *remodeling*, as emphasized by Basili [10].

References

[1]   Abowd, G., Bass, L., Clements, P., Kazman, R., Northrop, L., and Zaremski, A., "Recommended Best Industrial Practice for Software Architecture Evaluation," Carnegie Mellon University, Pittsburgh, USA CMU/SEI-96-TR-025, 1997, pp. 1-34.

[2]   Ackermann, C. and Lindvall, M., "Understanding Change Requests in Order to Predict Software Impact," In Proceedings of 30th NASA/IEEE Software Engineering Workshop (SEW 2006), Columbia, MD, USA, 2006.

[3]   Ahmed, M., Saliu, M. O., and AlGhamdi, J., "Adaptive Fuzzy Logic-Based Framework for Software Development Effort Prediction," *Information and Software Technology*, vol. 47, no. 1, pp. 31-48, 2005.

[4]   Aho, A. V. and Griffeth, N. D., "Feature Interaction in the Global Information Infrastructure," In Proceedings of 3rd ACM SIGSOFT Symposium on the Foundations of Software Engineering, Washington, DC, USA, 1995, pp. 2-5.

[5]   Akker, J. M., Brinkkemper, S., Diepen, G., and Versendaal, J. M., "Flexible Release Planning Using Integer Linear Programming," In Proceedings of 11th International Workshop on Requirements Engineering for Software Quality (REFSQ'05), Porto, Portugal, 2005, pp. 230-345.

[6]   Alghamdi, J. and Saliu, M. O., "Analysis and Theoretical Validation of Object-Oriented Coupling Metrics," In Proceedings of IASTED International Multi-Conference on Applied Informatics (AI'03), Innsbruck, Austria, 2003, pp. 1145 - 1152.

224

[7]   Arnold, R. S. and Bohner, S. A., "Impact analysis - Towards a Framework for Comparison," In Proceedings of IEEE International Conference on Software Maintenance, Montreal, Quebec, Canada, 1993, pp. 292-301.

[8]   Babar, M. A., Zhu, L., and Jeffrey, R., "A Framework for Classifying and Comparing Software Architecture Evaluation Methods," In Proceedings of Australian Software Engineering Conference, Melbourne, Australia, 2004, pp. 309-319.

[9]   Bagnall, A. J., Rayward-Smith, V. J., and Whittley, I. M., "The Next Release Problem," *Information and Software Technology*, vol. 43, no. 14, pp. 883-890, 2001.

[10]   Basili, V. R., "The Role of Experimentation in Software Engineering: Past, Current, and Future," In Proceedings of 18th International Conference on Software Engineering (ICSE'98), Berlin, Germany, 1996, pp. 442-449.

[11]   Bass, L., Clements, P., and Kazman, R., "Software Architecture in Practice," Second ed. Reading, MA.: Addison-Wesley, 2003.

[12]   Becerra, R. L. and Coello, C. A., "Solving Hard Multiobjective Optimization Problems using e-Constraint with Cultured Differential Evolution," In Proceedings of 9th International Conference on Parallel Problem Solving from Nature (PPSN IX), Reykjavik, Iceland, 2006, pp. 543-552.

[13]   Bengtsson, P. and Bosch, J., "Architecture Level Prediction of Software Maintenance," In Proceedings of 3rd European Conference on Software Maintenance and Reengineering (CSMR), Amsterdam, Netherlands, 1999, pp. 139-147.

[14]   Bengtsson, P., Lassing, N., Bosch, J., and van-Vliet, H., "Architecture-Level Modifiability Analysis (ALMA)," *The Journal of Systems and Software*, vol. 69, no. 1-2, pp. 129-147, 2004.

[15]   Berge, C., "Graphs and Hypergraphs." Amsterdam: North-Holland Publishing Company, 1976.

[16]   Bohner, S. A. and Arnold, R. S., "Software Change Impact Analysis." Los Alamitos, CA, USA: IEEE Computer Society Press, 1996.

[17]   Bondi, A. B., "Characteristics of Scalability and their Impact on Performance," In Proceedings of 2nd International Workshop on Software and Performance (WOSP2000), Ottawa, Ontario, Canada, 2000, pp. 195-203.

[18]   Briand, L. C., Daly, J. W., and Wust, J. K., " A Unified Framework for Coupling Measurement in Object-oriented Systems," *IEEE Transactions on Software Engineering*, vol. 25, no. 1, pp. 91-121, 1999.

[19]   Briand, L. C., Morasca, S., and Basili, V. R., "Property-Based Software Engineering Measurement," *IEEE Transactions on Software Engineering*, vol. 22, no. 1, pp. 68-86, 1996.

[20]   Briand, L. C. and Wieczorek, I., "Resource Estimation in Software Engineering," in *Encyclopedia of Software Engineering*, vol. 2, Marciniak, J. J. (Ed.) 2nd ed, New York, NY: Wiley, 2002, pp. 1160-1196.

[21]   Brooks, F. P., "No Silver Bullet: Essence and Accidents of Software Engineering," *Computer*, vol. 20, no. 4, pp. 10-19, 1987.

[22]   Calder, M., Kolberg, M., Magill, E. H., and Reiff-Marganiec, S., "Feature Interactions: a Critical Review and Considered Forecast," *Computer Networks*, vol. 41, no. 1, pp. 115-141, 2003.

[23] Carlshamre, P., "Release Planning in Market-Driven Software Product Development: Provoking an Understanding," *Requirements Engineering*, vol. 7, no. 3, pp. 139-151, 2002.

[24] Carlshamre, P., Sandahl, K., Lindvall, M., Regnell, B., and Nattoch Dag, J., "An Industrial Survey of requirements interdependencies in Software Release Planning," In Proceedings of 5th IEEE International Symposium on Requirements Engineering, Toronto, Canada, 2001, pp. 84-91.

[25] Chankong, V. and Haimes, Y. Y., "Multiobjective Decision Making: Theory and Methodology." New York: North-Holland, 1983.

[26] Chidamber, S. R. and Kemerer, C. F., "A Metrics Suite for Object-Oriented Design," *IEEE Transactions on Software Engineering*, vol. 20, no. 6, pp. 476-493, 1994.

[27] Christel, M. G. and Kang, K. C., "Issues in Requirements Elicitation," SEI, Carnegie Melon University, Pittsburgh, CA CMU/SEI-92-TR-12, 1992.

[28] Clark, B. K., "The Effects of Software Process Maturity on Software Development Effort," Department of Computer Science, University of Southern California, Los Angeles, 1997

[29] Clemen, R. T. and Winkler, R. L., "Combining Probability Distributions from Experts in Risk Analysis," *Risk Analysis*, vol. 19, no. 2, pp. 187-203, 1999.

[30] Clements, P., Bachmann, F., Bass, L., Garlan, D., Ivers, J., Little, R., Nord, R., and Stafford, J., "Documenting Software Architectures: Views and Beyond." Reading, MA: Addison-Wesley, 2002.

[31] CMMI, "Capability Maturity Model Integration (CMMI®) Version 1.1 Staged Representation," SEI, Carnegie Mellon University, Pittsburgh, PA 2002.

[32] Coello, C. A. C., Veldhuizen, D. A. V., and Lamont, G. B., "Evolutionary Algorithms for Solving Multi-Objective Problems." NY: Kluwer Academic Publishers, 2002.

[33] Collette, Y. and Siarry, P., "Multi-objective Optimization: Principles and Case Studies." NY: Springer-Verlag, 2004.

[34] Dahlstedt, A. G., Karlsson, L., Natt-och-Dag, J., Regnell, B., and Persson, A., "Market-Driven Requirements Engineering Processes for Software Products - A Report on Current Practices," In Proceedings of International Workshop on COTS and Product Software (RECOTS'03), Monterey Bay, CA, USA, 2003.

[35] Dahlstedt, A. G. and Persson, A., "Requirements Interdependencies - Moulding the State of Research into a Research Agenda," In Proceedings of 9th International Workshop on Requirements Engineering: Foundation for Software Quality (REFSQ'03), Klagenfurt/Velden, Austria, 2003, pp. 55-64.

[36] Datta, S. and Gentleman, R., "A Brief Overview of Hypergraphs: Theory and Potential Applications," Fred Hutchinson Cancer Research Center, Seattle, WA, USA, http://gentleman-lab.fhcrc.org/literature/hypergraphs, (Last Accessed: October 13, 2006, 2006).

[37] Dayani-Fard, H., "Quality-Based Software Release Management," PhD Thesis, Department of School of Computing, Queen's University, Canada, Kingston, Ontario, 2003

[38] Deb, K., "Multi-Objective Optimization Using Evolutionary Algorithms." UK: John Wiley & Sons, 2001.

[39] Denne, M. and Cleland-Huang, J., "The Incremental Funding Method: Data Driven Software Development," *IEEE Software*, vol. 21, no. 3, pp. 39-47, 2004.

228

[40]   Dennis, G., "Building a Trusted Computing Base for Air Traffic Control Software," Master's Thesis Thesis, Massachusetts Institute of Technology, Boston, MA, 2003

[41]   Denzinger, J. and Ruhe, G., "Decision Support for Software Release Planning using e-Assistants," *Journal of Decision Support Systems*, vol. 13, no. 4, pp. 399-421, 2004.

[42]   Dhama, H., "Quantitative Models of Cohesion and Coupling in Software," *Journal of Systems and Software*, vol. 29, no. 1, pp. 65-74, 1995.

[43]   Dobrica, L. and Niemela, E., "A Survey on Software Architecture Analysis Methods," *IEEE Transactions on Software Engineering*, vol. 28, no. 7, pp. 638-653, 2002.

[44]   Donzelli, P., "A Decision Support System for Software Project Management," *IEEE Software*, vol. 23, no. 4, pp. 67-75, 2006.

[45]   Duenas, J. C., de-Oliveira, W. L., and de-la-Puente, J. A., "A Software Architecture Evaluation Model," In Proceedings of 2nd International Workshop On Development and Evolution of Software Architectures for Product Families, Spain, 1998, pp. 148-157.

[46]   Ehrgott, M. and Gandibleux, X., "A Survey and Annotated Bibliography of Multiobjective Combinatorial Optimization," *OR Spektrum*, vol. 22, no. 4, pp. 425-460, 2000.

[47]   Eick, S. G., Graves, T. L., Karr, A. F., Marron, J. S., and Mockus, A., "Does Code Decay? Assessing the Evidence from Change Management Data," *IEEE Transactions on Software Engineering*, vol. 27, no. 1, pp. 1-12, 2001.

[48]   Erdogmus, H., "What's Good Software, Anyway?" *IEEE Software*, vol. 24, no. 2, pp. 5-7, 2007.

[49]   Erzberger, H., "The Automated Airspace Concept," In Proceedings of 4th USA/Europe Air Traffic Management R & D Seminar, Santa Fe, NM, USA, 2001, pp. 1-15.

[50]   Fandel, G., Spronk, J., and Matarazzo, B., "Multiple Criteria Decision Methods and Applications." Berlin: Springer-Verlag, 1985.

[51]   Feather, M. S., Cornford, S. L., and Gibbel, M., "Scalable Mechanisms for Requirements Interaction Management," In Proceedings of 4th International Conference on Requirements Engineering (ICRE'00), Schaumburg, IL, USA, 2000, pp. 119-129.

[52]   Fenton, N., "Software Measurement: A Necessary Scientific Basis," *IEEE Transactions on Software Engineering*, vol. 20, no. 3, pp. 199-206, Mar. 1994, 1994.

[53]   Figueira, J., Greco, S., and Ehrgott, M., "Multiple Criteria Decision Analysis: State of the Art Surveys." New York: Springer, 2005.

[54]   Forman, E. and Peniwati, K., "Aggregating Individual Judgments and Priorities with the Analytic Hierarchy Process," *European Journal of Operational Research*, vol. 108, no. 1, pp. 165-169, 1998.

[55]   Gall, H., Hajek, K., and Jazayeri, M., "Detection of Logical Coupling Based on Product Release History," In Proceedings of IEEE International Conference on Software Maintenance, Washington D.C., 1998, pp. 190-198.

[56]   Gall, H., Jazayeri, M., Klosch, R. R., and Trausmuth, G., "Software Evolution Observations Based on Product Release History," In Proceedings of International Conference on Software Maintenance (ICSM'97), Bari, Italy, 1997, pp. 160-166.

[57]   Gamma, E., Helm, R., Johnson, R., and Vlissides, J., "Design Patterns: Elements of Reusable Object-Oriented Design." Reading, MA: Addison-Wesley, 1994.

[58]   Garlan, D., "Research Direction in Software Architecture," *ACM Computing Survey*, vol. 27, no. 2, pp. 257-261, 1995.

[59]   Giroux, O. and Robillard, M. P., "Detecting Increases in Feature Coupling using Regression Tests," In Proceedings of 14th ACM SIGSOFT International Symposium on Foundations of Software Engineering (FSE 2006), Portland, Oregon, USA, 2006, pp. 163-174.

[60]   Graves, T. L., Karr, A. F., Marron, J. S., and Siy, H., "Predicting Fault Incidence Using Software Change History," *IEEE Transactions on Software Engineering*, vol. 26, no. 7, pp. 653-661, 2000.

[61]   Greer, D., "Decision Support for Planning Software Evolution with Risk Management," in *16th International Conference on Software Engineering and Knowledge Engineering (SEKE'04)*. Banff, Canada, 2004, pp. 503-508.

[62]   Greer, D. and Ruhe, G., "Software Release Planning: An Evolutionary and Iterative Approach," *Information & Software Technology*, vol. 46, no. 4, pp. 243-253, 2004.

[63]   Griffeth, N. D. and Lin, Y.-J., "Extending Telecommunications Systems: The Feature-Interaction Problem," *IEEE Computer*, vol. 26, no. 8, pp. 14-18, 1993.

[64]   Grubb, P. and Takang, A. A., "Software Maintenance: Concepts and Practice," 2nd ed: World Scientific, 2003.

[65]   Gursaran and Roy, G., "On the Applicability of Weyuker Property 9 to Object-Oriented Structural Inheritance Complexity Metrics," *IEEE Transactions on Software Engineering*, vol. 27, no. 4, pp. 381-384, 2001.

[66]   Hacknot, "The Top 10 Elements of Good Software Design," http://www.hacknot.info/hacknot/action/showEntry?eid=54, (Last Accessed: Aug. 6, 2006, 2006).

[67]   Haimes, Y. Y., Lasdon, L. S., and Wismer, D. A., "On a Bicriterion Formulation of the Problems of Integrated System Identification and System Optimization," *IEEE Transactions on Systems, Man, and Cybernetics*, vol. 1, no. 3, pp. 296-297, 1971.

[68]   Hassan, A. E. and Holt, R. C., "Predicting Change Propagation in Software Systems," In Proceedings of International Conference on Software Maintenance, Chicago, Illinois, USA, 2004, pp. 284-293.

[69]   Hassan, A. E. and Holt, R. C., "Studying the Chaos of Code Development," In Proceedings of Working Conference on Reverse Engineering (WCRE 2003), Victoria, Canada, 2003, pp. 123-133.

[70]   Henry, S. and Kafura, D., "Software Structure Metrics Based on Information Flow," *IEEE Transactions on Software Engineering*, vol. 7, no. 5, pp. 510-518, 1981.

[71]   Hochstein, L. and Lindvall, M., "Diagnosing Architectural Degeneration," In Proceedings of 28th NASA/IEEE Software Engineering Workshop (SEW-28), Greenbelt, MD, USA, 2003, pp. 137-142.

[72]   ILOG, "ILOG CPLEX 10.0 Reference Manual." Incline village, Nevada: ILOG CPLEX Division, 2006.

[73]   Jönsson, P. and Lindvall, M., "Impact Analysis," in *Engineering and Managing Software Requirements*, Aurum, A. and Wohlin, C. (Eds.), Heidelberg, Germany: Springer, 2005, pp. 116-142.

[74]   Jørgensen, M. and Shepperd, M., "A Systematic Review of Software Development Cost Estimation Studies," *IEEE Transactions on Software Engineering*, vol. 33, no. 1, pp. 33-53, 2007.

232

[75] Jung, H.-W., "Optimizing Value and Cost in Requirements Analysis," *IEEE Software*, vol. 15, no. 4, pp. 74-78, 1998.

[76] Karlsson, J. and Ryan, K., "A Cost-Value Approach for Prioritizing Requirements," *IEEE Software*, vol. 14, no. 5, pp. 67-74, 1997.

[77] Karlsson, J., Wohlin, C., and Regnell, B., "An Evaluation of Methods for Prioritizing Software Requirements," *Information and Software Technology*, vol. 39, no. 14-15, pp. 939-947, 1998.

[78] Karlsson, L., Dahlstedt, A. G., Natt-och-Dag, J., Regnell, B., and Persson, A., "Challenges in Market-Driven Requirements Engineering - an Industrial Interview Study," In Proceedings of 8th International Workshop on Requirements Engineering: Foundation for Software Quality (REFSQ'02), Essen, Germany, 2002.

[79] Karlsson, L., Dahlstedt, A. G., Regnell, B., Natt-och-Dag, J., and Persson, A., "Requirements Engineering Challenges in Market-Driven Software Development – An Interview Study with Practitioners," *Information and Software Technology*, vol. 49, no. 6, pp. 588-604, 2007.

[80] Kazman, R., "Software Architecture," in *Handbook of Software Engineering & Knowledge Engineering, Vol 1 Fundamentals*: World Scientific, 2001, pp. 47-67.

[81] Kazman, R., Asundi, J., and Klein, M., "Quantifying the Costs and Benefits of Architectural Decisions," In Proceedings of 23rd International Conference on Software Engineering (ICSE 2001), Toronto, Canada, 2001, pp. 297-306.

[82] Kazman, R., Bass, L., Klein, M., Lattanze, T., and Northrop, L., "A Basis for Analyzing Software Architecture Analysis Methods," *Software Quality Journal*, vol. 13, no. 4, pp. 329-355, 2005.

[83]   Kazman, R., Bass, L., Webb, M., and Abowd, G., "SAAM: A Method for Analyzing the Properties of Software Architectures," In Proceedings of 16th International Conference on Software engineering, Sorrento, Italy, 1994, pp. 81-90.

[84]   Kazman, R., Klein, M., Barbacci, M., Longstaff, T., H., L., and Carriere, J., "The Architecture Tradeoff Analysis Method," In Proceedings of International Conference on Engineering of Complex Computer Systems (ICECCS98), 1998, pp. 68-78.

[85]   Keck, D. O. and Kuehn, P. J., "The Feature and Service Interaction Problem in Telecommunications Systems: A Survey," *IEEE Transactions on Software Engineering*, vol. 24, no. 10, pp. 779-796, 1998.

[86]   Keeney, R. L., "Foundations for Making Smart Decisions," *IIE Solutions*, vol. 31, no. 5, pp. 24-30, 1999.

[87]   Keeney, R. L., "Value-Focused Thinking: A Path to Creative Decision-Making," Harvard University Press, 1992.

[88]   Keeney, R. L. and Raiffa, H., "Decisions with Multiple Objectives: Preferences and Value Trade-Offs." Cambridge, UK: Cambridge University Press, 2002.

[89]   Kelly, D., "A Study of Design Characteristics in Evolving Software Using Stability as a Criterion," *IEEE Transactions on Software Engineering*, vol. 32, no. 5, pp. 315-329, 2006.

[90]   Kim, I. Y. and de-Weck, O. L., "Adaptive Weighted-Sum Method for Bi-objective Optimization: Pareto front Generation," *Structural and Multidisciplinary Optimization*, vol. 29, no. 2, pp. 149-158, 2005.

[91]   Kitchenham, B. and Pfleeger, S. L., "Towards a Framework for Software Measurement Validation," *IEEE Transactions on Software Engineering*, vol. 21, no. 12, pp. 929-944, 1995.

[92]   Kitchenham, B., Pfleeger, S. L., and Fenton, N., "Towards a Framework for Software Measurement Validation," *IEEE Transactions on Software Engineering*, vol. 21, no. 12, pp. 929-944, Dec. 1995, 1995.

[93]   Krauskopf, J., "Elemental Concerns (Software Design)," *IEEE Potentials*, vol. 9, no. 1, pp. 13-15, 1990.

[94]   Larman, C. and Basili, V. R., "Iterative and Incremental Development: A Brief History," *IEEE Computer*, vol. 36, no. 6, pp. 47-56, 2003.

[95]   Laumanns, M., Thiele, L., and Zitzler, E., "An Efficient, Adaptive Parameter Variation Scheme for Metaheuristics Based on the Epsilon-Constraint Method," *European Journal of Operational Research*, vol. 169, no. 3, pp. 932-942, 2006.

[96]   Lehman, M. M., "Laws of Software Evolution Revisited," In Proceedings of 5th European Workshop on Software Process Technology (EWSPT'96), Nancy, France, 1996, pp. 108-124.

[97]   Lehman, M. M., "On Understanding Laws, Evolution and Conservation in the Large Program Life Cycle," *Journal of System and Software*, vol. 1, no. 3, pp. 213-221, 1980.

[98]   Lehman, M. M., Ramil, J. F., and Kahen, G., "A Paradigm for the Behavioural Modelling of Software Processes using System Dynamics," Department of Computing, Imperial College, London, Technical Report DTR018, 2001, pp. 1-11.

[99] Lehtola, L., Kauppinen, M., and Kujala, S., "Requirements Prioritization Challenges in Practice," In Proceedings of PROFES'2004, Kansai Science City, Japan, 2004, pp. 497-508.

[100] Li, M. and Smidts, C., "A Ranking of Software Engineering Measures Based on Expert Opinion," *IEEE Transactions on Software Engineering*, vol. 29, no. 9, pp. 811-824, 2003.

[101] Lin, J. G., "Multiple-Objective Problems: Pareto-Optimal Solutions by Method of Proper Equality Constraints," *IEEE Transactions on Automatic Control*, vol. 21, no. 5, pp. 641-650, 1976.

[102] Lin, J. G., "Proper Inequality Constraints and Maximization of Index Vectors," *Journal of Optimization Theory and Applications*, vol. 21, no. 4, pp. 505-521, 1977.

[103] Lindvall, M., "An Empirical Study of Requirements-Driven Impact Analysis in Object-Oriented Systems Evolution," PhD thesis Thesis, Department of Computer and Information Science, Linköping University, Linkoping, Sweden, 1997

[104] Lindvall, M., Rus, I., Donzelli, P., Memon, A., Zelkowitz, M., Betin-Can, A., Bultan, T., Ackermann, C., Anders, B., Asgari, S., Basili, V., Hochstein, L., Fellmann, J., Shull, F., Tvedt, R., Pech, D., and Hirschbach, D., "Experimenting with Software Testbeds for Evaluating New Technologies," *Empirical Software Engineering: An International Journal*, vol. 12, no. 4, pp. 417-444, 2007.

[105] Lindvall, M. and Sandahl, K., "How Well do Experienced Software Developers Predict Software Change?" *Journal of Systems and Software*, vol. 43, no. 1, pp. 19-27, 1998.

[106] Lindvall, M., Tesoriero, R., and Costa, P., "An Empirically-Based Process for Software Architecture Evaluation," *Empirical Software Engineering*, vol. 8, no. 1, pp. 83-108, 2003.

[107] Lock, S. and Kotonya, G., "An Integrated Framework for Requirement Change Impact Analysis," In Proceedings of 4th Australian Conference on Requirements Engineering, Sydney, Australia, 1999, pp. 29-42.

[108] Marler, R. T., "A Study of Multi-objective Optimization Methods for Engineering Applications," PhD Thesis, Department of Mechanical Engineering, The University of Iowa, Iowa City, IA, U.S.A., 2005

[109] Metzger, A., "Feature Interactions in Embedded Control Systems," *Computer Networks*, vol. 45, no. 5, pp. 625-644, 2004.

[110] Miodonski, P., Forster, T., Knodel, J., Lindvall, M., and Muthig, D., "Evaluation of Software Architectures with Eclipse," Institute of Experimental Software Engineering, Kaiserslautern, Germany, Technical Report IESE-Report 107.04/E, 2004.

[111] Mockus, A. and Weiss, D. M., "Predicting Risk of Software Changes," *Bell Labs Technical Journal*, vol. 5, no. 2, pp. 169-180, 2000.

[112] Natt-och-Dag, J., Regnell, B., Gervasi, V., and Brinkkemper, S., "A Linguistic-Engineering Approach to Large-Scale Requirements Management," *IEEE software*, vol. 22, no. 1, pp. 32-39, 2005.

[113] Ngo-The, A. and Ruhe, G., "A Systematic Approach for Solving the Wicked Problem of Software Release Planning," *International Journal of Soft Computing*, 2007.

[114] Ngo-The, A. and Saliu, M. O., "Measuring Dependency Constraint Satisfaction in Software Release Planning using Dissimilarity of Fuzzy Graphs," In Proceedings

of 4th IEEE International Conference on Cognitive Informatics (ICCI'05), Irvine, California, USA, 2005, pp. 301-307.

[115]   Nikora, A. P. and Munson, J. C., "Determining Fault Insertion Rates for Evolving Software Systems," In Proceedings of 9th International Symposium on Software Reliability Engineering, 1998, pp. 306-315.

[116]   Nuseibeh, B. and Easterbrook, S., "Requirements Engineering: A Roadmap," In Proceedings of 22nd International Conference on Software Engineering (ICSE 2000), Limerick, Ireland, 2000, pp. 35-46.

[117]   Obayashi, S., Sasaki, D., and Oyama, A., "Finding Tradeoffs by Using Multiobjective Optimization Algorithms," *Transactions of the Japan Society for Aeronautical and Space Sciences*, vol. 47, no. 155, pp. 51-58, 2004.

[118]   Ohlsson, M. C., Andrews, A. A., and Wohlin, C., "Modelling Fault-Proneness Statistically over a Sequence of Releases: A Case Study," *Journal of Software Maintenance and Evolution: Research and Practice*, vol. 13, no. 3, pp. 167-199, 2001.

[119]   Parnas, D., "On the Criteria to be Used in Decomposing Systems into Modules," *Communications of the ACM*, vol. 15, no. 12, pp. 1053-1058, 1972.

[120]   Parnas, D., Clements, P., and Weiss, D., "The Modular Structure of Complex Systems," In Proceedings of 7th International Conference on Software Engineering (ICSE'84), Orlando, FL, USA, 1984, pp. 408-417.

[121]   Penny, D. A., "An Estimation-Based Management Framework for Enhancive Maintenance in Commercial Software Products," In Proceedings of International Conference on Software Maintenance (ICSM'02), Montreal, Canada, 2002, pp. 122-130.

238

[122] Pfleeger, S. L. and Bohner, S. A., "A framework for software maintenance metrics," In Proceedings of IEEE Conference on Software Maintenance, San Diego, CA, USA, 1990, pp. 320-327.

[123] Porter, A. A. and Selby, R. W., "Empirically Guided Software Development using Metric-Based Classification Trees," *IEEE Software*, vol. 7, no. 2, pp. 46-54, 1990.

[124] Potts, C., "Invented Requirements and Imagined Customers: Requirements Engineering for Off-the-Shelf Software," In Proceedings of 2nd IEEE International Symposium on Requirements Engineering (RE'95), York, England, 1995, pp. 128-130.

[125] Rajlich, V., "Modeling Software Evolution by Evolving Interoperation Graphs," *Annals of Software Engineering*, vol. 9, no. 1-4, pp. 235-348, 2000.

[126] Regnell, B., Beremark, P., and Eklundh, O., "A Market-driven Requirements Engineering Process – Results from an Industrial Process Improvement Programme," *Requirements Engineering*, vol. 3, no. 20, pp. 121-129, 1998.

[127] ReleasePlanner[(R)], "Intelligent Decision Support Tool," Software Engineering Decision Support Lab, University of Calgary, Canada, http://www.releaseplanner.com, (Last Accessed: August 20, 2007).

[128] Rittel, H. and Webber, M., "Planning Problems are Wicked Problems," in *Developments in Design Methodology*, Cross, N. (Ed.), Chichester, UK: Wiley, 1984, pp. 135-144.

[129] Robinson, W. N., Pawlowski, S. D., and Volkov, V., "Requirements Interaction Management," *ACM Computing Surveys (CSUR)*, vol. 35, no. 2, pp. 132-190, 2003.

[130] Roy, B., "The Outranking Approach and the Foundations of ELECTRE Methods," *Theory and Decisions*, vol. 31, no. 1, pp. 49-73, 1991.

[131] Ruhe, G., "Software Engineering Decision Support – Methodology and Applications," in *Innovations in Decision Support Systems*, Tonfoni and Jain (Eds.), 2003, pp. 143-174.

[132] Ruhe, G., "Software Release Planning," in *Handbook of Software Engineering and Knowledge Engineering*, vol. 3, Chang, S. K. (Ed.): World Scientific Publishing, 2005.

[133] Ruhe, G. and Ngo-The, A., "Hybrid Intelligence in Software Release Planning," *International Journal of Hybrid Intelligent Systems*, vol. 1, no. 2, pp. 99-110, 2004.

[134] Ruhe, G. and Saliu, M. O., "The Art and Science of Software Release Planning," *IEEE Software*, vol. 26, no. 6, pp. 47-53, 2005.

[135] Ruhe, G. and Saliu, M. O., "Art and Science of System Release Planning," In Proceedings of (Tutorial) 7th International Conference on Product Focused Software Process Improvement (PROFESS 2006), Amsterdam, Germany, 2006, pp. 458-461.

[136] Saaty, T. L., "The Analytic Hierarchy Process," McGraw-Hill, New York, 1980.

[137] Saliu, M. O., "Software Release Planning for Evolving Systems," PhD Proposal Thesis, Department of Computer Science, University of Calgary, Canada, 2005

[138] Saliu, M. O., "Software Release Planning via Systematic Impact Analysis," In Proceedings of Doctoral Symposium, 14th IEEE International Requirements Engineering Conference (RE'06), Minneapolis, MN, USA, 2006.

[139] Saliu, M. O. and Ahmed, M., "Soft Computing Based Effort Prediction Systems - A Survey," in *Soft Computing in Software Engineering*, Damiani, E., Jain, L. C., and Madravio, M. (Eds.), Heidelberg, Germany: Springer-Verlag, 2004, pp. 151-182.

[140] Saliu, O. and Ruhe, G., "Making Judgment on Modifiability of Evolving Systems Components using Bayesian Networks," Software Engineering Decision Support Laboratory (SEDS), University of Calgary, Canada, Technical Report TR 063/2006, 2006, pp. 1-13.

[141] Saliu, O. and Ruhe, G., "Software Release Planning for Evolving Systems," *Innovations in Systems and Software Engineering - a NASA Journal*, vol. 1, no. 2, pp. 189-204, 2005.

[142] Saliu, O. and Ruhe, G., "Supporting Software Release Planning Decisions for Evolving Systems," In Proceedings of 29th IEEE/NASA Software Engineering Workshop (SEW-29), Greenbelt, MD, USA, 2005, pp. 14-26.

[143] Shaw, M., "Comparing Architectural Design Styles," *IEEE Software*, vol. 12, no. 6, pp. 27-41, 1985.

[144] Shaw, M. and Clements, P., "Toward Boxology: Preliminary classification of architectural styles," In Proceedings of Second International Software Architecture Workshop, San Francisco, USA, 1996, pp. 50-54.

[145] Shereshevsky, M., Ammari, H., Gradetsky, N., Mili, A., and Ammar, H. H., "Information Theoretic Metrics for Software Architectures," In Proceedings of International Computer Software and Applications Conference (COMPSAC 2001), Chicago, IL, USA, 2001.

[146] Simian, "Simian UI - The Code Similarity Analyzer," Redhill Consulting Pty Ltd, http://www.integility.com/simian_ui, (Last Accessed: November 15, 2006,

[147] Simon, H. A., "A Behavioral Model of Rational Choice," *The Quarterly Journal of Economics*, vol. 69, no. 1, pp. 99-118, 1955.

[148] Sneed, H. M., "Impact Analysis of Maintenance Tasks for a Distributed Object-Oriented System," In Proceedings of IEEE International Conference on Software Maintenance (ICSM'01), Florence, Italy, 2001, pp. 180-189.

[149] Standish, "CHAOS Report," Standish Group Research, 2002.

[150] Stratton, W., Sibol, D., Lindvall, M., and Costa, P., "Technology Infusion of the SAVE Tool into the Common Ground Software Development Process for NASA Missions at JHU/APL," In Proceedings of 2007 IEEE Aerospace Conference, Big Sky, MT, USA, 2007.

[151] Strigini, L., "Limiting the Dangers of Intuitive Decision-Making," *IEEE Software*, vol. 13, no. 1, pp. 101-103, 1996.

[152] Stuart, D., "Descriptive Decision Making: Comparing Theory with Practice," In Proceedings of 33rd Annual Conference of New Zealand Operational Research Society, Waikato University, Hamilton, 1998, pp. 99-108.

[153] Svahnberg, M., Wohlin, C., Lundberg, L., and Mattsson, M., "A Quality-driven Decision Support Method for Identifying Software Architecture Candidates," *International Journal of Software Engineering and Knowledge Engineering*, vol. 13, no. 5, pp. 547-573, 2003.

[154] Szidarovszky, F., Gershon, M. E., and Duckstein, L., "Techniques for Multiobjective Decision Making in Systems Management." NY: Elsevier, 1986.

[155] Turner, C. R., "Feature Engineering of Software Systems," PhD Thesis, Department of Department of Computer Science, University of Colorado, Boulder, 1998

[156] Turner, C. R., Fuggetta, A., Lavazza, L., and Wolf, A. L., "A Conceptual Basis for Feature Engineering," *Journal of Systems and Software*, vol. 49, no. 1, pp. 3-15, 1999.

[157] Van Scoy, R. L., "Software Development Risk: Opportunity, Not Problem," Software Engineering Institute, Pittsburgh (CMU/SEI-92-TR-30, ESC-TR-92-030), 1992.

[158] Walker, R. J., Holmes, R., Hedgeland, I., Kapur, P., and Smith, A., "A Lightweight Approach to Technical Risk Estimation via Probabilistic Impact Analysis," In Proceedings of ICSE Workshop on Mining Software Repositories (MSR'06), Shanghai, China, 2006, pp. 98-104.

[159] Weyuker, E. J., "Evaluating Software Complexity Measures," *IEEE Transactions on Software Engineering*, vol. 14, no. 9, pp. 1357-1365, 1988.

[160] Wild, C., Maly, K., Zhang, C., Roberts, C., Rosca, D., and Taylor, T., "Software Engineering Life Cycle Support – Decision Based Systems Development," In Proceedings of 9th International Conference on Computer Technology (TENCON'94), Singapore, 1994, pp. 781-784.

[161] Wilde, N. and Casey, C., "Early Field Experience with the Software Reconnaissance Technique for Program Comprehension," In Proceedings of International Conference on Software Maintenance, Monterey, CA, 1996, pp. 312-318.

[162] Wilde, N. and Scully, M. C., "Software Reconnaissance: Mapping Program Features to Code," *Journal of Software Maintenance: Research and Practice*, vol. 7, no. 1, pp. 49-62, 1995.

[163] Wolsey, L. A. and Nemhauser, G. L., "Integer and Combinatorial Optimization." New York: John Wiley, 1998.

[164] Wong, W. E., Gokhale, S. S., and Horgan, J. R., "Quantifying the Closeness between Program Components and Features," *The Journal of Systems and Software*, vol. 54, no. 2, pp. 87-98, 2000.

[165] Yau, S. S. and Collofello, J. S., "Some Stability Measurements for Software Maintenance," *IEEE Transactions on Software Engineering*, vol. 6, no. 6, pp. 545-552, 1980.

[166] Yellin, D. M., "Algorithms for Subset Testing and Finding Maximal Sets," In Proceedings of 3rd Annual ACM-SIAM Symposium on Discrete Algorithms, Orlando, FL, USA, 1992, pp. 386-392.

[167] Ying, A. T., Murphy, G. C., Ng, R., and Chu-Carroll, M. C., "Predicting Source Code Changes by Mining Change History," *IEEE Transactions on Software Engineering*, vol. 30, no. 9, pp. 574-586, 2004.

[168] Zhang, W., Mei, H., and Zhao, H., "Feature-Driven Requirement Dependency Analysis and High-Level Design," *Requirements Engineering*, vol. 11, no. 3, pp. 205-220, 2006.

[169] Zhang, Y., Harman, M., and Mansouri, S. A., "The Multi-Objective Next Release Problem," In Proceedings of Genetic and Evolutionary Computation Conference (GECCO 2007), London, UK, 2007.

[170] Zhao, J., Yang, H., Xiang, L., and Xu, B., "Change Impact Analysis to Support Architectural Evolution," *Journal of Software Maintenance and Evolution: Research and Practice*, vol. 14, no. 5, pp. 317-333, 2002.

[171] Zimmermann, T., Weissgerber, P., Diehl, S., and Zeller, A., "Mining Version Histories to Guide Software Changes," *IEEE Transactions on Software Engineering*, vol. 31, no. 6, pp. 429-445, 2005.

[172] Ziv, H., Richardson, D. J., and Klösch, R., "The Uncertainty Principle in Software Engineering," University of California, Irvine, CA, Technical Report UCI-TR-96-33, 1996.

Appendix A: UML Models for TSAFE Architectural Designs

A.1. High Level Coupling in TSAFE I

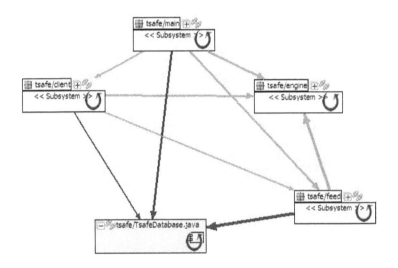

A.2. High Level Coupling in TSAFE II

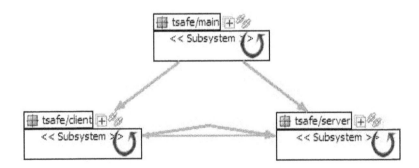

A.3. Low Level View of TSAFE I

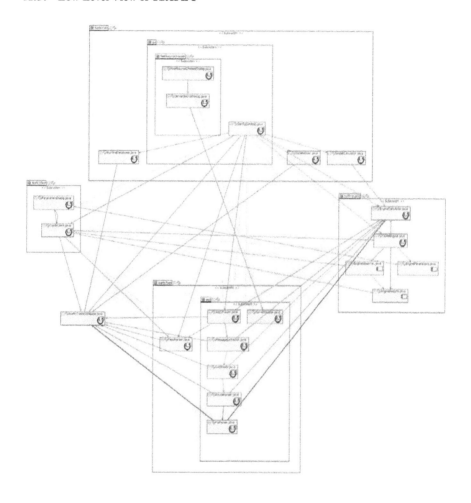

A.4. Low Level View of TSAFE II

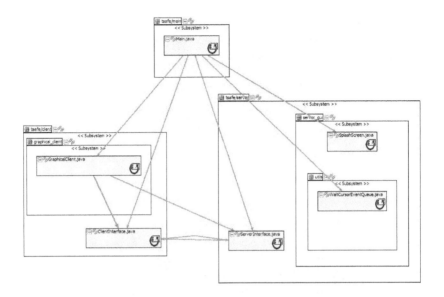

Appendix B: Empirical Validation Study I

B.1. **Relative Contribution of Component Characteristics to Modifiability – The Perspectives of 3 Experts**

Modifiability Characteristics	Experts Evaluation			Aggregated Result
	Expert-A	Expert-B	Expert-C	
Size	0.053	0.049	0.022	**0.046**
Complexity	0.114	0.083	0.473	**0.173**
Understandability	0.251	0.517	0.271	**0.330**
Health	0.394	0.091	0.173	**0.266**
Criticality	0.188	0.259	0.061	**0.184**

Consistency Ratio =	0.14	0.23	0.23
Importance =	0.5	0.3	0.2
W_e =	0.5276	0.2834	0.1890

B.2. **Results of the Evaluation of ReleasePlanner Components for Modifiability**

Ease of Modification (EoM) According to Expert-A										
	Reporting	Validator	IP Component	Java Brokers	Import/Export Component	Stakeholder Voting Analysis	DB Connectivity Class	Alternative Analysis Wizard	CR	1-CR
Size	0.189	0.060	0.025	0.038	0.136	0.190	0.040	0.321	0.09	0.91
Complexity	0.236	0.060	0.025	0.038	0.169	0.251	0.044	0.179	0.09	0.91
Understandability	0.186	0.031	0.063	0.143	0.189	0.206	0.070	0.113	0.09	0.91
Health	0.085	0.187	0.066	0.226	0.192	0.119	0.025	0.100	0.08	0.92
Criticality	0.049	0.109	0.219	0.223	0.043	0.043	0.275	0.039	0.07	0.93

Ease of Modification (EoM) According to Expert-B										
	Reporting	Validator	IP Component	Java Brokers	Import/Export Component	Stakeholder Voting Analysis	DB Connectivity Class	Alternative Analysis Wizard	CR	1-CR
Size	0.040	0.141	0.508	0.050	0.050	0.060	0.121	0.030	0.06	0.94
Complexity	0.025	0.216	0.482	0.095	0.036	0.041	0.083	0.023	0.09	0.91
Understandability	0.152	0.025	0.015	0.075	0.331	0.164	0.075	0.164	0.06	0.94
Health	0.130	0.065	0.015	0.098	0.426	0.143	0.015	0.108	0.13	0.87
Criticality	0.063	0.055	0.523	0.115	0.055	0.031	0.129	0.029	0.12	0.88

Ease of Modification (EoM) by Expert-C										
	Reporting	Validator	IP Component	Java Brokers	Import/Export Component	Stakeholder Voting Analysis	DB Connectivity Class	Alternative Analysis Wizard	CR	1-CR
Size	0.071	0.139	0.433	0.050	0.040	0.065	0.148	0.054	0.35	0.65
Complexity	0.061	0.199	0.458	0.055	0.092	0.045	0.034	0.056	0.21	0.79
Understandability	0.110	0.146	0.416	0.046	0.036	0.058	0.137	0.051	0.42	0.58
Health	0.062	0.136	0.403	0.048	0.035	0.075	0.147	0.093	0.43	0.57
Criticality	0.071	0.139	0.433	0.050	0.040	0.065	0.148	0.054	0.35	0.65

Final Aggregated Results								
	Reporting	Validator	IP Component	Java Brokers	Import/Export Component	Stakeholder Voting Analysis	DB Connectivity Class	Alternative Analysis Wizard
Size	0.006	0.005	0.011	0.002	0.004	0.006	0.004	0.009
Complexity	0.024	0.023	0.042	0.010	0.020	0.026	0.009	0.019
Understandability	0.054	0.015	0.031	0.035	0.071	0.057	0.027	0.040
Health	0.026	0.038	0.026	0.043	0.065	0.032	0.010	0.027
Criticality	0.010	0.018	0.063	0.030	0.009	0.008	0.039	0.007
EoM	0.120	0.098	0.174	0.121	0.169	0.129	0.089	0.102

Appendix C: Empirical Validation Study II

C.1. Table of Features, the Constraints and Resource Consumptions

	Features	Precedence & Coupling		Resource Consumption														
ID	Features	Precedes	Coupled to	Flash Dev.	Action Script Developers	Java Dev.	C++ Dev.	QA	PM	DBA	Product Manager	CAM	DB-server	Ash Gaming	Meadway (GDK)	Green Tube (EGT)	Game-servers	Technical Risk
1	Accounting			0	0	160	0	40	10	40	2.5	0	4	0	0	0	4	40
2	Archiving			0	0	160	0	40	10	40	2.5	0	4	0	0	0	4	40
3	Bonus			0	0	600	0	160	10	40	2.5	0	4	0	0	0	4	80
4	Build Process			0	0	560	0	160	40	40	0	0	2	0	0	0	5	80
5	Common Wallet Cleanup			0	0	160	0	10	10	5	2.5	0	1	0	0	0	1	10
6	Configuration			0	0	320	0	80	10	5	2.5	0	4	0	0	0	4	80
7	CSR Support			0	0	240	0	60	10	80	2.5	0	4	0	0	0	4	60
8	CyberBanx (Banking Optimization)			0	0	400	0	100	10	80	2.5	0	4	0	0	0	4	100
9	CyberEye			0	0	120	0	30	10	80	2.5	0	4	0	0	0	4	30
10	Internationalization			0	0	200	0	50	10	0	2.5	0	4	0	0	0	4	50
11	Progresive Jackpot			0	0	200	0	50	10	40	2.5	0	4	0	0	0	4	50
12	Marketing/COGNOS			0	0	640	0	160	10	80	2.5	0	4	0	0	0	4	80
13	Optimizations			0	0	320	0	80	10	40	2.5	0	4	0	0	0	4	80
14	Payment Processors			0	0	80	0	20	10	40	2.5	0	4	0	0	0	4	20
15	Promotion			0	0	480	0	120	10	40	2.5	0	4	0	0	0	4	120
16	Registration			0	0	120	0	30	10	40	2.5	0	4	0	0	0	4	30
17	Replay			0	0	200	0	80	10	40	2.5	0	4	0	0	0	4	50
18	Reporting			0	0	400	0	100	10	40	2.5	0	4	0	0	0	4	100
19	Responsible Gaming			0	0	240	0	60	10	40	2.5	0	4	0	0	0	4	60
20	SDK			0	0	160	0	20	10	40	2.5	0	4	0	0	0	4	20
21	Security & Auditing			0	0	240	0	60	10	40	2.5	0	4	0	0	0	4	60
22	Special Users/Revamp Affiliate			0	0	400	0	60	10	40	2.5	0	4	0	0	0	4	60
23	Usability			0	0	280	0	70	10	40	2.5	0	4	0	0	0	4	70
24	Reporting-CashLiability			0	0	160	0	40	10	40	2.5	0	4	0	0	0	4	40
25	Reporting-retwin			0	0	160	0	40	10	40	2.5	0	4	0	0	0	4	40
26	LuckyHoliday	5, 30,		324	332	452.5	0	80	10	0	0	0	4	0	0	0	4	80
27	Neptune Gold	31,		320	320	320	0	80	10	0	0	0	4	0	0	0	4	80
28	6 FOG games (via GDK)			20	20	120	0	80	10	10	0	0	4	0	0	0	4	320
29	meadway 6 games (via GDK)			20	20	120	0	80	10	10	0	0	4	0	0	0	4	320
30	LuckyHoliday reskins part 1	12,		320	0	0	0	80	0	0	0	0	4	0	0	0	4	80
31	Netune Gold reskins			320	0	178	0	80	0	0	0	0	4	0	0	0	4	80
32	GDK optimization	11,		0	0	160	0	40	20	0	0	0	4	0	0	0	4	80
33	GDK developer program	28,		80	160	320	0	160	160	0	0	0	4	0	0	0	33	320
34	Multiplayer Games			1920	1920	3840	0	960	1920	0	640	0	4	0	0	0	8	960
35	Tournaments			160	160	640	0	320	160	160	0	0	8	0	0	0	8	640
36	Jackpot on GDK games			80	0	640	0	640	320	80	320	0	4	0	0	0	4	320
37	PlayerHandle Security			0	320	640	0	120	120	0	0	0	4	0	0	0	4	160
38	Summarize Group Win - Affiliate/Bonus Integration			0	0	40	0	10	2	0	2	0	4	0	0	0	4	20
39	Player Managed Bonus - Affiliate/Bonus Integration			0	0	320	0	80	16	0	16	0	4	0	0	0	4	160
40	Allow Umlauts			0	0	40	0	10	2	0	2	0	4	0	0	0	4	20
41	Audit			0	0	80	0	20	4	0	4	0	4	0	0	0	4	40
42	Chat Search			0	0	80	0	20	4	0	4	0	4	0	0	0	4	40
43	Poker on televison - Client & Server Enhancements			0	0	0	80	20	4	0	4	0	4	0	0	0	4	160
44	Enhancements			320	0	0	80	100	20	0	20	0	4	0	0	0	4	800
45	Show NL & PL - Client Enhancements			0	0	0	80	20	4	0	4	0	4	0	0	0	4	160
46	Player color coding - Client Enhancements			0	0	0	80	20	4	0	4	0	4	0	0	0	4	160
47	Player Notes - Client Enhancements			0	0	0	80	20	4	0	4	0	4	0	0	0	4	160
48	Date Range for Deposits and Withdrawals			0	0	0	80	20	4	0	4	0	4	0	0	0	4	160
49	Combine Player Totals - Client Enhancements			0	0	0	80	20	4	0	4	0	4	0	0	0	4	160
50	Login by Day & Name - Client Enhancements			0	0	0	80	20	4	0	4	0	4	0	0	0	4	160
51	Allow image changes - Client Enhancements			0	0	0	80	20	4	0	4	0	4	0	0	0	4	160
52	New Table Designs - Client Enhancements			0	0	0	120	30	6	0	6	0	4	0	0	0	4	240
53	Game Server 2.1 - Client Enhancements			0	0	0	160	40	8	0	8	0	4	0	0	0	4	320
54	Resizable C++ Client - Client Enhancements			0	0	0	320	80	16	0	16	0	4	0	0	0	4	640
55	Show player actions (tt7405) - Client Enhancements			0	0	0	120	30	6	0	6	0	4	0	0	0	4	240
56	Avatars - Client Enhancements			0	0	0	160	40	8	0	8	0	4	0	0	0	4	320
57	Buddy lists - Client Enhancements			0	0	0	160	40	8	0	8	0	4	0	0	0	4	320
58	Japanese Clients - Client Enhancements			0	0	0	160	40	8	0	8	0	4	0	0	0	4	320
59	New Summary Report - Client Enhancements			0	0	0	80	20	4	0	4	0	4	0	0	0	4	160
60	Add Rake to Hand History - Client Enhancements			0	0	0	80	20	4	0	4	0	4	0	0	0	4	160
61	Reconciliation for ECM - Client Enhancements			0	0	0	160	40	8	0	8	0	4	0	0	0	4	320
62	Korean Client - Client Enhancements			0	0	0	160	40	8	0	8	0	4	0	0	0	4	320
63	Italian Client - Client Enhancements			0	0	0	120	30	6	0	6	0	4	0	0	0	4	240
64	Collusion Catcher			0	0	120	0	30	6	0	6	0	4	0	0	0	4	240
65	Rake Reports by Game Type			0	0	120	0	30	6	0	6	0	8	0	0	0	8	240
66	Game Play Disconnect by Hour			0	0	160	0	40	8	0	8	0	8	0	0	0	8	320
67	Report player online by SubLicensee			0	0	160	0	40	8	0	8	0	8	0	0	0	8	320
68	Add instance id to tournament History report			0	0	80	0	20	4	0	4	0	4	0	0	0	4	160
69	Add tournament name and link			0	0	80	0	20	4	0	4	0	4	0	0	0	4	160
70	Add Winner Screen Name to Hand History			0	0	80	0	20	4	0	4	0	4	0	0	0	4	160

#	Description															
71	Move all URLs to URL manager			0	0	80	0	20	4	0	4	0	4	0	0	0	4	160
72	Show STT tourn id in game client			0	0	80	0	20	4	0	4	0	4	0	0	0	4	160
73	Add Bonus type under points and Tournament			0	0	80	0	20	4	0	4	0	4	0	0	0	4	160
74	Web Page for all Poker Client Link Info			0	0	80	0	20	4	0	4	0	4	0	0	0	4	160
75	New Casino Tab - Client Enhancements			0	0	80	0	20	4	0	4	0	4	0	0	0	4	160
76	Better internationalization			0	0	80	0	20	4	0	4	0	4	0	0	0	4	160
77	Time Zone selection			0	0	40	0	10	2	0	2	0	4	0	0	0	4	80
78	Mac and Linux Support - Client Enhancements			0	0	80	0	20	4	0	4	0	4	0	0	0	4	160
79	Add Hand History Link - Client Enhancements			0	0	80	0	20	4	0	4	0	4	0	0	0	4	160
80	Support for Common Wallet			0	0	320	0	80	16	0	16	0	8	0	0	0	8	640
81	Multi-Currency Support			0	0	480	0	120	24	0	24	0	8	0	0	0	8	960
82	CyberBoss Integration			0	0	160	0	40	8	0	8	0	4	0	0	0	4	320
83	Deactivate Sub Licensee			0	0	80	0	20	4	0	4	0	4	0	0	0	4	160
84	Marketing fee			0	0	160	0	40	8	0	8	0	4	0	0	0	4	320
85	multiple license per login			0	0	320	0	80	16	0	16	0	4	0	0	0	4	640
86	Payment Processing			0	0	80	0	20	4	0	4	0	4	0	0	0	4	160
87	Player IP history			0	0	160	0	40	8	0	8	0	4	0	0	0	4	320
88	Push Data to Poker DB			0	0	80	0	20	4	0	4	0	4	0	0	0	4	160
89	Block duplicate IP			0	0	120	0	30	6	0	6	0	4	0	0	0	4	240
90	Turkish Draw			0	0	320	0	80	16	0	16	0	8	0	0	0	8	640
91	Satellite Tournaments			0	0	320	0	80	16	0	16	0	4	0	0	0	4	640
92	Bad Beat Jackpots			0	0	320	0	80	16	0	16	0	4	0	0	0	4	640
93	Add IP to Initial PDU			0	0	80	0	20	4	0	4	0	2	0	0	0	2	160
94	SSL Security			0	0	80	0	20	4	0	4	0	2	0	0	0	2	160
95	Failover			0	0	640	0	160	32	0	32	0	8	0	0	0	8	1280
96	Rebuys and Add-ons			0	0	320	0	80	16	0	16	0	4	0	0	0	4	640
97	Other MTT game Types			0	0	320	0	80	16	0	16	0	4	0	0	0	4	640
98	startup/shutdown			0	0	80	0	20	4	0	4	0	4	0	0	0	4	160
99	sub licensee email			0	0	80	0	20	4	0	4	0	4	0	0	0	4	160
100	Sub License Support			0	0	120	0	30	6	0	6	0	4	0	0	0	4	240
101	sublicense enable/disable player			0	0	160	0	40	8	0	8	0	6	0	0	0	6	320
102	Support Datafeed			0	0	80	0	20	4	0	4	0	2	0	0	0	2	160
103	Support Fund Types			0	0	80	0	20	4	0	4	0	2	0	0	0	2	160
104	Show player registered for STT or MTT			0	0	80	0	20	4	0	4	0	2	0	0	0	2	160
105	Show names of tournaments played in			0	0	80	0	20	4	0	4	0	2	0	0	0	2	160
106	MTT Table Copy			0	0	320	0	80	16	0	16	0	8	0	0	0	8	640
107	Add Limit Buy search criteria - Tournament Enhancement			0	0	160	0	40	8	0	8	0	4	0	0	0	4	320
108	Games: Bingo			80	0	480	0	80	60	0	16	0	8	0	0	0	8	80
109	games: Keno			40	0	200	0	80	60	0	16	0	8	0	0	0	4	40
110	Games: Poker			0	0	480	0	120	48	0	24	0	4	0	0	0	4	160
111	Games: Scratch Card			40	0	180	0	40	80	0	21.333	0	4	0	0	0	4	40
112	Games: add jackpot to slots			0	0	200	0	50	20	0	10	0	2	0	0	0	2	320
113	CyberBoss Mobile			0	0	346.667	0	96.667	34.667	0	17.333	0	4	0	0	0	4	320
114	Security			0	0	160	0	40	16	0	8	0	2	0	0	0	2	80
115	Enhance Architecture			0	0	373.33	0	93.33	37.33	0	18.67	0	4	0	0	0	4	106.67
116	MIDP 2.0			0	0	160	0	40	16	0	8	0	4	0	0	0	4	80
117	Notification and distributed automated build			0	0	480	0	120	48	0	24	0	6	0	0	0	6	120
118	Projects: Interwetten			0	0	160	0	40	16	0	8	0	4	0	0	0	4	320
119	SVG			0	0	480	0	120	48	0	24	0	4	0	0	0	4	160
120	Projects: RyanAir			0	0	160	0	40	16	0	8	0	2	0	0	0	2	640
121	Viral Distribution			40	0	640	0	120	160	0	16	0	2	0	0	0	2	120
122	Support Bonus/affiliate programs			0	0	320	0	80	32	0	16	0	3	0	0	0	3	160
123	Projects: Gala/Eurobet			146.67	0	146.67	0	36.67	14.67	0	7.33	0	2	0	0	0	2	40
124	Network Operator config support and testing			0	0	0	0	0	0	0	0	0	0	0	0	0	0	640
125	Projects: UK Betting			0	0	40	0	10	4	0	2	0	1	0	0	0	1	640
126	Authorization			0	0	800	0	40	80	0	20	0	1	0	0	0	1	80
127	Bingo look and feel			480	480	80	0	80	60	0	0	0	1	0	0	0	0	0
128	Bingo Replay			0	0	320	0	80	80	40	0	0	4	0	0	0	2	0
129	Bingo Game Play			10	0	80	0	80	10	0	0	0	2	0	0	0	2	0
130	Bingo Extra Game Functions			480	480	640	0	160	80	0	80	0	1	0	0	0	6	0
131	Bingo Configuration			0	0	640	0	80	80	40	0	0	6	0	0	0	4	0
132	Bingo Reports			0	0	320	0	40	40	40	40	0	4	0	0	0	4	0
133	Bingo Community			0	0	480	0	80	80	0	80	0	4	0	0	0	4	0
134	Game Profile Stakes			0	0	200	0	40	20	0	6	0	3	0	0	0	3	40
135	Premium SMS			0	0	200	0	40	20	0	6	0	2	0	0	0	2	80
136	Junit testing			0	0	200	0	40	20	0	6	0	2	0	0	0	2	40
137	Mediae use			0	0	200	0	40	20	0	6	0	2	0	0	0	2	40
138	Enhance Architecture using MVC pattern	185.		0	0	320	0	40	20	0	0	0	3	0	0	0	3	40
139	Xlets			0	0	320	0	40	20	0	6	0	3	0	0	0	3	40
140	Internationalization			0	0	400	0	40	20	0	6	0	1	0	0	0	2	40
141	Netbean processor blocks			0	0	200	0	40	20	0	0	0	1	0	0	0	2	40
142	Wbxml use in protocol			0	0	160	0	40	20	0	6	0	1	0	0	0	2	40
143	Jsr 177 + jsr 229			0	0	200	0	40	20	0	6	0	1	0	0	0	2	40
144	On device debugging			0	0	200	0	40	20	0	0	0	1	0	0	0	2	40
145	Flatten 3d arrays			0	0	50	0	20	20	0	0	0	2	0	0	0	2	40
146	Use midlet-data-size			0	0	80	0	20	20	0	0	0	2	0	0	0	2	40
147	Profiling and reuse hot code			0	0	160	0	40	20	0	6	0	2	0	0	0	1	40
148	Age Verification			8	0	400	0	80	120	0	0	0	1	0	0	0	0	120
149	Batch Play			40	0	720	0	40	120	0	0	0	1	0	0	0	0	80
150	Mobile & Mobile MyAccount			0	0	0	0	0	0	0	0	0	0	0	0	0	0	40
151	Mobile Registration			0	0	0	0	0	0	0	0	0	0	0	0	0	0	40
152	GPMS	153.		0	0	0	0	0	0	0	0	0	0	0	0	0	0	40
153	Refactor 90-ball bingo			0	0	400	0	160	0	0	6	0	0	0	0	0	0	40
154	Multiplayer Table Poker			40	0	200	0	80	100	0	80	0	1	0	0	0	1	40
155	Progressive Live Jackpot			0	0	240	0	40	80	0	60	0	1	0	0	0	1	40
156	Bull's eye Bucks			40	0	120	0	24	16	0	16	0	1	0	0	0	1	40
157	Hot Race (Phase I)			120	0	560	0	80	80	0	80	0	1	0	0	0	1	40
158	Casino Stud Poker			24	0	160	0	24	40	0	16	0	1	0	0	0	1	40
159	3 cards poker			24	0	200	0	40	40	0	16	0	1	0	0	0	1	40
160	Mad Madathorn			60	0	280	0	60	80	0	24	0	1	0	0	0	1	40
161	Fruit Party			40	0	160	0	24	40	0	16	0	1	0	0	0	1	40
162	Linux Smartphones			24	0	120	0	40	40	0	40	0	1	0	0	0	1	40
163	Palm Smartphones			24	0	120	0	40	40	0	40	0	1	0	0	0	1	40
164	Windows Smartphones			24	0	160	0	40	40	0	40	0	1	0	0	0	1	40
165	Blackberry Smartphones			24	0	80	0	24	40	0	40	0	1	0	0	0	1	40
166	240/290			16	0	40	0	8	16	0	6	0	1	0	0	0	1	40
167	132*176			16	0	40	0	8	16	0	8	0	1	0	0	0	1	40
168	352*416			16	0	40	0	8	16	0	8	0	1	0	0	0	1	40
169	176*192			16	0	40	0	8	16	0	6	0	1	0	0	0	1	40
170	176*208			16	0	40	0	8	16	0	6	0	1	0	0	0	1	40

171	240*320			16	0	40	0	8	16	0	8	0	1	0	0	0	1	40
172	208*208			16	0	40	0	8	16	0	8	0	1	0	0	0	1	40
173	Mobile MIDP registration & payment			8	0	440	0	120	40	0	40	0	1	0	0	0	1	40
174	Pay while you Play for fun			80	0	360	0	120	80	0	80	0	1	0	0	0	1	40
175	SMS Payment			40	0	240	0	120	40	0	80	0	1	0	0	0	1	40
176	Players Preferences			80	0	760	0	160	120	0	80	0	1	0	0	0	1	40
177	Mobile "My Account"			8	0	480	0	80	80	0	40	0	1	0	0	0	1	40
178	Download Bonus			40	0	320	0	80	80	0	80	0	1	0	0	0	1	40
179	Infection/Referral Bonus			80	0	400	0	80	80	0	80	0	1	0	0	0	1	40
180	Loyalty Bonus			40	0	280	0	80	80	0	80	0	1	0	0	0	1	40
181	Mobile Specific Business Reports			0	0	400	0	120	40	0	40	0	1	0	0	0	1	40
182	Multiple Operator Testing			0	0	80	0	240	0	0	0	0	1	0	0	0	1	40
183	Gigaspace	15.		0	0	360	0	160	80	0	0	0	1	0	0	3	40
184	Cognos	12.		0	0	360	0	160	40	0	40	0	1	0	0	1	40
185	Dynamic Provisioning			0	0	320	0	120	0	0	0	0	1	0	0	0	0
186	Betfair Performance Fixes			0	0	400	0	80	0	0	0	0	0	0	0	0	0
187	Merge CVS trunk			0	0	320	0	120	0	0	0	0	0	0	0	0	0
188	Setup Maven and			0	0	80	0	0	0	0	0	0	0	0	0	0	0
189	Metrics Program setup			0	0	120	0	0	0	0	0	0	0	0	0	0	0
190	CleanUp Logs			0	0	80	0	0	0	0	0	0	0	0	0	0	0

C.2. The Available Resource Capacities

Resources			Resource Capacities				
Resource Name	Resource Type	Resource Units	Release 1	Release 2	Release 3	Release 4	Release 5
Flash Developers	Effort	Person Hours	1725	1725	1725	1725	1725
Action Script Developers	Effort	Person Hours	1380	1380	1380	1380	1380
Java Developers	Effort	Person Hours	10000	10000	14145	14145	14145
C++ Developers	Effort	Person Hours	690	690	690	690	690
QA	Effort	Person Hours	3450	3450	3450	3450	3450
PM	Effort	Person Hours	1380	1380	1380	1380	1380
DBA	Effort	Person Hours	1035	1035	1035	1035	1035
Product Manager	Effort	Person Hours	1380	1380	1380	1380	1380
CAM (Client Account Manager)	Effort	Person Hours	1380	1380	1380	1380	1380
Hardware-db-server	Servers	CPU weeks	520	624	624	624	624
Ash Gaming (GDK) (Number of Games)	Effort	Games	3	6	6	6	6
Meadway (GDK)	Effort	Games	6	6	6	6	6
Green Tube (EGI)	Effort	Games	5	5	5	5	5
Hardware-game-servers	Servers	CPU weeks	2860	3432	3432	3432	3432
Technical Risk	risk	risk	2000	2000	2000	2000	2000

C.3. Stakeholders and their Weight of Importance

ID	Stakeholder E-mail	Stakeholder Name	Weight
S_1	stakeholder-1@company.com	Any Bet	1
S_2	stakeholder-2@company.com	Aspiritus	3
S_3	stakeholder-3@company.com	Bet and Win ? 6 Skins	9
S_4	stakeholder-4@company.com	Bet at Home	6
S_5	stakeholder-5@company.com	Bet Shop ? 2 Skins	2
S_6	stakeholder-6@company.com	Bingo.com	3
S_7	stakeholder-7@company.com	Boyle Sports	2
S_8	stakeholder-8@company.com	CashPoint	2
S_9	stakeholder-9@company.com	Cheeky Moon	1
S_{10}	stakeholder-10@company.com	Colony	1
S_{11}	stakeholder-11@company.com	Eurobet ? 3 Skins	7
S_{12}	stakeholder-12@company.com	Global Casinos	1
S_{13}	stakeholder-13@company.com	Gold Bet	1
S_{14}	stakeholder-14@company.com	Inside Gaming - ADVFN	1
S_{15}	stakeholder-15@company.com	Inside Gaming ? Betfair	1
S_{16}	stakeholder-16@company.com	Inside Gaming ? Fox Poker Club	1
S_{17}	stakeholder-17@company.com	Inside Gaming ? Heaven	1
S_{18}	stakeholder-18@company.com	Inside Gaming - Lukto	1
S_{19}	stakeholder-19@company.com	Interwetten	6
S_{20}	stakeholder-20@company.com	Luminar	1
S_{21}	stakeholder-21@company.com	Meadway ? 4 Skins	2
S_{22}	stakeholder-22@company.com	MY Bet	1
S_{23}	stakeholder-23@company.com	Paradise Bet	4
S_{24}	stakeholder-24@company.com	Point Bet	2
S_{25}	stakeholder-25@company.com	Sandpiper	1
S_{26}	stakeholder-26@company.com	Sporting Bet ? 4 Skins	1
S_{27}	stakeholder-27@company.com	Stan James	4
S_{28}	stakeholder-28@company.com	Total Bet	1
S_{29}	stakeholder-29@company.com	Uk Betting	6
S_{30}	stakeholder-30@company.com	Victor Chandler ? 9 skins	6
S_{31}	stakeholder-31@company.com	Project Prioritization	9
S_{32}	stakeholder-32@company.com	chart_strategy	9
S_{33}	stakeholder-33@company.com	chart_revenue	9

C.4. Values of the Features from the Perspectives of all the Stakeholders

Value of features — Stakeholders

ID	Features
1	Accounting
2	Archiving
3	Bonus
4	Build Process
5	Common Wallet Cleanup
6	Configuration
7	CSR Support
8	CyberBanx (Banking Optimization)
9	CyberEye
10	Internationalization
11	Progresive Jackpot
12	Marketing/COGNOS
13	Optimizations
14	Payment Processors
15	Promotion
16	Registration
17	Replay
18	Reporting
19	Responsible Gaming
20	SDK
21	Security & Auditing
22	Special Users/Revamp Affiliate
23	Usability
24	Reporting-CashLiability
25	Reporting-netwin
26	LuckyHoliday
27	Neptune Gold
28	6 FOG games (via GDK)
29	meadwby 6 games (via GDK)
30	LuckyHoliday reskins part 1 (2 games)
31	Netune Gold reskins
32	GDK optimization
33	GDK developer program
34	Multiplayer Games
35	Tournaments
36	Progressive Jackpot on GDK games
37	PlayerHandle Security
38	Summarize Group Win - Affiliate/Bonus Integration
39	Player Managed Bonus - Affiliate/Bonus Integration
40	Allow Unfauts
41	Audit
42	Chat Search
43	Poker on televison - Client & Server Enhancements
44	Telesina - Client & Server Enhancements
45	Show NL & PL - Client Enhancements
46	Player color coding - Client Enhancements
47	Player Notes - Client Enhancements
48	Withdrawals - Client Enhancements
49	Combine Player Totals - Client Enhancements
50	Login by Day & Name - Client Enhancements
51	Allow image changes - Client Enhancements
52	New Table Designs - Client Enhancements
53	Game Server 2.1 - Client Enhancements
54	Resizable C++ Client - Client Enhancements
55	Show player actions (tt7408) - Client Enhancements
56	Avatars - Client Enhancements
57	Buddy lists - Client Enhancements
58	Japanese Clients - Client Enhancements
59	New Summary Report - Client Enhancements
60	Add Rake to Hand History - Client Enhancements
61	Reconciliation for ECM - Client Enhancements
62	Korean Client - Client Enhancements
63	Italian Client - Client Enhancements
64	Collusion Catcher - Client Enhancements
65	Rake Reports by Game Type - Client Enhancements
66	Game Play Disconnect by Hour - Client Enhancements
67	Report player online by SubLicensee - Client Enhancements
68	Add instance id to tournament History report - Client Enhancements
69	Add tournament name and link - Client Enhancements
70	Add Winner Screen Name to Hand History - Client Enhancements
71	Move all URLs to URL manager - Client Enhancements
72	Show STT tourn Id in game client - Client Enhancements
73	Add Bonus type under points and Tournament - Client Enhancements
74	Web Page for all Poker Client Link Info - Client Enhancements
75	New Casino Tab - Client Enhancements
76	Better internationalization - Client Enhancements
77	Time Zone selection - Client Enhancements
78	Mac and Linux Support - Client Enhancements
79	Add Hand History Link - Client Enhancements
80	Support for Common Wallet

#	Item									
81	Multi-Currency Support			9	9	9	9	9		9	7	1
82	CyberBoss Integration		9	9	9	9	9	9			9	9	1
83	Deactivate Sub Licensee Support		2	9	9	9	9	9	9		9	7	1
84	Marketing fee			9	9	9	9	9			9	7	1
85	multiple license per login			9	9	9	9	9			9	7	1
86	Payment Processing			9	9	9	9	9			9	7	1
87	Player IP history		5	9	9	9	9	9			9	7	1
88	Push Data to Poker DB		4	9	9	9	9	9	6		9	7	1
89	Block duplicate IP - Server Enhancements		5	9	9	9	9	9	9		9	7	1
90	Turkish Draw - Server Enhancements										9	7	1
91	Satellite Tournaments - Server Enhancements		5					5			9	7	1
92	Bad Beat Jackpots - Server Enhancements										9	7	1
93	Add IP to initial PDU - Server Enhancements		9	9	9	9	9	5			9	7	1
94	SSL Security - Server Enhancements										9	7	1
95	Failover - Server Enhancements		9	9	9	9	9	9			9	7	1
96	Rebuys and Add-ons (66696) Server Enhancements										9	7	1
97	Other MTT game Types - Server Enhancements		9	9	9	5	5				9	7	1
98	status shutdown		9	9	9	9	9	5			9	7	1
99	sub licensee email		9	9	9	9	9	5			9	7	1
100	Sub Licensee Support		9	9	9	9	9				9	7	1
101	authorise enable/disable player		5	9	9	9	9	9			9	7	1
102	Support Detailed		9	9	9	9	9	9			9	7	1
103	Support Fund Types		9	9	9	9	9				9	7	1
104	Show player registered for STT or MTT -Tournament Enhancement		9	9	9	9	9				9	7	1
105	Show names of tournaments played in - Tournament Enhancement		9	9	9	9	9	9			9	7	1
106	MTT Table Copy - Tournament Enhancement		5	9	9	9	9	5			9	7	1
107	Add Limit Buy search criteria - Tournament Enhancement		9	9	9	9	9	5			9	7	1
108	Games: Bingo	9		9					5		9	5	2
109	Games: Keno	9		9					5		9	5	2
110	Games: Poker	9		9					5		9	5	2
111	Games: Scratch Card	9		9							9	5	1
112	Games: add jackpot to slots	9		9					5		9	5	2
113	CyberBoss Mobile	9		9					3		9	6	1
114	Security	9		9					9		9	5	1
115	Enhance Architecture	9		9							9	5	1
116	MIDP 2.0	9		9					9		7	5	1
117	Notification and distributed automated build	9		9					5		9	5	1
118	Projects: Intervarion			9							9	5	1
119	SVG			9							9	5	1
120	Projects: RyanAir	9		9							9	5	1
121	Viral Distribution	9		9					9		9	5	2
122	Support Bonus/affiliate programs	9		9					9		9	5	1
123	Projects: GalaSkanbet			9							9	6	1
124	Network Operator config support and testing	9		9					5		9	5	1
125	Projects: UK Betting	9		9					9		9	5	1
126	Authorization	9		9							9	5	1
127	Bingo look and feel										9	1	1
128	Bingo Replay										9	1	1
129	Bingo Game Play										9	1	1
130	Bingo Extra Game Functions										9	1	1
131	Bingo Configuration										9	1	1
132	Bingo Reports										9	1	1
133	Bingo Community										9	1	1
134	Game Profile Stakes										9	1	1
135	Premium SMS										9	1	1
136	Junit testing										9	1	1
137	Mobile use										9	1	1
138	Enhance Architecture using MVC pattern										9	1	1
139	Xlets										9	1	1
140	Internationalisation										9	1	1
141	Netbeari processor blocks										9	1	1
142	Where to use in protocol										9	1	1
143	Mw 177 o for 229										9	1	1
144	On device debugging										9	1	1
145	Flatten 2d arrays										9	1	1
146	Use midlet data size										9	1	1
147	Profiling and reuse hot code										9	1	1
148	Age Verification										9	1	1
149	Reich Play										6	5	1
150													
151	Mobile Payment & Mobile MyAccount / Mobile Registration										9	5	1
152	XiPMS										9	5	1
153	Refrator 90-ball bingo										9	5	1
154	Multiplayer Table Poker										9	5	1
155	Progressive Live Jackpot										9	5	1
156	Bull's eye Busto										9	5	1
157	Hot Rope (Phase II)										9	5	1
158	Casino Stud Poker										6	5	1
159	9 cards poker										9	5	1
160	Mad Mettachan										9	5	1
161	Fruit Party										3	5	1
162	Lunux Smartphones										9	5	1
163	Palm Smartphones										9	5	1
164	Windows Smartphones										7	5	1
165	Blackberry Smartphones										6	5	1
166	UIQ 260										7	5	1
167	133*176										7	5	1
168	262*416										7	5	1
169	176*208										7	5	1
170	176*220										7	5	1
171	240*320										7	5	1
172	208*208										7	5	1
173													
174	Mobile MIDP registration & payment / Play while you Play for fun										9	5	1
175	SMS Payment										9	5	1
176	Players Preferences										5	5	1
177	Mobile "My Account"										9	5	1
178	Download Bonus										5	5	1
179	Reload/Reload Bonus										7	5	1
180	Loyalty Bonus										7	5	1
181	Mobile Specific Business Reports										5	5	1
182	Multiple Operator Testing										7	5	1
183	Obsolesce										9	5	2
184	Cronos										9	9	2
185	Dynamic Provisioning												
186	Setfigi Performance Fixes												
187	Merge CVS trunk												
188	Setup Maven and												
189	Metrics Program setup												
190	CleanUp Logs												

C.5. System Values of Features (Before and After Generation of Release Plans)

ID#	Recalculated System Values						Number of SD-coupled Features					
	Release Plan Alternatives					Initial Approximation	Release Plan Alternatives					Initial Approximation
	SP1	SP2	SP3	SP4	SP5		SP1	SP2	SP3	SP4	SP5	
1	6.307	7.368	6.423	4.599	5.763	30.69	11	12	15	7	9	53
2	6.621	10.739	12.694	11.947	6.893	39.153	22	32	37	36	19	114
3	10.157	16.091	8.193	8.715	4.979	54.389	30	46	22	22	13	150
4	3.861	4.729	3.389	2.151	1.856	36.508	10	11	8	6	5	94
5	8.734	15.323	16.607	15.794	15.916	44.797	29	46	50	50	50	135
6	12.137	19.405	21.65	12.213	13.643	67.871	33	46	52	30	31	166
7	11.272	18.465	20.553	21.666	21.214	62.53	34	46	53	54	53	162
8	9.364	4.019	3.464	0.583	3.62	25.311	17	7	6	1	7	51
9	9.276	12.801	13.547	13.35	14.224	37.587	22	34	37	37	38	94
10	12.238	19.299	21.79	20.743	20.587	62.076	34	49	54	54	53	163
11	8.155	13.724	18.73	17.33	9.253	50.141	27	43	48	50	25	142
12	12.049	16.059	11.354	5.849	5.799	57.201	32	45	31	15	14	161
13	15.631	22.907	24.575	15.423	14.17	81.426	36	51	55	32	32	179
14	12.742	19.319	21.358	22.327	23.004	64.906	32	47	52	56	56	164
15	2.824	5.08	4.018	1.087	7.854	29.136	5	9	7	2	13	51
16	9.55	13.701	13.56	14.912	15.156	44.956	30	43	46	49	51	138
17	7.236	12.287	14.235	6.443	6.393	43.636	23	36	42	20	20	127
18	11.581	8.76	8.289	5.909	6.551	50.592	34	27	26	16	17	150
19	16.16	21.846	24.293	25.773	25.22	79.228	37	50	55	57	56	174
20	8.305	11.39	13.156	13.642	14.108	42.794	28	39	44	45	45	139
21	10.243	14.98	17.344	9.664	9.293	52.135	31	47	53	27	28	155
22	9.046	8.318	2.619	4.86	5.905	36.9	15	14	4	8	9	63
23	15.81	19.867	12.51	22.165	10.801	54.845	39	47	31	54	25	158
24	7.839	10.706	11.718	12.744	5.434	37.166	23	33	37	40	16	111
25	15.012	22.083	24.196	24.463	24.674	75.519	35	49	53	55	55	174
26	13.29	18.757	19.962	21.403	21.6	66.205	36	49	53	56	55	172
27	7.402	13.025	6.435	5.553	3.197	39.086	26	42	20	18	10	119
28	16.371	17.602	17.225	16.959	16.482	69.899	42	40	39	39	38	166
29	15.526	15.713	15.323	15.042	15.127	54.466	42	41	40	40	40	153
30	13.549	19.349	20.486	21.562	21.959	65.673	36	50	53	55	54	166
31	11.675	12.04	10.167	10.807	4.96	51.857	31	32	29	28	14	152
32	16.927	22.323	24.127	23.754	24.896	77.317	35	49	54	55	55	176
33	10.243	9.155	9.155	9.151	9.151	35.9	18	16	16	16	16	63
34	16.123	17.237	16.822	17.069	16.689	64.792	46	44	44	44	43	165
35	11.112	9.923	10.111	9.312	8.712	34.193	28	24	24	22	21	91
36	6.724	5.016	4.698	21.056	21.154	76.038	17	11	10	46	46	168
37	10.336	9.555	3.225	3.803	3.325	50.074	33	28	9	12	10	150
38	15.854	22.917	25.824	25.773	25.376	60.737	34	49	55	56	55	173
39	5.221	2.351	1.708	8.806	8.633	39.659	14	8	5	30	29	123
40	10.531	16.991	18.312	19.007	19.221	57.645	31	47	51	52	52	154
41	9.489	16.148	17.008	16.887	18.543	50.18	31	48	52	53	52	147
42	8.76	10.684	12.338	3.905	5.644	30.69	16	19	22	7	10	55
43	10.231	9.937	8.733	9.761	9.544	38.102	26	24	22	24	23	107
44	19.081	18.238	18.247	18.115	18.199	74.168	46	44	44	44	44	173
45	4.979	5.073	7.128	6.793	7.326	67.363	12	11	16	14	16	166
46	3.122	2.999	3.648	2.561	2.762	54.309	9	9	12	7	8	155
47	15.87	15.028	3.367	3.571	3.592	54.979	42	40	9	10	10	151
48	3.774	4.604	4.368	4.392	5.044	66.089	11	11	12	11	13	160
49	4.581	3.694	4.085	4.396	4.018	60.147	12	11	12	12	12	161
50	3.936	2.904	3.168	3.049	3.449	49.704	11	8	8	8	9	145
51	5.331	8.794	14.389	14.428	13.076	79.276	12	19	33	32	31	178
52	17.681	16.896	16.292	16.484	3.794	66.141	44	42	42	42	10	166
53	17.743	16.376	16.246	15.848	15.546	62.144	44	42	41	40	40	162
54	19.526	19.756	19.383	19.549	19.018	71.079	45	45	45	45	44	166
55	10.399	9.66	9.063	9.72	9.42	34.714	24	21	20	21	20	89
56	20.65	19.16	19.23	19.199	19.306	80.718	48	44	44	44	44	177
57	13.494	12.797	12.23	12.664	12.647	47.784	39	36	35	36	36	146
58	10.946	9.99	9.226	9.34	9.123	34.399	29	27	25	25	24	106
59	3.877	3.775	3.902	3.464	3.159	55.06	10	10	11	11	11	153
60	3.462	1.657	1.958	1.948	2.524	47.316	9	6	7	7	8	145
61	9.566	9.677	6.474	9.137	8.587	30.853	17	15	15	16	15	55
62	7.941	7.396	7.941	6.854	7.854	29.138	14	13	14	12	13	51
63	20.375	20.14	20.431	3.853	3.565	76.899	47	46	46	10	10	176
64	9.802	9.847	10.001	9.734	9.384	41.361	33	31	30	30	29	128
65	18.462	3.605	18.166	3.834	3.246	66.863	47	10	45	10	10	170
66	14.416	13.68	13.086	13.351	13.689	54.935	40	38	36	37	37	155
67	22.439	20.869	21.034	20.756	20.763	78.736	47	45	45	45	45	175
68	10.502	9.869	9.307	9.3	9.3	29.901	18	16	15	15	15	52
69	4.728	4.972	7.823	15.195	15.376	81.798	11	11	16	32	33	176
70	3.574	3.54	3.553	3.646	3.156	53.961	12	11	12	10	10	154
71	4.485	2.982	3.203	3.341	3.531	54.579	12	9	9	9	11	152
72	4.62	5.14	5.494	7.487	7.571	70.77	12	12	12	16	17	170
73	4.444	3.514	4.668	3.494	3.572	59.087	11	11	12	10	10	162
74	6.19	6.373	5.027	4.453	4.656	63.517	17	17	12	11	11	161
75	2.874	8.657	2.496	7.805	7.372	39.057	9	25	8	23	22	113
76	6.335	6.513	8.774	7.731	7.682	79.782	13	19	18	16	17	177
77	13.586	10.471	11.392	11.611	18.154	56.675	41	30	30	31	52	161
78	8.784	7.69	6.583	6.583	6.033	34.946	16	14	12	12	11	61
79	2.112	2.567	2.441	1.771	2.071	44.441	8	7	8	6	7	136
80	17.769	16.72	16.511	16.39	16.44	65.617	42	40	40	40	40	165
81	19.804	18.941	18.38	18.07	17.47	66.244	45	43	43	43	42	168
82	16.545	15.709	16.286	15.387	16	64.257	41	38	38	37	38	161
83	3.7	4.014	4.1	4.238	4.066	59.838	11	11	12	10	10	158
84	18.285	17.481	17.989	17.336	17.972	73.203	44	42	43	42	43	169
85	6.905	6.76	9.269	6.466	6.168	57.51	22	21	22	20	19	91
86	3.415	2.469	3.426	2.252	2.891	51.412	10	9	10	8	9	151
87	12.195	12.257	12.206	11.572	11.139	40.076	34	33	33	31	30	114
88	2.789	7.724	7.724	7.72	7.17	32.279	5	13	13	13	12	57
89	12.125	10.853	11.458	10.196	9.961	44.021	33	30	30	26	27	124
90	16.926	17.595	16.766	16.741	16.713	67.631	42	39	37	37	37	164

91	11.332	10.26	10.27	10.343	10.793	41.678		33	29	29	29	29	121
92	13.86	12.303	12.879	12.356	12.091	50.519		36	32	34	33	32	148
93	3.727	3.633	3.15	2.861	3.239	50.444		10	10	8	8	9	146
94	8.954	9.156	7.662	6.397	6.417	74.987		20	20	16	14	14	172
95	8.854	7.771	7.745	7.196	7.196	35.955		16	14	14	13	13	64
96	4.866	4.341	4.866	4.424	4.424	24.105		9	8	9	8	8	43
97	20.659	19.975	20.071	18.949	19.112	72.579		47	46	45	45	45	175
98	3.764	3.282	4.572	3.698	3.642	59.083		11	10	12	10	10	160
99	1.68	9.869	9.307	9.3	9.3	29.901		3	16	15	15	15	52
100	20.34	19.792	4.253	5.287	5.128	79.581		45	44	10	12	12	171
101	21.363	19.706	19.467	19.893	19.715	80.671		46	43	42	43	43	173
102	2.786	1.977	5.845	5.928	5.828	33.383		7	5	16	16	15	86
103	10.882	9.82	10.244	9.608	10.275	40.243		29	26	27	26	27	114
104	6.665	7.115	7.115	7.4	7.1	30.695		15	15	15	15	14	77
105	5.1	5.101	5.365	6.915	7.009	72.881		11	11	12	15	15	166
106	15.316	14.781	14.308	14.1	14.339	58.947		42	40	38	39	39	156
107	13.408	12.59	12.239	12.446	12.774	52.845		39	36	34	34	34	145
108	21.087	14.663	14.414	14.134	13.918	80.037		45	33	32	32	32	176
109	11.333	15.782	15.985	16.826	16.412	47.555		29	44	47	50	50	141
110	1.648	6.124	6.133	5.671	5.671	30.428		3	11	11	10	10	54
111	6.187	11.045	13.401	7.968	6.693	40.979		25	36	41	22	19	123
112	17.908	13.358	12.508	12.525	23.432	71.126		43	33	33	30	55	170
113	10.647	10.003	9.008	9.178	6.728	44.424		36	33	32	31	30	139
114	11.62	7.192	6.984	3.715	7.627	44.545		33	23	23	11	23	129
115	16.851	6.296	10.699	6.151	6.27	66.702		41	17	29	14	13	163
116	8.353	8.318	2.619	4.86	5.905	36.9		15	14	4	8	9	63
117	2.866	3.423	9.551	2.148	2.467	37.114		8	9	24	7	8	95
118	17.791	17.25	17.317	17.321	17.021	64.316		46	44	45	44	43	166
119	18.707	3.643	3.964	7.028	7.113	68.531		44	11	12	16	16	166
120	15.103	13.924	13.881	13.063	12.699	56.062		40	37	37	36	35	159
121	7.242	6.41	5.597	3.528	3.32	53.736		19	18	13	10	10	150
122	7.573	8.297	8.506	3.982	4.207	65.731		19	20	16	12	12	168
123	9.836	9.114	9.017	9.093	9.093	33.343		23	21	21	21	21	86
124	13.175	11.713	11.954	11.178	10.728	48.109		38	34	34	33	32	143
125	10.946	9.99	9.226	9.34	9.123	34.399		29	27	25	25	24	108
126	7.966	8.203	7.112	6.391	14.011	69.206		20	19	15	15	34	168
127	14.665	17.966	18.749	19.808	19.963	55.651		41	47	51	54	54	156
128	13.338	18.666	18.784	20.585	20.842	67.28		35	49	54	54	53	167
129	15.069	20.428	23.196	23.414	24.362	79.953		35	48	54	55	54	173
130	12.687	8.343	9.319	8.08	8.284	52.283		36	27	27	24	24	148
131	15.88	18.256	19.36	9.63	8.922	56.608		40	45	48	27	25	157
132	8.274	13.078	14.521	14.354	15.035	43.899		30	42	47	48	48	137
133	11.847	16.678	18.758	20.729	20.22	61.759		33	46	51	55	55	161
134	17.976	19.089	21.242	21.863	21.659	67.632		43	49	54	56	55	169
135	16.352	5.786	4.516	9.925	10.537	58.597		40	15	12	26	27	154
136	12.758	10.848	8.95	16.379	15.996	49.047		40	33	30	50	50	151
137	10.66	8.912	7.756	14.825	14.87	50.323		37	27	24	51	51	147
138	5.186	5.497	6.825	8.607	8.272	50.808		14	15	26	25	56	151
139	5.521	4.99	6.193	7.477	8.997	45.044		17	16	26	23	25	132
140	19.067	14.894	13.894	23.151	23.376	72.776		44	35	33	56	55	174
141	4.296	4.123	6.767	7.022	7.394	36.78		12	12	22	20	21	112
142	17.672	12.083	21.232	21.41	20.7	66.829		43	33	54	55	54	166
143	3.92	4.62	4.764	4.622	4.307	32.45		10	11	11	12	12	83
144	4.159	4.878	3.466	7.423	8.619	34.945		7	8	6	13	15	61
145	3.6	7.792	6.546	15.764	15.438	40.744		10	21	20	43	43	114
146	12.2	7.26	16.649	16.088	15.844	46.983		34	23	48	47	47	137
147	16.453	11.573	21.533	21.775	21.586	66.084		42	32	54	56	55	168
148	20.273	8.463	7.666	7.584	14.092	78.952		48	20	17	16	33	178
149	3.208	3.116	3.582	4.361	4.272	44.333		10	10	11	12	12	132
150	17.78	20.168	22.716	22.266	21.598	64.092		43	48	52	54	53	160
151	17.729	18.716	20.891	20.783	21.583	67.682		42	48	52	53	53	166
152	19.694	22.258	24.47	24.715	24.718	73.81		44	51	55	56	55	173
153	15.931	12.347	12.019	12.499	12.618	59.304		41	31	30	30	31	155
154	19.488	20.996	23.363	22.881	23.147	73.185		38	28	25	51	52	150
155	13.691	10.878	8.724	16.555	17.237	52.207		22	20	17	18	19	83
156	7.98	8.244	6.997	7.606	7.935	33.132		18	16	13	23	25	152
157	6.635	6.241	5.369	7.876	8.689	53.193		30	23	23	22	23	129
158	9.1	7.149	5.995	6.96	7.83	42.221		38	29	50	51	51	155
159	13.949	10.422	16.736	16.941	17.757	54.471		10	9	8	5	4	54
160	5.575	4.936	4.374	2.666	2.199	30.428		11	30	52	55	54	160
161	4.428	10.263	18.4	19.367	18.844	59.262		13	8	9	5	6	48
162	7.18	4.423	4.989	2.792	3.309	28.515		24	17	17	16	12	91
163	8.199	5.563	5.545	5.692	4.505	33.736		42	47	52	54	54	159
164	17.416	19.002	20.9	21.219	20.947	62.529		40	50	55	57	56	174
165	19.596	22.57	24.9	24.437	24.521	77.508		44	47	53	54	54	169
166	16.609	17.661	20.441	20.07	20.469	64.005		12	12	9	7	9	53
167	6.842	7.368	5.239	4.599	5.783	30.69		41	49	54	55	54	167
168	18.625	21.65	23.773	24.599	24.385	72.266		32	41	44	47	48	126
169	11.346	13.555	14.979	15.772	16.083	42.085		12	5	4	6	5	50
170	6.656	2.758	2.188	3.304	2.755	28.436		39	47	50	54	54	157
171	14.147	15.739	17.389	19.194	19.072	56.374		17	8	10	20	19	84
172	9.378	4.976	5.575	11.063	10.454	35.955		41	30	29	27	55	165
173	16.475	12.119	11.729	11.427	22.763	67.455		19	31	30	31	52	169
174	7.821	12.296	12.063	12.794	20.973	66.453		42	33	53	56	56	183
175	15.516	11.888	19.118	20.169	19.983	61.504		18	6	4	7	6	81
176	9.933	3.514	2.199	3.932	3.336	34.232		19	19	29	29	29	164
177	7.416	7.972	11.589	11.791	11.156	66.398		21	33	53	55	55	175
178	8.942	14.613	24.387	24.46	25.061	77.766		45	34	55	55	55	172
179	19.695	15.32	23.36	23.32	23.551	72.471		18	30	29	53	30	156
180	6.701	10.089	9.443	17.909	11.816	56.408		12	33	31	55	54	172
181	5.003	13.367	12.664	21.931	22.026	72.048		43	51	55	56	55	174
182	19.949	23.196	25.575	26.544	25.181	81.178		22	21	22	20	22	116
183	6.686	7.246	7.253	6.187	7.556	39.034		15	20	11	7	9	63
184	9.046	11.384	6.22	3.843	5.905	36.9		6	5	3	13	12	49
185	3.398	2.821	1.616	7.507	6.924	27.242		37	47	51	53	53	151
186	14.068	15.399	17.523	18.925	18.764	57.148		23	19	31	33	33	91
187	9.396	7.102	11.859	12.694	12.661	36.403		39	48	52	54	53	162
188	15.19	17.312	18.668	19.7	20.207	60.896		42	50	55	55	54	168
189	17.907	21.819	23.633	23.151	22.82	71.431		38	45	50	52	53	141
190	11.654	13.32	15.318	15.946	16.112	43.671							

C.6. Structure of 5 Release Plans Generated by SoRPES for the 190 Features

	f1	f2	f3	f4	f5	f6	f7	f8	f9	f10	f11	f12	f13	f14	f15	f16	f17	f18	f19	f20	f21	f22	f23	f24	f25	f26	f27	f28	f29	f30	f31	f32	f33
SP1	1	1	1	3	1	1	1	2	1	1	1	1	1	1	1	1	1	1	1	1	1	1	2	1	1	1	1	6	6	1	1	1	6
SP2	2	1	1	3	1	1	1	3	1	1	1	1	1	1	2	1	1	2	1	1	1	2	1	1	1	1	6	6	1	2	1	1	6
SP3	1	1	2	3	1	1	1	3	1	1	1	2	1	1	3	1	1	2	1	1	3	2	1	1	1	2	6	6	1	2	1	1	6
SP4	2	1	2	4	1	2	1	5	1	1	1	3	2	1	5	1	2	3	1	1	2	3	1	1	1	2	6	6	1	2	1	1	6
SP5	2	2	3	4	1	2	1	6	1	1	2	3	2	1	6	1	2	3	1	1	2	3	2	2	1	1	3	6	6	1	3	1	6

	f34	f35	f36	f37	f38	f39	f40	f41	f42	f43	f44	f45	f46	f47	f48	f49	f50	f51	f52	f53	f54	f55	f56	f57	f58	f59	f60	f61	f62	f63	f64	f65	f66
SP1	6	6	3	1	1	3	1	1	2	6	6	4	5	6	4	4	4	5	6	6	6	6	6	6	4	4	6	6	6	6	6	6	6
SP2	6	6	4	2	1	5	1	1	1	6	6	4	5	6	4	4	3	6	6	6	6	6	6	6	4	5	6	6	6	6	6	5	6
SP3	6	6	5	3	1	5	1	1	1	6	6	3	4	5	4	4	5	2	6	6	6	6	6	6	4	5	6	6	6	6	6	6	6
SP4	6	6	6	3	1	6	1	1	2	6	6	3	5	4	4	4	5	2	6	6	6	6	6	6	4	5	6	6	6	5	6	5	6
SP5	6	6	6	5	1	6	1	1	2	6	6	3	5	4	3	4	5	2	6	6	6	6	6	6	4	5	6	6	6	5	6	5	6

	f67	f68	f69	f70	f71	f72	f73	f74	f75	f76	f77	f78	f79	f80	f81	f82	f83	f84	f85	f86	f87	f88	f89	f90	f91	f92	f93	f94	f95	f96	f97	f98	f99
SP1	6	6	5	4	5	5	5	3	5	4	2	6	4	6	6	6	4	6	6	5	6	4	6	6	6	6	5	3	6	6	6	5	5
SP2	6	6	4	4	5	4	5	3	6	3	2	6	5	6	6	6	4	6	6	5	6	6	6	6	6	6	5	3	6	6	6	5	6
SP3	6	6	3	4	5	4	4	4	5	3	2	6	5	6	6	6	4	6	6	5	6	6	6	6	6	6	5	3	6	6	6	4	6
SP4	6	6	2	5	5	3	4	4	6	3	2	6	5	6	6	6	4	6	6	5	6	6	6	6	6	6	5	3	6	6	6	4	6
SP5	6	6	2	5	4	3	4	4	6	3	1	6	5	6	6	6	4	6	6	5	6	6	6	6	6	6	5	3	6	6	6	4	6

	f100	f101	f102	f103	f104	f105	f106	f107	f108	f109	f110	f111	f112	f113	f114	f115	f116	f117	f118	f119	f120	f121	f122	f123	f124	f125	f126	f127	f128	f129	f130	f131	f132
SP1	6	6	3	6	6	5	6	6	2	1	4	1	2	6	2	2	2	3	6	6	6	3	3	6	6	6	3	2	1	1	2	2	1
SP2	6	6	5	6	6	4	6	6	2	1	6	1	2	6	2	3	2	3	6	4	6	3	3	6	6	6	3	1	1	1	2	1	1
SP3	5	6	6	6	6	4	6	6	2	1	6	1	2	6	2	2	3	6	6	4	6	3	3	6	6	6	3	1	1	1	2	1	1
SP4	4	6	6	6	6	3	6	6	2	1	6	2	2	6	3	3	3	4	6	3	6	4	4	6	6	6	3	1	1	1	2	2	1
SP5	4	6	6	6	6	3	6	6	2	1	6	2	1	6	2	3	3	4	6	3	6	4	4	6	6	6	2	1	1	1	2	2	1

	f133	f134	f135	f136	f137	f138	f139	f140	f141	f142	f143	f144	f145	f146	f147	f148	f149	f150	f151	f152	f153	f154	f155	f156	f157	f158	f159	f160	f161	f162	f163	f164	f165
SP1	1	2	6	2	2	3	3	2	3	2	3	3	3	2	2	6	5	2	2	2	2	2	3	2	2	3	4	2	2	2	2	2	2
SP2	1	1	3	2	2	3	3	2	3	2	3	3	2	2	2	3	4	1	1	1	2	1	2	3	2	2	3	2	2	3	2	1	1
SP3	1	1	3	2	2	2	2	2	2	2	1	3	3	2	1	1	3	4	1	1	1	2	1	2	3	2	1	3	1	2	2	1	1
SP4	1	1	2	1	1	2	2	1	2	1	2	2	1	1	1	3	3	1	1	1	2	1	2	2	2	1	3	1	2	2	1	1	1
SP5	1	1	2	1	1	2	2	1	2	1	1	1	3	2	1	1	2	1	1	2	1	1	2	3	2	1	1	1	3	1	2	1	1

	f166	f167	f168	f169	f170	f171	f172	f173	f174	f175	f176	f177	f178	f179	f180	f181	f182	f183	f184	f185	f186	f187	f188	f189	f190	F1	F2
SP1	2	2	2	2	2	2	2	2	3	2	2	3	3	2	3	4	2	1	1	3	2	2	2	2	2	214873	9488.43
SP2	1	2	1	1	2	1	2	2	2	2	3	3	2	2	2	2	1	2	1	3	1	2	1	1	1	211997	11576.38
SP3	1	2	1	1	2	1	2	2	2	1	3	2	1	1	2	2	1	2	2	3	1	1	1	1	1	206321	12775.73
SP4	1	2	1	1	2	1	1	2	2	1	3	2	1	1	1	1	1	2	2	2	1	1	1	1	1	197759	13167.21
SP5	1	2	1	1	2	1	1	1	1	1	3	2	1	1	2	1	1	2	3	2	1	1	1	1	1	189189	13293.34

C.7. Structure of 5 Release Plans Generated by ReleasePlanner for 190 Features

	f1	f2	f3	f4	f5	f6	f7	f8	f9	f10	f11	f12	f13	f14	f15	f16	f17	f18	f19	f20	f21	f22	f23	f24	f25	f26	f27	f28	f29	f30	f31	f32	f33
RP1	1	1	1	2	2	5	6	2	1	2	1	6	2	1	4	6	6	3	3	4	1	2	2	1	2	2	2	6	6	2	2	1	6
RP2	1	1	1	2	4	4	6	2	1	2	1	6	2	1	4	6	4	3	3	4	1	2	2	1	2	2	2	6	6	2	2	1	6
RP3	1	1	1	2	4	4	5	2	1	2	1	6	2	1	4	6	4	3	3	4	1	2	2	1	2	2	2	6	6	2	2	1	6
RP4	1	1	1	2	2	5	6	2	1	2	1	6	2	4	6	6	6	3	3	4	1	2	2	1	2	2	2	6	6	2	2	1	6
RP5	1	1	1	2	2	5	6	2	1	2	1	6	2	4	6	6	6	3	3	4	1	2	2	1	2	2	2	6	6	2	2	1	6

	f34	f35	f36	f37	f38	f39	f40	f41	f42	f43	f44	f45	f46	f47	f48	f49	f50	f51	f52	f53	f54	f55	f56	f57	f58	f59	f60	f61	f62	f63	f64	f65	f66
RP1	6	6	6	3	4	6	6	5	6	5	6	6	3	2	6	3	4	1	6	6	6	6	6	6	5	5	6	6	4	6	6	6	6
RP2	6	6	6	3	6	6	6	5	5	5	6	6	3	2	6	3	4	1	6	6	6	6	6	6	5	5	6	6	4	6	6	6	6
RP3	6	6	6	3	5	6	6	5	6	5	6	6	3	2	6	3	4	1	6	6	6	6	6	6	5	5	6	6	4	6	6	6	6
RP4	6	6	6	3	1	6	6	6	6	6	6	6	3	2	6	3	4	1	6	6	6	6	6	6	5	5	6	6	4	6	6	6	6
RP5	6	6	6	3	1	6	6	6	6	6	6	6	3	2	6	3	4	1	6	6	6	6	6	6	5	5	6	6	4	6	6	6	6

	f67	f68	f69	f70	f71	f72	f73	f74	f75	f76	f77	f78	f79	f80	f81	f82	f83	f84	f85	f86	f87	f88	f89	f90	f91	f92	f93	f94	f95	f96	f97	f98	f99
RP1	6	3	4	3	5	4	3	5	4	3	1	5	5	6	6	6	4	6	6	2	6	5	6	6	6	6	4	3	6	6	6	4	3
RP2	6	3	4	3	5	4	3	5	4	3	1	5	5	6	6	6	4	6	6	2	6	5	6	6	6	6	4	3	6	6	6	4	3
RP3	6	3	4	3	5	4	3	5	4	3	1	5	5	6	6	6	4	6	6	2	6	5	6	6	6	6	4	3	6	6	6	4	3
RP4	6	3	4	3	5	4	3	5	4	3	1	5	5	6	6	6	4	6	6	2	6	5	6	6	6	6	4	3	6	6	6	4	3
RP5	6	3	4	3	5	4	3	5	4	3	1	5	5	6	6	6	4	6	6	2	6	5	6	6	6	6	4	3	6	6	6	4	3

	f100	f101	f102	f103	f104	f105	f106	f107	f108	f109	f110	f111	f112	f113	f114	f115	f116	f117	f118	f119	f120	f121	f122	f123	f124	f125	f126	f127	f128	f129	f130	f131	f132
RP1	6	6	5	5	6	6	6	6	2	3	1	4	2	6	2	2	2	3	6	3	6	4	5	6	6	6	6	6	2	1	1	1	1
RP2	6	6	5	5	6	4	6	6	2	3	1	4	2	6	2	2	2	3	6	3	6	6	6	6	6	6	6	6	2	2	1	1	1
RP3	6	6	5	5	6	4	6	6	2	3	1	4	2	6	2	2	2	3	6	3	6	6	5	6	6	6	6	6	2	2	1	1	1
RP4	6	6	5	5	1	4	6	6	2	3	1	4	2	6	2	2	2	3	4	3	6	6	5	6	6	6	6	1	2	1	1	1	1
RP5	6	6	5	5	1	4	6	6	2	3	1	4	2	6	2	2	2	3	4	3	6	6	5	6	6	6	6	1	2	1	1	1	1

	f133	f134	f135	f136	f137	f138	f139	f140	f141	f142	f143	f144	f145	f146	f147	f148	f149	f150	f151	f152	f153	f154	f155	f156	f157	f158	f159	f160	f161	f162	f163	f164	f165
RP1	1	1	1	2	1	1	1	4	1	1	1	6	1	1	4	5	3	1	1	2	2	6	1	1	2	1	6	2	1	1	4	1	1
RP2	1	1	1	2	1	1	1	4	1	1	1	6	1	1	5	5	3	1	1	2	2	4	1	1	2	1	6	2	1	1	1	1	1
RP3	1	1	1	2	1	1	1	4	1	1	1	6	1	1	4	5	3	1	1	2	2	4	1	1	2	1	6	2	1	1	1	1	1
RP4	1	1	1	2	1	1	1	4	1	1	1	6	1	1	6	5	3	1	1	2	2	6	1	1	2	1	6	2	1	1	1	1	6
RP5	1	1	1	2	1	1	1	4	1	1	1	6	1	1	6	5	3	1	1	2	2	6	1	1	2	1	6	2	1	1	1	1	6

	f166	f167	f168	f169	f170	f171	f172	f173	f174	f175	f176	f177	f178	f179	f180	f181	f182	f183	f184	f185	f186	f187	f188	f189	f190	F1
RP1	6	6	6	6	4	1	6	2	1	6	2	5	1	2	1	2	1	2	2	1	1	1	1	2	1	165773
RP2	1	6	1	1	1	1	6	2	1	6	2	4	1	2	1	2	1	2	2	1	1	1	1	2	1	166805
RP3	1	6	1	1	1	1	6	2	1	6	2	4	1	2	1	2	4	2	2	1	1	1	1	2	1	166805
RP4	1	6	1	1	1	1	6	2	1	6	2	6	1	2	1	2	4	2	2	1	1	1	1	2	1	162428
RP5	6	6	6	6	1	5	6	2	1	6	2	4	1	2	1	2	1	2	2	1	1	1	1	2	1	162482

VDM publishing house ltd.

Scientific Publishing House

offers

free of charge publication

of current academic research papers, Bachelor´s Theses, Master's Theses, Dissertations or Scientific Monographs

If you have written a thesis which satisfies high content as well as formal demands, and you are interested in a remunerated publication of your work, please send an e-mail with some initial information about yourself and your work to *info@vdm-publishing-house.com.*

Our editorial office will get in touch with you shortly.

VDM Publishing House Ltd.
Meldrum Court 17.
Beau Bassin
Mauritius
www.vdm-publishing-house.com